JOURNEY TO JESUS

WORSHIP AND WITNESS

The Worship and Witness series seeks to foster a rich, interdisciplinary conversation on the theology and practice of public worship, a conversation that will be integrative and expansive. Integrative, in that scholars and practitioners from a wide range of disciplines and ecclesial contexts will contribute studies that engage church and academy. Expansive, in that the series will engage voices from the global church and foreground crucial areas of inquiry for the vitality of public worship in the twenty-first century.

The Worship and Witness series demonstrates and cultivates the interaction of topics in worship studies with a range of crucial questions, topics, and insights drawn from other fields. These include the traditional disciplines of theology, history, and pastoral ministry—as well as cultural studies, political theology, spirituality, and music and the arts. The series focus will thus bridge church worship practices and the vital witness these practices nourish.

We are pleased that you have chosen to join us in this conversation, and we look forward to sharing this learning journey with you.

SERIES EDITORS:

John D. Witvliet
Noel Snyder
Maria Cornou

JOURNEY TO JESUS

Faith Formation into Christ and Community

Kent Jorgen Burreson
Rhoda Grever Schuler

Forewords by
Maxwell E. Johnson *and* Arthur A. Just Jr.

CASCADE *Books* • Eugene, Oregon

JOURNEY TO JESUS
Faith Formation into Christ and Community

Worship and Witness

Copyright © 2025 Wipf and Stock. All rights reserved. Except for brief quotations in critical publications or reviews, no part of this book may be reproduced in any manner without prior written permission from the publisher. Write: Permissions, Wipf and Stock Publishers, 199 W. 8th Ave., Suite 3, Eugene, OR 97401.

Cascade Books
An Imprint of Wipf and Stock Publishers
199 W. 8th Ave., Suite 3
Eugene, OR 97401

www.wipfandstock.com

PAPERBACK ISBN: 978-1-6667-6480-2
HARDCOVER ISBN: 978-1-6667-6481-9
EBOOK ISBN: 978-1-6667-6482-6

Cataloguing-in-Publication data:

Names: Burreson, Kent Jorgen, author. | Schuler, Rhoda Grever, author. | Johnson, Maxwell E., and Just, Arthur A., Jr., forewords.

Title: Journey to Jesus : faith formation into Christ and community / Kent Jorgen Burreson and Rhoda Grever Schuler.

Description: Eugene, OR: Cascade Books, 2025 | Series: Worship and Witness | Includes bibliographical references and index.

Identifiers: ISBN 978-1-6667-6480-2 (paperback) | ISBN 978-1-6667-6481-9 (hardcover) | ISBN 978-1-6667-6482-6 (ebook)

Subjects: LCSH: Discipling (Christianity). | Catechumens. | Initiation rites—Religious aspects—Christianity.

Classification: BV811.3 J70 2025 (print) | BV811.3 (ebook)

Scripture quotations are from New Revised Standard Version Bible, copyright © 1989 National Council of the Churches of Christ in the United States of America. Used by permission. All rights reserved worldwide.

Diagram "The Structure of Apostolic Genius" is from Alan Hirsch, *The Forgotten Ways: Reactivating the Missional Church,* Brazos Press, a division of Baker Publishing Group, copyright © 2006. Used by permission.

A shorter version of chapter 4 appeared as "Voyage to Belonging and Renewal through the Adult Catechumenate" in *Currents in Theology and Mission* (April 2022) and is reprinted by permission of the journal.

Portions of chapter 6 appeared as "Mentoring in the Pews: Fostering a Missional Habitus" in *Lutheran Mission Matters* (May 2022) and are reprinted by permission of the journal.

Dedicated
to faithful teachers and professors who inspired our learning,
to Spirit-filled preachers whose sermons
broke open the word of God for us in profound ways,
to grace-filled liturgists whose voices, movements, and gestures
brought us into Christ's presence,
and to our faithful spouses, Cindy and Mark,
without whose support and love
our lives would be incomplete,
and this book would still be a work in progress.

CONTENTS

Foreword by Maxwell E. Johnson ix

Foreword by Arthur A. Just Jr. xi

Acknowledgments xv

1 Introducing the Journey 1

Introduction to Part I: Context Is Everything 13

2 St. John: Drawing People into Christ's Orbit through Pastoral Care 19

3 Living Faith: Heart-to-Heart Combat against Sin, Death, and the Power of the Devil 40

4 St. Mary's: Creating a Sense of Belonging 56

5 Redeemer: Receiving, Teaching, Celebrating, and Sharing Christ Jesus 72

Introduction to Part II: Common Themes across Uncommon Contexts 95

6 Fostering a Missional *Habitus* 99

7 The Path of Conversion: Belonging, Believing, Behaving 123

8 Ritual: Enacting and Rehearsing the Christian Story 142

9 Epilogue: Catechumenal Signs of Resilience 169

Appendix 1: Research Design and Methods 177

Appendix 2: Scripture Study/Reflection: An Aural Method/The African Method 185

Chart: The Stages of the Adult Catechumenate and the Ritual Transitions 190

Glossary 192

Bibliography 199

Index 205

FOREWORD

As this excellent study by Kent Burreson and Rhoda Schuler makes abundantly clear, the overall importance of the modern restoration of the adult catechumenate for the faith and life of the contemporary church cannot be overestimated. With specific regard to the current Roman Catholic *Ordo of Christian Initiation of Adults* (OCIA),[1] a Benedictine liturgical scholar and strong advocate of this ritual process wrote several years ago:

> What the Roman documents contain are not merely specific changes in liturgical rubrics, but a restored and unified vision of the Church.... One may turn an altar around and leave *reform* at that. But one cannot set an adult catechumenate in motion without becoming necessarily involved with *renewal* in the ways a local church lives its faith from top to bottom. For members of an adult catechumenate must be secured through evangelization; they must be formed to maturity in ecclesial faith through catechesis both prior to baptism and after it; and there must be something to initiate them into that will be correlative to the expectations built up in them throughout their whole initiatory process. This last means a community of lively faith in Jesus Christ dead, risen, and present actually among his People. In this area, when one change occurs, all changes.[2]

---

1. Note from authors Burreson and Schuler: Although the new translation of the Roman Catholic catechumenate (OCIA) is now available, throughout this book we reference the former translation, the *Rite of Christian Initiation of Adults*, and use its familiar acronym, RCIA, for two reasons. First, the parishes we researched, insofar as they referenced or used the RCIA, were using this original translation. Second, the new translation was published after we had submitted our manuscript for publication.

2. Kavanagh, "Christian Initiation in Post-Conciliar Catholicism," 7–8, emphasis in original.

Foreword

In short, because of the need for the active involvement of the whole faith community in the process of adult initiation (baptism, confirmation, and first communion) all attempts at restoring the adult catechumenate in a variety of different denominations today, Lutheran, Roman Catholic, Episcopal, Methodist, Presbyterian, etc., do not so much offer a new way to do sacramental ritual as much as they offer a new way to be and do church.

Putting their doctoral formation especially in sixteenth-century Lutheran baptismal rites (Burreson) and Lutheran confirmation rites in the United States (Schuler) to good use, these authors introduce us to this exciting process of adult formation and discipleship in a variety of diverse Lutheran ecclesial contexts (urban, suburban, and multicultural). In doing so they show us, indeed, by means of personal interviews, participant observation, and solid theological reflection, that where this adult catechumenal process is embraced there is, in the words of Kavanagh, that "*renewal* in the ways a local church lives its faith."

Of equal importance is the fact that this study is solidly "Lutheran" in its theological approach. While some Lutheran critics of the adult catechumenate have seen it as an attack on Lutheran baptismal theology associated with the importance of infant baptism, Burreson and Schuler show us that this is not the case. Lutherans may embrace the adult catechumenal process without thereby denigrating the importance and theology of infant initiation in the least as Lutherans seek to do evangelism in a post-Christendom world, where infant baptism and church membership can no longer be assumed on the part of several who may come seeking Christ and his body the church.

Thanks, Kent and Rhoda, for doing this important work. May it inspire many to investigate the gift of the catechumenate and its importance in the life of the church.

Maxwell E. Johnson
Emeritus Professor of Theology (Liturgical Studies)
University of Notre Dame
Notre Dame, Indiana

FOREWORD

TWENTY-FIVE YEARS AGO, I was invited by *Lutheran Forum* to write an introduction to the catechumenate entitled "Journey to Life in Christ." At that time, I had high hopes that the ancient catechumenate could transform our churches as they organized their communal life around baptism and the mission of the church. Lutherans had just completed "Catechumenate Training Days," a joint project between the Evangelical Lutheran Church in America (ELCA) and the Lutheran Church–Missouri Synod (LCMS), where church leaders came together to engage in learning about the catechumenate and then seeing it modeled and embodied in its four stages: inquiry, the catechumenate, enlightenment, and mystagogy. These training sessions, held around the country, led to the publication of *Welcome to Christ* by Augsburg Fortress (1997), and the more modest document by the LCMS, *Make Disciples Baptizing and Teaching: Resources and Ideas for Renewing the Lutheran Catechumenate* (2003). What a kairotic moment for the catechumenate to enliven our churches. Unfortunately, that journey ended with a whimper.

What a delight to see Kent Burreson and Rhoda Schuler revive this journey with the support and encouragement of the Calvin Institute of Christian Worship (CICW) and the Hoffmann Institute at Concordia University, St. Paul, Minnesota. Through their determination during a pandemic, they now offer us this important resource: *Journey to Jesus: Faith Formation into Christ and Community.* I am deeply honored to write a foreword to a book that I hope, once again, will capture the imagination of our churches to the genius of the adult catechumenate of the early church.

In my own teaching of both MDiv and DMin students, I am witnessing an openness to the catechumenate that I have never seen before. My DMin course entitled "A Lutheran Catechumenate for the Postmodern World" is well attended and the enthusiasm is high among the pastors who understand that their ministry and mission is much different than that of the modern world of their parents and grandparents. Today's world is more like the world early Christians confronted, where people are asking questions about God, church, and life that are basic and foundational. Instruction in the faith in a classroom setting and format may not be the most appropriate way to form new converts into a life in Christ. The ancient pattern of making Christians through evangelization, baptism, Eucharist, and mystagogical catechesis seems particularly timely in our increasingly unchurched world. This is especially true when those seeking God are allowed time in their process of formation to ask basic questions and be formed gradually by Scripture, liturgy, and catechism, the three sources of catechesis for life in Christ.

Some of my students for their DMin projects implemented a form of the catechumenate in their parishes. Each one was different, but none of them really captured what the ancient catechumenate was about. Perhaps one of the reasons is that there were no models of the catechumenate to show them the way. But that is not true anymore. Kent and Rhoda have now provided us a resource of four congregations who have captured how the catechumenate can be the overarching purpose for their life together in Christ, offering people a journey to Jesus that joins them to his body, the church, through the three BEs: believing, belonging, and behaving.

These four congregations appropriate the catechumenate in different ways, sensitive to their own contexts of ministry and mission, showing that the catechumenate is intended to be adaptable to each parish. But in all four congregations you see the catechumenate as the "way" a catechumen follows Jesus and travels with him along the catechetical road to Jerusalem and to the cross and empty tomb. By journeying along the same way that Christ traveled, the catechumen becomes prepared to enter the mysteries of baptism and the Lord's Supper in a community constituted by believing, belonging, and behaving. This journey to Jesus provides an opportunity for the entire congregation to be renewed in its own baptismal journey to the heavenly Jerusalem. The adult catechumenate offers the church a process of evangelization and catechesis that is biblical and historical in its form and substance. Kent and Rhoda reflect theologically on each congregation's appropriation of the catechumenate through the vast amount of literature available to us on how the catechumenate has been revived to serve our postmodern world.

Foreword

Journey to Jesus: Faith Formation into Christ and Community is a rich and indispensable primer on what the catechumenate looks like in congregations that have been shaped by its ancient wisdom. This will be the first book my students read as they contemplate how the catechumenate may be the key to the revitalization of their congregation's ministry and mission.

Arthur A. Just Jr.
Professor of Exegetical Theology
Concordia Theological Seminary
Fort Wayne, Indiana

ACKNOWLEDGMENTS

IT IS NOT HYPERBOLE to say that without the support of the Calvin Institute of Christian Worship (CICW) this book never would have been birthed. Shortly after we heard that our grant proposal submitted to a different funding source was rejected, Kent shared our disappointment with Dr. John Witvliet, a friend and colleague from graduate school. John, recognizing the value of research on adult faith formation, encouraged Kent to rewrite the grant and submit it to CICW, where John serves as the director. Yes, perhaps the old adage is true. It's not what you know; it's who you know. In our case, we prefer to believe that it is a both/and rather than either/or, and that John not only had confidence in Kent's character and passion for the topic but also that he was well aware of Kent's academic credentials. Funded first through a CICW Vital Worship Grant for worshiping communities, the importance of our research was confirmed when CICW funded a second Vital Worship Grant for teacher-scholars. We give thanks to God for John, for CICW and its board (which makes the funding decisions), and for all the gracious staff at the Calvin Institute of Christian Worship, whose encouragement, especially through the pandemic, bolstered our work. We are grateful also for the support of the Hoffmann Institute at Concordia University, St. Paul, Minnesota, under the direction of Dr. Mark Koschmann, who invited us to give the annual Hoffmann Lecture in October 2019, and who approved partial funding through the Hoffmann Institute for Rhoda's course release in fall 2020.

We also want to name publicly and thank various individuals who contributed to this project. To our student workers: Madi Patrow, undergraduate student at Concordia University, St. Paul, who transcribed Rhoda's handwritten interview notes with efficiency, attention to detail, and genuine interest in the project; and Sarah Rusche, graduate student in the deaconess program at Concordia Seminary, St. Louis, who transcribed

Acknowledgments

Kent's hand-scribbled, nearly illegible notes with aplomb—no small, mean task. We thank God for Madi and Sara and pray that God will bless their ministry among God's people! We also thank colleagues in academia and pastoral ministry for their consultations on this project: Rev. Paul E. Hoffman, who consulted on the initial grant project and facilitated the online and in-person gathering of pastors and lay leaders from our model and mentored congregations, for his enthusiastic support of our initial project and continued words of encouragement and prayers; Dr. Alisa Potter Mee, whom we consulted when preparing our interview questions, for her probing queries about our topic and thoughtful wordsmithing of our questions, and for her review and suggested edits to the appendix on research and design methods; Dr. Laura Wangsness Willemsen, whom we consulted on the craft of "memo writing," i.e., transforming raw interview data into a narrative arc, for her affirmations of our early efforts that gave us confidence to move forward with the book. We thank God for these friends and colleagues, for their generous sharing of time and skills to promote this project, and for their love of Christ's church.

And we give thanks to God for the willing spirit of the pastors, congregations, and laity from the participating congregations, who took a risk and responded affirmatively to an email request seeking help with our research project. Those in the pastoral ministry know well that there is always work enough to do; yet these pastors agreed to open their doors and welcome us into their midst, arranging interviews, following up with folks to track down consent forms, answering questions via emails and phone calls, and reviewing manuscripts for accuracy. Our lives have been enriched throughout the research process and writing of this book, especially by the relationships we now have with these fellow laborers in our Lord's vineyard. We pray that our readers will be as inspired by their stories as we have been.

1

INTRODUCING THE JOURNEY

Audrey, living out her faith by "welcoming the stranger" in her midst, drew Fritz and Dagny toward the path to life in Christ when she befriended this new family on her block in a heavily churched suburban community. Fritz and Dagny began their journey to Jesus when Audrey invited them to St. John's Advent dinners, which eventually led to attending church services. Here they encountered an environment where, in the words of Fritz, "everyone was welcoming" and where they discovered "a good fit for us."[1] When the time came to commit to attending the weekly adult faith formation classes, Audrey smoothed the path of their journey by volunteering to provide childcare, assuring Fritz and Dagny that she would personally care for their son with special needs.

Having been married for more than a decade, Fritz and Dagny's life together had been one without church, without Christ—until they met Audrey. Fritz's childhood church experiences in the Baptist tradition never took hold in his life. Hints that Dagny dropped about her faith journey indicate a more complicated story. She alluded to "baggage" she "carried" about decisions she'd made earlier in her life and questions she had about joining the church. In many ways their story is emblematic of the grim statistics facing faith communities. According to a 2020 Gallup poll, the percentage

---

1. Fritz and Dagny (pseudonyms), interview by Rhoda Schuler, August 8, 2018. All interviews for this project were conducted in confidentiality, and the names of the lay interviewees are withheld according to standard protocols for research on human subjects. Subsequent quotations and summaries of Fritz and Dagny are from this interview, unless otherwise noted.

of adults living in the United States who "have a formal membership with a specific house of worship" (church, synagogue, or mosque) has dropped precipitously in the last two decades from 70 percent to 47 percent.² Although those who self-identify as "Christian" in 2021 remain a majority of the adult population (63 percent), that figure is down significantly in the last decade, when it was 75 percent, according to Pew Research. Protestant denominations of all types are suffering losses; the percentage of the US adult population who self-identify as evangelical Protestants and non-evangelical Protestants both declined by 6 percent between 2007 and 2021.³

When parsed by generations, the quantitative research supports anecdotal stories of devout older Christians who lament the abandonment of the faith by their children and grandchildren. According to the Gallup poll, "31% of millennials have no religious affiliation. . . . Similarly, 33% of the portion of Generation Z that has reached adulthood have no religious preference."⁴ These "nones," those with no religious affiliation, the fastest growing category in surveys about religious identification, were 29 percent of the US adult population in 2021, up from 16 percent in 2007.⁵

This changing religious landscape is the backdrop for our research on the adult catechumenate, which included hearing from Fritz and Dagny about their journey to Jesus through the adult faith formation at St. John. Dagny shared that a private conversation with the pastor had lifted the weight of the "baggage" she carried from earlier in her life. Fritz recounted how the adult faith formation seeped into their home life. When they began to discuss the readings they brought home, it was, he said, "weird—something we weren't used to," to which Dagny added, "Talking about our faith." Because the resources were there, Dagny could initiate the conversations, and that, Fritz said, "took down the barrier" for him. As they shared memories from Fritz's baptism at the Easter Vigil, Dagny called it a "momentous occasion." And then she looked at Fritz and said, "It was a big deal for you to be baptized, [and] something I wanted for a long time." As they spoke of his baptism, Dagny again named Audrey, whose "winsome witness" (to use the words of their pastor) drew them to this faith community.

Their journey to Jesus was one of many that we heard as we interviewed folks from four congregations with strong adult catechumenates.

2. Jones, "U.S. Church Membership Falls Below Majority for First Time."
3. Smith, "About Three-in-Ten U.S. Adults Are Now Religiously Unaffiliated."
4. Jones, "U.S. Church Membership Falls Below Majority for First Time."
5. Smith, "About Three-in-Ten U.S. Adults Are Now Religiously Unaffiliated."

Introducing the Journey

Our research on the practice of adult faith formation is deeply personal yet undertaken for the sake of the church and world. First, the personal side of our research interest. Kent is a member of Generation X, an ordained pastor, and seminary professor; Rhoda is a baby boomer, a consecrated deaconess, and professor emerita at a church-related university. We are both "cradle" Midwestern Lutherans, children of devout parents who handed on the Christian faith through their active membership in Lutheran congregations and faith practices in the home. Experiencing gracious worship practices that communicated the good news of Jesus Christ as youth and young adults led us both into graduate work in the field of liturgical studies. These studies introduced us to the adult catechumenate of the early church, with its many rituals, and to the liturgical reforms of the Second Vatican Council, which found inspiration from the early church as it developed the Rite of Christian Initiation for Adults (RCIA), a program of faith formation that is part of every Roman Catholic parish.[6] As graduate students at different institutions, we met in 1998 at the annual meeting of the North American Academy of Liturgy, forging a friendship based on a mutual passion for worship and liturgy. Yet we also share a commitment to Jesus Christ as Savior of the world and to our denomination as that place where Jesus was made known to us in preaching, teaching, and the sacraments. Thus, our research is ultimately for the sake of the church and the world—the world so beloved by God that God sent his only Son to live in the world and make known the Father and his love—a world full of people like Fritz and Dagny, whose lives were made whole through the proclamation of the good news of Jesus.

To connect with the Fritz and Dagnys of the world today is complicated by our current cultural context, and thus our research is also for the sake of the church, which is called to proclaim the saving message of Jesus to the world. Having experienced firsthand the seismic cultural shifts in North America that have moved the church from a respected part of society to an institution on its margins, viewed by some with suspicion, by others as superfluous, and by yet others with open scorn, we recognize that those serving as pastors and other professional workers in the church, as

---

6. Although the new translation of the Roman Catholic catechumenate (OCIA) is now available, throughout the book we reference the former translation, the *Rite of Christian Initiation of Adults*, and use its familiar acronym, RCIA, for two reasons. First, the parishes we researched, insofar as they referenced or used the RCIA, were using this original translation. Second, the new translation was published after we had submitted our manuscript for publication.

well as students preparing for service in the church, face different challenges and opportunities than we did when we finished our formal training for ministry. To use the language of theologians and religious scholars, we in the West live in a post-Christendom world,[7] a reality that we view as an opportunity to introduce an adult catechumenal process. One of the greatest challenges Christian leaders face in this post-Christendom context is to discover authentic ways of engaging with the world, particularly those generations in which the "nones" predominate. Research indicates that anxiety, fear, loneliness, and isolation are common maladies of our times across age groups, but particularly among millennials and Gen Z.[8] Scott Bruzek, pastor of one of the congregations we studied, frames this challenge as an opportunity. According to Pastor Bruzek, the question people respond to is not "what do you think?" But "how do you feel?" For those who feel anxious, fearful, unloved, and lonely, the good news of Jesus, manifested as the body of Christ in a local congregation, is the remedy. Jesus, the Word made flesh, reveals the God on whom the anxious can "cast all [their] cares" (1 Pet 5:7) and embodies the God who is love (1 John 4:16). The risen Christ, who "lives to silence all our fears,"[9] is found in the Christian community, the antidote for loneliness.

Our knowledge of church history assures us that the twenty-first century is not the first era in which the church was on the margins of society, where Christians were viewed with suspicion and outright scorn. Such was the world of early Christianity, and historians such as Alan Kreider have looked to history for clues and guidance to revive a missional spirit today. Kreider argues that initially "the church grew because it was addressing people's needs and liberating them from the compulsions that were disfiguring their society," offering the lessons of early Christian history as a model for what the church might be today.[10] Asking the question "how

---

7. See, for example, Kreider, *Change of Conversion*; McLeod and Ustorf, eds., *Decline of Christendom*; Murray, *Post-Christendom*.

8. See DeSilver, "Concerns and Challenges of Being a U.S. Teen"; Substance Abuse and Mental Health Services Administration, *Key Substance Use and Mental Health Indicators in the United States*, 31–32. This report shows the steady increase from 2009 through 2019 among the US population ages eighteen to twenty-five experiencing a "major depression episode" (MDE), "any mental illness" (AMI), and "serious mental illness" (SMI). In all three categories, those ages eighteen to twenty-five had the highest percentage of population—MDE: 10.3 percent ; AMI: 30.6 percent; SMI: 8.6 percent.

9. The phrase is the first line from the hymn "I Know that My Redeemer Lives" (stanza five, found in many hymnals).

10. Kreider, *Change of Conversion*, 106–7.

do you feel?" to reveal people's perceived needs and the weight of societal expectations is an opportunity for a missional response on the part of the church, a response that takes place through an adult faith formation process that makes space to explore the questions of those seeking liberation "from the compulsions disfiguring" today's world.

As liturgical scholars, we view the tradition of the adult catechumenate, developed by early Christian leaders, as wisdom to be mined for its riches that can be applied to our similar context. We believe that an adult faith formation process can be an entry point into—or back into—a life of faith in Christian community through both of its major components—catechetical formation and instruction and a strong emphasis on ritual markers throughout the process. Having long understood the power of ritual, we find hope in the major epistemological shift of the last fifty years—a shift away from privileging reason and pure intellectual thought as the way in which humans come to know what is true. We agree with those philosophers who recognize that we come to know what is true and understand who we are and how we relate to the world through "embodied practices."[11] On a mundane level, many will recognize that we "know" how to do many tasks (how to bake cookies, mow a lawn, plant a garden, drive a car) not because we observed others doing these tasks or thought about them, but because we engaged in them ourselves—we embodied these practices and can do them reflexively. The same holds true for the most profound truths about God and all the "ultimate questions" that philosophers and theologians have pondered with their intellects. Embodied practices—for us, Christian rituals—transmit ultimate truths in a more profound way than a theological treatise can. As one ritual theorist and theologian said, "ritual knowledge is . . . corporeal [rather than] cerebral, praxiological rather than speculative, engaged rather than detached."[12]

What follows is an idealized description of an adult catechumenal model based on materials produced by Roman Catholics and Protestants since the Second Vatican Council and inspired by early church literary sources.[13] It is a process that is adaptable to learning styles for adults in

---

11. See, for example, Merleau-Ponty, *Phenomenology of Perception*; Bourdieu, *Logic of Practice*; Johnson, *Meaning of the Body*. For more accessible works, see James K. A. Smith's series, Cultural Liturgies, vol. 1–3, especially volumes 1 and 2, *Desiring the Kingdom* and *Imagining the Kingdom*.

12. Jennings Jr., "On Ritual Knowledge," 332.

13. Contemporary sources include the following: *Rite of Christian Initiation of Adults*; *Go Make Disciples*; *Welcome to Christ: A Lutheran Catechetical Guide*; and *Welcome to*

our current cultural context and one that can make use of rituals to deepen participants' understanding of the faith and to foster a sense of belonging within a Christian community.

In present-day adult faith formation, there are four distinct stages or periods, each punctuated with a public ritual marking one's passage from one stage to the next. The stage of inquiry, as an opportunity for the seeker to begin exploring Christianity and for the church to introduce the seeker to Christ, is a very open-ended and informal period. Its inspiration comes from early church practices when adult baptism was normative, and catechesis, that is, formal instruction in the faith, preceded the rite of baptism, which in many parts of the ancient world took place at the great Vigil of Easter. One fourth-century source describes the first step for those seeking to become catechumens. The writer, Egeria, a pilgrim in Jerusalem, depicts a process in which candidates for baptism appeared with witnesses before the bishop, who examined their character before admitting them to the catechumenate.[14] The contemporary context, as noted earlier, is informal and a time of exploration and questioning for inquirers; in one sense, it is a reversal of the early church pattern—an adaptation that recognizes the lack of trust in institutions by many people today and the desire of the church to bear witness to Christ to those with little understanding of Christianity.

Central to this period are three elements: introduction to the living God in Jesus Christ, to Scripture that bears witness to the Triune God, and to the life of faith, all three of which are experienced within the life of the local congregation. In weekly meetings the catechumenal leaders shape the encounter with the Christian faith on the seekers' terms. It is a period of focused listening on the part of the catechumenal leaders. What questions do the seekers have? What has their spiritual journey looked like? What encounters have they had with the church before this? What are they seeking? This stage allows those questions to be engaged in an encounter with Christ through Scripture. Primary biblical narratives are read and discussed, especially the Gospel accounts appointed in the church's Sunday lectionary, and the seekers are asked to reflect on what they have heard. This allows the catechumenal leaders to listen actively to seekers and then bear witness to Christ in relation to the seekers' response to what they have heard. The experience of the liturgy and the community in action also allow

---

Christ: Lutheran Rites for the Catechumenate. Early church sources include: *Pilgrimage of Egeria*; Cyril of Jerusalem, "Five Catechetical Lectures to the Newly Baptized."

14. *Pilgrimage of Egeria*, 188–89.

Introducing the Journey

opportunities for reflection. What have they seen and experienced in Sunday liturgy and in the community's life together? What sense do they make of it? How does it influence what they are seeking? What does it tell them about God in this community? What questions do they have?

After a period ranging from several weeks to several months, those ready to commit to the full faith formation process are welcomed to the second stage, the catechumenate, through a public rite of welcome in the Sunday assembly, which marks the transition from inquirer or seeker to a new status, that of a catechumen, one who is ready to be instructed in the faith of the church and formed to be a disciple of Jesus Christ by its practices. The ritual in *Welcome to Christ* includes signing of the candidates with the cross and the signing of the other bodily senses, one of the most moving and richly symbolic rites in the entire catechumenal process.[15] This marking indicates that the candidates belong to Christ and are moving toward baptism (or affirmation of baptism), where they will receive the benefits of forgiveness, life, and salvation and be united to Christ. They also begin willingly to answer Christ's call to take up their cross and follow him, learning how to live a life that bears witness to Jesus. The signing of the senses claims every part of the body and all the senses as redeemed by Christ Jesus' passion and resurrection, oriented in service to his kingdom, and directed toward the final renewal in the new heaven and new earth. Because it is witnessed by those assembled for worship, it also draws the whole congregation into this faith formation process as they pray for the catechumens and publicly welcome them into this faith community. The weekly gatherings for faith formation and instruction, involving a lay catechist, sponsors for each catechumen, and the pastor, continue. In the words of one twenty-first-century source, the catechumens have entered an "open-ended period of apprenticeship, and formation in worship, prayer, reflection on scripture, and ministries of service and justice to others in need."[16] Each catechumen, their sponsors, the catechists, and the pastors navigate a path of discernment as to when each catechumen is ready to cross the threshold with the intention of preparing for baptism.

The end of the catechumenate stage is marked by the Rite of Election for Initiation (RCIA) or Enrollment for Candidates for Baptism (*Welcome to Christ*). Early church sources from the fourth and fifth centuries describe this intense time of daily instruction during the forty days of Lent, referring

---

15. *Welcome to Christ: Lutheran Rites*, 9–12.
16. *Go Make Disciples*, 94.

to it as the period of enlightenment.[17] The RCIA has adopted similar language for this third stage: purification and enlightenment. Gathering weekly with their sponsors, catechist, and pastor for study and discussion, "the Elect" seek to purify desires and to be enlightened by the Holy Spirit and formed for a life of faith in Christ lived in community. Formation and instruction in this period are intended to feed and support spiritual preparation. This turn, out of the period of the catechumenate into intense preparation, usually (but not exclusively) during Lent, focuses the Elect on spiritual preparation for baptism and incorporation into the body of Christ.

Go Make Disciples describes this stage as a time for candidates to reflect on their "readiness to renounce self-centeredness and evil and to commit to Christ and his direction in daily life," during which they "bring all of their attitudes, wounds, yearnings, and commitments into the light of Christ." Continued study of God's word leads to "encountering Jesus and accepting his call to belong to the reign of God."[18] This stage is distinguished from the previous one by weekly rituals for candidates with their sponsors in the Sunday liturgy; in addition to a blessing of the candidates, these rituals include presenting to them tangible symbols of the faith (the creed, Lord's Prayer, a worship book) and intercessions for them by the whole community of faith.[19] Supported by their sponsors and the Christian community, the candidates approach the culminating ritual at the Vigil of Easter, mirroring the practice of the early church, when the Vigil lasted throughout the night and concluded at first light—the time of the Christ's resurrection. Many Protestant churches have introduced the Vigil of Easter since its renewal by Roman Catholics in the twentieth century. The baptismal imagery of Romans 6, dying to sin and rising to new life, informs this choice of the Easter Vigil as an optimal time for baptism and affirmation of baptism for the candidates.

The fourth and final stage is called mystagogy, again drawing on the language of the early church, where the focus of this stage was teaching about the "mysteries," or sacraments, as we in the Western church call them. Having experienced baptism or affirmation of baptism in the dramatic setting of the Vigil of Easter and, for some, partaking in the Lord's Supper for

---

17. See, for example, the reference to "candidates for enlightenment" in Procatechesis by Cyril of Jerusalem, quoted in Whitaker, *Documents of the Baptismal Liturgy*, 27.

18. *Go Make Disciples*, 108.

19. *Rite of Christian Initiation of Adults*, 77–122; *Welcome to Christ: Lutheran Rites*, 22–34.

the first time, the mystagogical gatherings are the ideal time to reflect on the meaning of the sacraments for the life of these disciples of Jesus. It is a time to deepen the neophytes' understanding of the faith of the church and to reflect on how one's identity as a Christian informs a person's daily life of witness, worship, fellowship, and service.[20]

Using the Emmaus story (Luke 24) as the paradigm, Bryon Hansen describes a process of "ritual catechesis" for the stage of mystagogy that revolves around these three questions: "What did you experience? What does it mean?" and "What is God now calling you to do about it?"[21] Hansen notes that Ambrose and other early church leaders followed this pattern of *not* explaining the ritual prior to experiencing it. By beginning with the neophytes' experience, the church acknowledges that "we believe that God is at work in persons' lives." If the first question honors the person's experience through which God is working, the second one is the opportunity, in Hansen's words, "to do some solid teaching and exploration of the tradition." Thus, the mystagogy requires leaders who are well trained in Scripture, the rites, and sacramental theology.

As another author points out, the role of "traditional" teaching is most effective in the latter stages of adult faith formation, when "the people who are learning *already love* God," so that the teaching functions to deepen the faith already present in the heart.[22] Reflecting on the ritual experiences and unpacking the depth of sacramental theology and other core Christian beliefs through teaching leads to the final task of mystagogy: guiding the neophytes to explore how God is calling each one to live out their baptismal calling in the world.[23] How does God's call to daily dying and rising in Christ shape a person's relationships with family, friends, and co-workers?[24] How does this calling from God shape work, leisure, and life in Christian community? Where and how is one called to witness to the love of God through Christ in daily life? Thus, good mystagogical reflection will draw the person into patterns of prayer and worship that point one back to the

---

20. For a summary of the stages and rituals, see the chart, "The Stages of the Adult Catechumenate and the Ritual Transitions," 190–91.

21. Hansen, "Emmaus Journey."

22. Macalintal, *Your Parish Is the Curriculum*, 96, emphasis in original.

23. Hansen, "Emmaus Journey."

24. For a rich interpretation of baptism as daily dying and rising, see Luther, *Large Catechism*, 464–67, paras. 64–86.

grace of God given in baptism, to the living water that is always available for cleansing and renewal.

To reach those of all generations who are looking for meaning in their lives, the church is called to build community with and among seekers, to provide catechesis that allows for exploration of questions, and to foster faith formation through ritual. We became convinced of the transformative power of an adult faith formation process not through reading the many resources about the adult catechumenate (ancient or contemporary) but primarily through our case study research. Our study of four Lutheran congregations, each with a robust adult catechumenate, demonstrates the power of this process. Through interactions with the pastors, lay leaders, and participants in the catechumenates and our participation in key liturgical celebrations, we are convinced that this process has the potential not only to form adults into active disciples of Christ but also to bring forth a missional mindset within the congregation, as exemplified by Audrey. She was the first witness of Christ's love to Fritz and Dagny, a witness they experienced again and again at the parish. As Dagny expressed it, "There's something really special about this church; I want to be that way too." Audrey was also a model of service to them, removing the last barrier on their path to discipleship and instilling in them the desire to emulate her life of witness and service. For Dagny especially, the journey meant much more than filling a pew on Sundays; it is, in her words, about "bringing [my faith] into the world," just as Audrey had done for them.

We make no claims of a magic bullet to save declining congregations, nor do we offer a step-by-step "program" to implement an adult catechumenate in congregations. Instead, our research has led us to be descriptive, not prescriptive; we narrate stories of individual lives changed and of congregations with an ethos of outreach in order to inspire pastors and other church professionals committed to making disciples to think in new ways. We tell the stories of four very different congregations in different types of communities served by pastors with differing gifts. While there are several commonalities, such as strong pastoral care and a commitment by the pastor and whole congregation to the adult catechumenate, our primary finding is the contextual nature of the adult faith formation process in each congregation. We tell these inspiring individual stories of faith formation and present the missional mindset of congregations in the hope that the creative power of the Spirit will spark imaginative thinking among pastors, other church professionals, and lay leaders.

Introducing the Journey

Although the research is descriptive, all the congregations are deeply engaged in that which is prescriptive, according to Christ Jesus. All of the congregations are committed to following the Great Commission, making lifelong disciples by baptizing and teaching; they are committed to his new commandment to love one another as Christ has loved them and to lift up the Crucified One, who promises to draw all people to himself.

INTRODUCTION TO PART I
Context Is Everything

Our research at four congregations with a robust adult catechumenate supports the claim of Paul Hoffman, whose book describes the adult catechumenate in a Lutheran congregation located in the northwest United States. Hoffman asserts that a strong adult faith formation process not only forms the faith of individuals but also that of the whole congregation.[1] Our research has revealed the contextual quality of this process; each of the four congregations, under the leadership of their pastors, has developed an adult faith formation process that is unique to the history and size of the congregation, to the gifts and skills of the pastor, and that is shaped by the socioeconomic and demographic makeup of each congregation and the community in which it is located. In Part I we introduce the four Lutheran congregations we visited and studied.

To develop a taxonomy for our findings, we have drawn on the research and language of two scholars, Alan Kreider and Diana Butler Bass. Kreider describes conversion in the early church as "a process of multidimensional change" that "involved changes in *belonging, belief, and behavior*—in the context of an experience of God that . . . for some people must have been very powerful."[2] Butler Bass, a church historian who studies trends in contemporary American culture, uses the Gospels to argue that just as *belonging* preceded *believing* in the lives of those whom Jesus encountered, so our current cultural context calls Christians to follow the same missional pattern. "Christianity," she writes, "began with an invitation

---

1. Hoffman, *Faith Forming Faith*, 5.
2. Kreider, *Change of Conversion*, xv, emphasis added.

Introduction to Part I: Context is Everything

into friendship, into creating a new community, into forming relationships based on love and service."[3]

Located in the highly educated and strongly churched community of Wheaton, Illinois, St. John Lutheran Church is the subject of chapter 2, "Drawing People into Christ's Orbit through Pastoral Care." Pastor Bruzek, senior pastor of a ministry team with three ordained leaders, has crafted an adult faith formation process that dovetails with the well-organized pastoral care work distinctive of this congregation. After weathering a difficult and contentious period in the congregation's history, Pastor Bruzek has emphasized love as the "primary virtue" that defines the congregation. In this affluent community where "people feel a need to keep up appearances," the pastors strive to love and serve the members of the flock so that people can be free to voice their vulnerabilities to their shepherds. In a community that measures success by wealth and prestige, living out the grace of God through pastoral care is one way to express this primary virtue.

Pastor Bruzek has shaped an adult catechumenate around "Scripture, prayer, liturgy and Eucharist, tithing and alms, and thorough mercy and a winsome witness" that resonates with the well-educated population drawn to St. John's. As the lead teacher for the faith formation classes, he has structured the class around the liturgy, bringing resources from contemporary culture, theological and philosophical history, and literary works to his teaching. The faith formation process leads with the love of God in Christ for sinful humanity that moves people to faith in Christ and love of neighbor.

The title of Chapter 3, "Heart-to-Heart Combat against Sin, Death, and the Power of the Devil," reflects both classic Lutheran language and the social context of Living Faith Lutheran Church, Cumming, Georgia. Pastor Timothy Droegemueller challenges individual and corporate sin and frequently uses colorful binary language to contrast those who are part of the kingdom of God from those who are still part of "the devil's playground." Such language resonates with people living in the Bible Belt, attracting many new disciples to this congregation that was a mission started in 1999 and has grown to over three hundred baptized members.[4]

3. Butler Bass, *Christianity after Religion*, 205.

4. The language of spiritual combat and battle used throughout chapter 3 is reflective of the language that Pastor Droegemueller and Living Faith use in their catechumenate. It should not be interpreted in a geopolitical or physical sense. It references Christian engagement in the spiritual realm for a life of faith. It is a spiritual battle for trust in God and for the spiritually generated behavior that flows from that faith.

INTRODUCTION TO PART I: CONTEXT IS EVERYTHING

Over a decade ago Pastor Droegemueller began using a discipleship formation process aligned with the ancient catechumenate, borrowing the outline of the process and language of its stages from a book by Arthur Just.[5] The process begins with weekly gatherings that engage participants first in the study of Scripture, recognizing that many people in the community already accept the Bible as authoritative in their lives. In the season of Epiphany, they study Martin Luther's *Small Catechism* as the basis for separation from life outside of Christ to life in Christ. Introducing adult catechumens to the basics of Lutheran theology early in the process is important in an area of the United States where Lutherans are not a dominant denomination, and illustrates the priority of believing in the faith formation process of this congregation.

The essential theme of their catechumenate and congregational life is heart-to-heart combat. Catechumenal formation leads those incorporated into congregational life to ongoing, lifelong learning that shapes life in Christ and prepares neophytes for the spiritual battle to bear witness to Christ in the world. Central to Pastor Droegemueller's teaching and preaching is the language of Psalm 1, which sets forth the choice of two ways, the way of sinners, leading to death, and the way of the righteous, which comes through faith in Christ. His theology resonates with this middle-class community, many of whom are seeking theological clarity and certainty in a changing cultural landscape.

Chapter 4, "Creating a Sense of Belonging," describes the adult catechumenate at St. Mary's Lutheran Church, located in a working-class neighborhood in the northeastern area of the US, which is attracting younger families because of affordable housing and good schools. As the smallest of the congregations we researched (average weekly attendance of seventy-two, pre-pandemic), St. Mary's, with a century of history in its community, was introduced to an innovative process of adult faith formation by Pastor M, a new seminary graduate, during her first year as their pastor. To assist with the staffing of the catechumenal process, Pastor M recruited a longtime lay member of the congregation, Pearl, with a deep commitment for sharing the gospel.

Blessed with an accessible preaching style and warm down-to-earth presence, Pastor M touched the hearts of members and new visitors alike. The occasional visitors were drawn into the faith formation process led by the team that brought together Pastor M's youthful energy and warmth

---

5. Just Jr., *Heaven on Earth*; see chapter 8.

Introduction to Part I: Context is Everything

with Pearl's wisdom and teaching skills. The early stages of the catechumenal process were constructed to listen to the stories of the participants, building trust and community within the group, and modeling prayer for one another. During the latter stage in the season of Lent, they all participated in weekly rituals during the Sunday worship that introduced them publicly and cemented a sense of belonging between catechumens and congregation.

As a smaller congregation, the intergenerational catechumenal team mirrored the makeup of the catechumens, who ranged from millennials to members of the Greatest Generation. The faith formation process fostered a sense of belonging across the typical generational divides, as the participants were formed into lifelong disciples of Jesus Christ.

Chapter 5, titled "Receiving, Teaching, Celebrating, and Sharing Christ Jesus," unfolds the riches of faith formation at Redeemer Evangelical Lutheran Church. Located in the Bronx, one of the poorest and most ethnically diverse zip codes in New York City, Redeemer congregation brings together gracious liturgy, gospel-oriented preaching, and well-structured adult and youth faith formation that equips these saints of God to survive and thrive in all walks of life and throughout all stages of faith development. In an ever-changing community where many struggle with day-to-day existence, Redeemer Evangelical Lutheran Church and its staff, Pastor Taylor and Deaconess Rojas, offer stability—Pastor Taylor has served Redeemer since 2001—and hope in Christ, whose life of prayer and works of healing connect with the needs and longings of many in the Bronx.

In a context where many rarely encounter beauty and grace, the faith formation process at Redeemer marks each stage in the catechumenal process with robust rituals that set apart the participants from destructive ways of living and mark them as ones claimed by Christ crucified. Liturgy, as the core of Redeemer's identity—with a minimum of five full services every week—is the source that creates and nurtures community. Thus, there is a natural synergy between the rituals that mark the catechumens' transitions from one stage of the process to the next and the rich liturgical life of the whole congregation, which witnesses and participates with joy in the faith journey of those who are on the road to discipleship.

A visit to each of these four congregations on a Sunday would reveal differences in styles of worship, preaching, and communal expressions—all part of the contextualization of the ministry in these disparate congregations. But they share a commitment to a holistic faith formation process

Introduction to Part I: Context is Everything

that has shaped the missional ethos of each congregation in similar ways. We invite the reader to delve deeper into the narrative of each congregation, told from the perspective of the pastoral and lay leaders and of those who were formed into a pattern of lifelong discipleship through the adult catechumenate at St. John, Living Faith, St. Mary's, and Redeemer congregations.

2

ST. JOHN

Drawing People into Christ's Orbit through Pastoral Care

Implicitly referencing the Great Commission (Matt 28:18–19), Pastor Scott Bruzek, senior pastor at St. John Lutheran Church since 1997, declared, "We don't need more members; but we definitely need more disciples."[1] If the Great Commission is the goal, Jesus' "New Commandment" to "love one another as I have loved you" (John 13:34) is the means to attain that goal, shaping the ethos of St. John Lutheran Church and serving as the guiding principle for adult faith formation. Pastor Bruzek, speaking broadly about St. John's adult catechumenate, first discussed the classic method of catechesis, which emphasizes passing on the content of the Christian faith. Rather than this narrow "data dump" approach, he asked, "How can [the catechumens] have an experience where they feel completely loved, welcomed?" He revealed the deeper context of that statement at one of our virtual conferences on adult faith formation, saying, "When I was young, we used to ask people what they thought; now people ask, 'How do you feel?'" People today respond that they feel "empty, lost, broken, listless, betrayed, miserable, angry, loveless, afraid, victimized,

---

1. Rev. Dr. Scott Bruzek, interview by Rhoda Schuler, August 8, 2018. Subsequent quotations and summaries of Pastor Bruzek are from this interview, unless otherwise noted.

Part I: Context is Everything

alienated, oppressed, in despair"—all of which can be compressed into the statement "I feel alone and unloved."[2]

The adult catechumenate at St. John is only one way—albeit a primary one—through which the pastors and church leaders model faithfulness to Jesus' command to "love one another" in their flock, creating a sense of belonging that fills the void of being alone and unloved. When asked to name three words or phrases that describe the congregation, Pastor Bruzek first responded, "We focus on love as the primary virtue." Like the gravitational pull of a star on a planet, the love of God, experienced through the pastors and the preschool director[3] at St. John, draws people into orbit around the Sun of Righteousness, Jesus Christ; in the congregation's catechumenal process, those drawn into this orbit explore more deeply the love of God in Christ and the faith of the church in its Lutheran expression. Commenting on what made Pastor Bruzek's catechetical teaching meaningful, Susan referenced the prodigal son, and continued by saying, it was the "teaching that I am loved" that made a profound impact on her. "Everything," she said, is "seen through the lens that God loves you; God touches you and chooses you."[4]

Describing the pastoral team, George declared, "It's love with a capital L."[5] For twenty-five years the gravitational effect of God's love embodied through the preaching, teaching, and pastoral care at St. John has drawn people into the catechumenate, birthing a congregational ethos where love truly is "the primary virtue." To trace the power of God's love transforming catechumens into disciples who "love one another," this chapter will 1) describe the context of the community of Wheaton, Illinois, note some important pastoral practices at St. John Lutheran Church, and provide a brief taxonomy of those interviewed; 2) discuss the central role of pastoral care in relation to the four stages of the catechumenate, followed by a section that hypothesizes the role of the Easter Vigil in the catechumenal process; 3) explore the catechetical classes from the perspective of the

---

2. "Painting a Vision for Forming Lutheran Christians," panel discussion with Pastors Scott Bruzek, Timothy Droegemueller, and Dien Ashley Taylor, October 20–22, 2020.

3. The role of the preschool teacher, Val Gaede, is discussed in greater detail in chapters 6 and 8.

4. Susan (pseudonym), interview by Rhoda Schuler, August 7, 2018. Subsequent quotations and summaries of Susan are from this interview, unless otherwise noted.

5. George and Gail (pseudonyms), interview by Rhoda Schuler, January 20, 2019. Subsequent quotations and summaries of George and Gail are from this interview, unless otherwise noted.

participants to highlight the core value of passing on the content of the Christian beliefs (in their Lutheran expression). This section focuses on "the Friendlies," a term coined by Pastor Bruzek for those who, after completing the catechumenal process, have found such treasures therein that the wisdom of the catechetical teaching has drawn them back to the classes a second and even third time. The chapter continues with a discussion of worship life at St. John, showing the importance of the Sunday liturgy in the catechetical process, particularly for the stage of mystagogy. To return to the theme of "love as the primary virtue" comes the story of Keith, whose comments on the Holy Thursday liturgy at St. John created an opening to delve into this powerful ritual moment of Jesus' sacrificial love for salvation of the world as experienced by other "catechumens." If Jesus' command to "make disciples" governs the shape of the catechumenate, its corollary is the summary of St. John's unofficial mission statement: "making disciples and making them stronger,"[6] illustrated with narratives of "the Friendlies" who chart their course from "catechumens" to disciples who "love because he first loved us" (1 John 4:19). We conclude with a reflection on the three BEs of conversion, believing, behaving, and belonging.

ST. JOHN LUTHERAN CHURCH IN WHEATON, AN "EVANGELICAL ENCLAVE"

Wheaton, a well-established and well-heeled suburb of Chicago,[7] is home to Wheaton College, an evangelical institution founded in 1860, that is respected both by the evangelical community and those outside it. Its presence defines this suburb, according to author and pastor Jason Byassee, as an "evangelical enclave,"[8] one that is also highly educated. Among people twenty-five years old and older, over 94 percent have completed high school; nearly two-thirds (64.5 percent) have a bachelor's degree or higher.[9] Pastor Bruzek described the community as "very churched" when

---

6. Quoted both by Pastors Buchs and Bruzek.

7. According to the 2020 US Census Bureau, the median household income is $108,737; the population is around 53,000, and it is racially homogeneous, with 82.1 percent of the population reported as "White alone"; 7.1 percent as Hispanic or Latino; 6.6 percent as Asian; 6 percent as "Two or more races"; and 3.5 percent as "Black or African American alone"; "QuickFacts: Wheaton (city), Illinois."

8. Byassee, "From the Sacristy," 168.

9. "QuickFacts: Wheaton (city), Illinois."

he first came to Wheaton but "less so now." As a "bounded community," it is stable with some growth. With three full-time pastors (at the time of our research) and about five hundred family units, the staff of St. John has developed a disciplined and effective means of tracking church attendance and connecting with members and visitors. Thirty minutes prior to each Sunday liturgy, all three pastors are vested and at the doors of the gathering space, welcoming people as they enter. Like many congregations, St. John has attendance folders in every pew, and people attending Sunday worship—members and visitors—are asked to register their name; visitors also provide contact information; and people also use the form to register to receive Holy Communion that day.

The office is closed on Monday, but by Tuesday morning all the information from the registration forms has been recorded into the database, and each pastor has access to the attendance list. They go through it and make additions of those with whom they spoke (but didn't sign the registration form), thus increasing the accuracy of the attendance database, which is programmed to generate reports of families who have been absent for several weeks.[10] The pastoral staff then follows up with these families. On the one hand, as one who was deeply impacted by Orwell's *1984* in high school, I was more than a little creeped out by this "Big Brother" system of tracking attendance; but on the other hand, I was won over to this practice by the multitude of positive comments from interviewees of the attentive pastoral care at St. John. The database is also used to generate another weekly list: Each pastor receives the names and addresses of ten family units and each handwrites a personal note to those families that week. Over the course of a calendar year, each family unit receives three personal notes from their pastors. Technology is neither inherently good nor evil but can be used to promote one or the other. St. John uses its database for good; the ultimate goal is to remind all that they are loved and not alone.

Those interviewed for our research included three paid staff: two of the three full-time pastors (the third was on sabbatical when I visited) and the preschool director; and fifteen people who had completed or were currently in the catechumenal process (three individuals, and six couples). Everyone interviewed in the latter group of "catechumens" falls into one of four categories: "cradle" LCMS folks, all of whom were required to complete

---

10. The database is programed with information about each family unit's regular attendance pattern. Pastor David Buchs, interview by Rhoda Schuler, July 24, 2018. Subsequent quotations and summaries of Pastor Buchs are from this interview, unless otherwise noted.

the six-month catechumenal process;[11] evangelical Christians, from the plethora of evangelicals in and around the community of Wheaton; those with connections to the Roman Catholic Church, who find continuity between their prior worship experiences and St. John's weekly Eucharist and traditional liturgy; and finally, some "nones," whose spouse or partner fits into one of the other categories. Fritz and Dagny, whose story was told in the introduction, illustrate this pattern.

STAGES OF THE CATECHUMENATE: LIMINAL MOMENTS OF PASTORAL CARE

Many who were interviewed either named pastoral care or the pastors themselves as a strength of the congregation, or described a way in which one or more of the pastors made them feel welcomed or provided spiritual care to them. Dennis, a cradle LCMS Lutheran, said that he has "had many pastors—these pastors are exceptional—all three."[12] Unlike St. Mary's or Redeemer Lutheran, which are rich in rituals that mark the transitions between the stages of the catechumenate, St. John has no public ritual of welcome, no ritual of signing a "book of the Elect," no presentation of creed, hymnal, or other symbol of Christian discipleship. Baptisms, confirmations, and reception of members are done at the Easter Vigil, marking the end of the third stage of the adult catechumenate. Instead of public rituals, the transitions—the liminal moments that mark the passage from one stage to another—are woven into the pastoral care patterns and the usual ebb and flow of a congregation's calendar.

The stage of inquiry, that open-ended and informal period, is ongoing, deliberate, and centered in pastoral care. As people visit Sunday worship, make a connection to St. John through family and friends, or enroll a child in the preschool, family units are added to the [Big Brother] database in the category of "prospects." One or more of the pastors will form a relationship

---

11. Not all LCMS folks who express interest in joining St. John are willing to do this; they find another church home. Ken and Phyllis reported that their first response to this requirement was "Are you kidding?" Ken noted that the requirement is "part intentional—if it's too onerous, St. John is not for you." Ken and Phyllis (pseudonyms), interview by Rhoda Schuler, August 8, 2018. Subsequent quotations and summaries of Ken and Phyllis are from this interview, unless otherwise noted.

12. Grace and Dennis (pseudonyms), interview by Rhoda Schuler, January 20, 2019. Subsequent quotations and summaries of Grace and Dennis are from this interview, unless otherwise noted.

PART I: Context is Everything

with the family; all make an effort to know people by name—a practice noted by several interviewees[13]—and to find ways to connect them with others at St. John. One couple recalled being invited to the pastor's home for dinner with other couples of their generation; a woman with children commented that it was easy to find friends through the many programs and activities for mothers and young families; Pastor Bruzek linked a retired person with a working group that oversees maintenance projects in the facility.[14] Curt and Lucille, who came from a large evangelical church, spoke of the contrast between that congregation, where pastoral care is done by assistant pastors and lay leaders, and St. John, where, as Lucille said, the "pastors know you, provide care." In naming three strengths of the congregation, Curt said, "The pastoral care is phenomenal," noting that all three pastors know the names of the members.

These connections are made and strengthened continuously, and when the typical summer hiatus from "regular" church activities ends in September, those on the "prospective" list are invited (through various means, including personal emails, announcements in the newsletter, and face-to-face conversations) to join the adult catechumenate that meets on Saturday mornings from early/mid-October until Easter. In the words of Pastor Bruzek, St. John's catechumenal process works well because it "draws the deeply wounded and the really committed" and "because people *love* enough." The invitation stresses the low stakes involved; in his conversations with people contemplating the adult catechumenate, Pastor Bruzek declares, "We date before we kiss."[15] That is, come and see; get to know St. John and its pastors; learn what being a disciple means, why the congregation worships as it does, and what the LCMS believes before making a

13. Curt and Lucille (pseudonyms), interview by Rhoda Schuler, August 8, 2018; they were impressed that Pastor Buchs knew the names of scores of students at the Sunday school opening for kindergartners through third graders. Subsequent quotations and summaries of Curt and Lucille are from this interview, unless otherwise noted. Grace and Dennis felt very welcomed by Pastor Buchs because he remembered their names on their second visit.

14. Gail and George; Susan; Keith (pseudonym), interview by Rhoda Schuler, August 7, 2018. Subsequent quotations and summaries of Keith are from this interview, unless otherwise noted.

15. Said by him in our interview; also quoted by Lester and Nancy (in unison, followed by laughter), an indication of his common use of this phrase in connection with the adult catechumenate. Lester and Nancy (pseudonyms), interview by Rhoda Schuler, August 8, 2018. Subsequent quotations and summaries of Lester and Nancy are from this interview, unless otherwise noted.

commitment. And he adds, "If you decide this isn't the place for you, you get to keep the donuts."[16]

With only public announcements to the congregation and without any public ritual in the worshiping community, the second stage, the catechumenate, begins with little fanfare on a Saturday morning in the fall. Sessions last for ninety minutes, with breakfast and childcare provided. Even before people commit to attending the classes, they are "under the care" of the pastors, who are available for family emergencies and for spiritual counsel.[17] Several people shared the affirming quality of this spiritual counsel. Gail reported that she felt "safe talking [with Pastor Buchs] about my doubt and challenges. I never felt like I would be rejected." Katherine, whose ex-fiancé was also attending the catechumenate classes, told me that because Pastor Buchs "wants to understand our story," he met separately with them to hear each one's perspective.[18] Dagny also shared that a pastoral conversation had lifted the weight of "baggage" she had carried for some time.[19] Dennis described Pastor Buchs as his "confessor," seeking the pastor's counsel about his prayer life and the application of Scripture in daily life.

Those attending the classes are also expected to attend Sunday worship, and in most cases have already been regularly participating in the weekly service of word and sacrament. Attendance tracking by the database flags families when there are changes in attendance patterns, so that one of the pastors can reach out, as such a change often indicates the need for pastoral care.[20] One couple in the catechumenal process commented that the

---

16. Pastor Bruzek's words here were quoted by Curt and Lucille.

17. Ken and Phyllis quoted Pastor Bruzek as saying, "If you commune here, you're under our pastoral care." Pastor Buchs said something similar in his interview. For clarification, Pastor Bruzek wrote, "Our way of saying it is: If you are willing to come under our care, then we are willing to be your pastors—for as long as it takes—through the Catechumenate—and beyond—even if that means going through it a time or two (the record is 4 times!—and he did finally join!)—but we also need to teach most folks what it means for me to be a pastor and for them to have a pastor—we are not ecclesiastical vending machines—but we are those willing to care for your soul—with all that this means." Email to Rhoda Schuler, January 26, 2023.

18. Katherine (pseudonym), interview by Rhoda Schuler, January 19, 2019. Subsequent quotations and summaries of Katherine are from this interview, unless otherwise noted.

19. Fritz and Dagny (pseudonyms), interview by Rhoda Schuler, August 8, 2018. Subsequent quotations and summaries of Fritz and Dagny are from this interview, unless otherwise noted.

20. Pastor David Buchs, who stated, "It's a system meant to attend to those who are not present."

pastors "always notice when we're not here," and that because of their child's health issues they "sometimes miss several weeks." But, she continued, "we always hear from them when we miss."[21]

Admittance to the Lord's Supper illustrates both the centrality of pastoral care to the adult catechumenate and the flexible approach at St. John. Those raised in and confirmed by the LCMS are welcomed to the Lord's table immediately (Dennis and Grace reported communing on their first visit); conversation with one of the pastors is the path leading to reception of the Lord's Supper for others.[22] Lucille, whose background is evangelical, reported that after sitting in with her sons' first communion instruction, she was invited to the eucharistic table because, in her words, the pastors had "decided I knew enough and could commune." Susan's narrative is similar. Pastor Bruzek initiated a conversation with her, confirming that because she "believes this is the body of Christ," she would be welcome at the table. For others—a minority of those interviewed (Fritz and Dagny; Gail and George)—first communion took place at the Vigil. Unlike the Roman Catholic RCIA, where the normative practice of the "first communion" is a shared experience by all catechumens and candidates at the Easter Vigil, this liminal moment for most at St. John is not a public ritual but a private, pastoral meeting that culminates for the individual on the next Sunday by coming forward with the whole assembly to the altar. Susan reported that friends she had made said to her, "I saw you took communion today," a comment that gave her a sense of belonging.

A similar pastoral practice marks the transition from the catechumenate stage to the third stage, purification and enlightenment, as described by those interviewed. There is no change in the teaching methods or content covered in the Saturday morning class time, but during Lent, the pastors have conversations with individuals and couples in the process. For Susan, that conversation happened earlier, when she was admitted to the Lord's Supper; she remembered Pastor Bruzek saying, "If you're still around," that is, if you plan to go through reception into formal church membership at the Vigil, there were "certain expectations" of membership; she reported "tithing, attending regularly, and acts of mercy" as examples. Ken and Phyllis recalled "paperwork" that had to be completed for those

---

21. Gail and George, confirming the practice described by Pastor Buchs.

22. Regarding reception of the Lord's Supper: the Sunday bulletin "encourages" visitors who are LCMS members "to commune. Other guests wishing to join our confession and receive this Holy Sacrament are asked to meet with a pastor in the weeks before communing for the first time." Sunday worship folder, July 25, 2021, 13.

"becoming members." They also noted that not everyone who participates in the catechumenal classes opts into full membership, describing a split decision for one couple—one person officially joined St. John but the spouse did not.[23] It seems that Pastor Bruzek's assurance (as reported by Ken and Phyllis) that "it's fine either way" is perceived as genuine and the process is "low pressure," enveloped in pastoral care.

Celebrating the Easter Vigil as the ritual transition from the third to the final stage of the catechumenal process, mystagogy, is standard practice in Roman Catholic parishes and most Protestants congregations with a similar adult faith formation model. Although St. John celebrates the Easter Vigil, baptizing children and adults, confirming youth, and receiving adults into membership, one might argue that St. John has no final stage, no mystagogy. The catechumenal classes end before the Easter season of the church year begins, and those who gathered for six months on Saturday mornings never reconvene as a group. If there is no "fourth stage" to St. John's adult catechumenate, this reality begs the question, how does the Vigil function for these adult catechumens?

VIGIL OF EASTER: THE QUEEN OF FEASTS

Although most interviewees described the Vigil of Easter as a major service at St. John, they remembered few, if any, details of the liminal rituals traditionally associated with the catechumenate (baptism, adult confirmation, and reception into membership) at the Vigil.[24] Ken's comment may explain why; he described the whole Vigil as "98 percent high feast day, 2 percent acceptance of new members," which was a ritual that took "less than five minutes." The comments of others about the Vigil echo a similar sentiment, and some included comments about the party afterwards. Phyllis (Ken's wife) said that the Vigil "*is as high as Easter* [Sunday morning], higher than Christmas" (emphasis added). When asked what made the greatest impression on them, Curt replied, "the liturgy and the way it's done well here," and Lucille added, "Then there's a big party; they ran out of cake." Susan, who

23. Those who continue to attend remain "under the pastoral care" of the staff. The ritual for membership at the Vigil is to become a voting member of the congregation.

24. As the interviewer—and one with a strong interest in ways that ritual shapes the theology of participants—I often gave additional prompts to draw out people's memories of the rite associated with the catechumenal process at the Vigil. My interpretation here is based on the paucity of details in spite of my efforts to elicit more information from interviewees.

sang at the Vigil, could articulate more details of the service, although she remembered little about the baptism of her own children. She also spoke of the totality of the service, recalling the movement of the service "from darkness to light," noting the engagement of "all the senses" and "the triumphant music" heralding the resurrection at the end. Of the post-vigil party she said, "It's lavish, [celebrating] *the biggest day of the year*, with kegs of beer and wine" (emphasis added)—a bit of a surprise, she shared, for someone raised in an evangelical tradition and who had had no alcohol at her wedding reception.

If the first part of Ken's comment ("98 percent high feast day . . .") encapsulates the impression of many, the second part of Ken's comment—"2 percent acceptance of new members"—is echoed in details of the Vigil from Keith. He had few concrete, specific memories of the Vigil, saying he "just became a member" and it was "a nice service; then a party after." As if to emphasize the "membership" side of the ritual, Keith also recalled Pastor Bruzek jokingly saying to him, "You got the secret handshake and now you can enter." If few experienced the ritual at which they officially became voting members of the congregation as meaningful or memorable, perhaps this is a deliberate shaping of the Vigil service, one reflecting the opening words of this chapter: "We don't need more members; but we definitely need more disciples."

A deeper look at the catechetical teaching and the worship life of St. John will reveal ways in which the unfolding of "the mysteries"—the sacramental life of the church—is integral to the third stage, the catechumenal classes. We turn first to descriptions of the catechetical classes developed over twenty-five years by Pastor Bruzek, a master teacher.

CATECHESIS: BELIEFS THAT RESOUND IN THE EAR

"Ted Talks for Lutherans," the phrase Ken and Phyllis dropped to describe the catechetical teaching of Pastor Bruzek, is a synecdoche for a style of teaching that is lecture-based, polished, engaging, and content-rich in Lutheran theology. But even that phrase does not capture all the nuances of this master teacher. Unlike a recorded Ted Talk, Pastor Bruzek encourages questions and uses a vast array of resources from church fathers, art, poetry, rap music, newspaper articles and opinion writings, cartoons, and everyday examples to illustrate his teaching.[25] When I asked Curt and Lucille about

---

25. Some items listed here were named by Phyllis; Ken added that these resources "make you realize how Christianity is working everywhere."

the curriculum used, they collectively burst out in laughter, saying that Pastor Bruzek "uses a million disconnected handouts; there's a table like this [referring to the six-foot long one at which we were seated] with piles . . ." But there *is* a curriculum, Luther's *Small Catechism*,[26] unfolded through the framework of the Sunday liturgy, as Pastor Bruzek himself told me, and as some participants recognized. Curt commented that Bruzek "goes through the Catechism, but not everybody knows it." Ken and Phyllis recognized that the classes are "structured around the liturgy."[27]

Curt and Lucille also described his teaching as "very natural; very conversational"; and Curt commented that Pastor Bruzek is "very intelligent but presents it in an easy way." Nancy spoke of his ability to break down the complex, making it easier to understand; she also said that he repeats ideas "so they stick with you. He makes it fun." Phyllis quoted Pastor Bruzek: "The only simplicity to be trusted is that on the far side of complexity." Continuing to quote him, she said, "If you can't say it in five words or less, you don't know what you're talking about." The picture painted by these three couples ("the Friendlies") reveals a knowledgeable teacher with specific learning goals, a multitude of resources from which to draw, and the ability to "read the room," adjusting his style and content to his audience.[28] Curt and Lucille, coming from an evangelical background, said much the same thing: Pastor Bruzek is "willing to go off script, based on the needs of the group." They gave the example of Pastor Bruzek providing a more thorough review of Lutheran baptismal theology for the sake of evangelicals in the room. They continued, "He doesn't bash other denominations," but makes "clear distinctions" about "why we believe what we believe." Lester used the word "organic" to describe Bruzek's teaching style.

Others also commented on specific content from the classes. George stated that he heard "a lot of law" in the tradition in which he was raised,

---

26. Martin Luther's *Small Catechism* was first published in 1529 as a pamphlet; it was often included in other publications such as hymnals, Bibles, and prayer books. Its "Six Chief Parts" are the Ten Commandments, Apostles' Creed, Lord's Prayer, Baptism, the Lord's Supper, and (added in 1531) Confession and Absolution. The format is Q & A, and Luther's explanations are brief, accessible, and yet profound. It remains the primary catechetical "textbook" in Lutheran churches throughout the world nearly five hundred years after its first publication and is included in the confessional writings subscribed to by Lutheran pastors.

27. This is an accurate statement, confirmed in Pastor Bruzek's interview. He also said that the first three weeks cover the invocation and confession and absolution, the liturgical sections that begin the Sunday liturgy.

28. The phrase in quotations marks was said by Ken.

but, he said, in the teaching and preaching at St. John he hears a "good law/gospel balance."[29] The staying power of Pastor Bruzek's use of materials from contemporary culture is illustrated by one lesson, recounted in two separate interviews. Both Susan and the couple, Lester and Nancy, described a cartoon of roadkill (a dead raccoon, according to Lester and Nancy) with the caption "Get well soon." Susan unfolded this image, saying that it drove home the "total depravity" of the human condition, that "you're dead in sin." Lester said the same, adding that you "can't make yourself better," to which Nancy added, "Jesus does it to you." A cradle LCMS Lutheran, she went on to quote from the confession of sins in the LCMS hymnal ("We are by nature sinful and unclean . . .") and from Luther's *Small Catechism* ("I believe that I cannot by my own reason or strength believe in Jesus Christ my Lord or come to him . . ."). Nancy also recalled playing "phone tag" to illustrate the importance of creeds that pass on the faith of the church, "so teachings don't drift off" course. After Lester had commented at length on Pastor Bruzek's gifts as a teacher, Nancy, verbalizing the St. John ethos of love, spontaneously added, "We love him." Keith also affirmed his teaching skills, commenting that Pastor Bruzek can interject humor, Scripture, and everyday living into teaching, which is his "greatest gift."

As a master teacher, Pastor Bruzek connects well with his audience, responds to their needs, and communicates the content of the faith (*fides quae*) effectively while also deepening the personal faith (*fides qua*), the faith of the heart of participants. Susan's experience epitomizes the power of Pastor Bruzek's catechetical teaching. When asked what had been most beneficial for her faith formation from the pastor, her first response was "his teaching that I'm loved." Earlier in the interview she had spoken of the "works righteousness" she had picked up in her life, naming societal expectations and her evangelical upbringing as sources of this disordered theology. One Saturday she missed the class; but she shared that the next week, while she was substitute teaching in the public school system, she used her lunch break to watch the video recording of the missed class. To do so was, she said, "such a gift."

---

29. In the Lutheran tradition, a law/gospel hermeneutic is the key to scriptural interpretation. George had prior exposure to this peculiar Lutheran term as an undergraduate at an LCMS university.

LITURGY AND/AS CATECHESIS: UNFOLDING THE SACRAMENTAL MYSTERIES

In contrast with many LCMS congregations, St. John Lutheran Church offers Holy Communion at every service on every Sunday.[30] But its practice of "daily Eucharist" at 7:40 AM from Tuesday through Friday (the church is closed on Mondays) mark the congregation as an outlier in the denomination.[31] Clearly, the centrality of the sacraments is a presupposition in the congregational life of St. John, and—because the structure of the catechetical classes is the Sunday liturgy—this weekly liturgy of word and sacrament is part of the ongoing, imbedded "stage" of mystagogy. The rite of confession and absolution typically follows the entrance hymn—and this first part of the liturgy is the topic that opens catechetical classes in the fall.[32] That the sacrament of baptism can "replace" the rite of confession and absolution[33] indicates a faithfulness to baptismal theology, for Luther claims that "baptism . . . comprehends also the third sacrament, formerly called penance, which is really nothing else than baptism. . . . If you live in repentance, therefore, you are walking in baptism."[34] Thus, every Sunday liturgy encompasses both sacraments, and the mystagogical unpacking of their meaning is an ongoing part of the catechetical teaching.

St. John is also a liturgical "outlier" by the formality of the Sunday worship (what some would characterize as "high church"), which begins each Sunday with a procession of vested clergy and lay leaders and ends with their procession out of the nave, both led by the crucifer. There are no screens or projectors in the sanctuary, and the liturgy is uninterrupted by

---

30. Through the influence of ecumenical liturgical renewal and faithfulness to the Lutheran Confessions, the trend in LCMS congregations for the last sixty years has been to offer the Lord's Supper more frequently—from four times a year early in the twentieth century; to once a month by mid-century; then to twice a month, which is still a common practice. Today in larger communities, one can find some LCMS congregations with weekly Eucharist.

31. Information from the home page of St. John Lutheran Church, Wheaton, Illinois.

32. Stated by Scott Bruzek; confirmed by Lester and Nancy and by Susan.

33. Comparison of worship folders: On July 25, 2021, the Divine Service included the rite of confession and absolution after the processional hymn, its traditional place in the LCMS Divine Service. Two service folders (August 5, 2018, 8:30 AM service, and February 25, 2024, 8:30 AM service) have no rite of confession and absolution; instead, the rite of Holy Baptism is in its place in both services, immediately after the processional hymn of the Divine Service.

34. Luther, *Large Catechism*, 465–66, paras. 74–75.

prompts such as, "we stand and sing hymn number . . ."; all necessary information is printed in the service folder in an easy-to-follow format for those familiar with the classic shape of word and sacrament worship. The Sunday Divine Service[35] includes the use of incense every week. As Pastor Bruzek noted (in a tangent during our interview), incense is "like a dog marking its territory," and according to Exodus, this is God's way of placing boundaries around what is divine, and thus is proscribed for use "in your tabernacle, not your home." Interviewees familiar with Roman Catholic worship noted their sense of affinity with the liturgy at St. John.[36]

Surprisingly, the formal liturgy is also appreciated by cradle LCMS people and those from an evangelical background. In the former group are Lester and Nancy, who described church shopping when they moved to the area. St. John was their "third try" of local LCMS congregations, and it happened to be St. Michael and All Angels (a minor feast day on the liturgical calendar), but at St. John, "They pulled out all the stops." Among the words Lester and Nancy named to describe the strengths of St. John were "eucharistic" and "liturgy." Appreciation of the historic liturgy was a recurring theme with Curt (who attended a Lutheran elementary school) and Lucille (raised a Methodist).[37] Their teenaged boys "like the printed liturgy" and its "predictability." Curt named "meaningful liturgy" as a strength of St. John. Early in the interview he made this poignant statement: "I came for the sacramental theology and discovered side benefits I can't imagine living without." Lucille commented that "it's special to participate in something so historic," using the phrase "the tradition" to describe "how the first Christians did it," adding "the pastors are always talking about it [the tradition] even in the liturgy." She also expressed an appreciation for the liturgical calendar—a change from their experience with evangelical worship. Susan, raised in the evangelical tradition, was the most remarkable; she introduced the topics of baptism, Eucharist, and confession and absolution in response to a variety of questions throughout her interview. And she commented that Pastor Bruzek always addressed her "why" questions about worship practices in the catechetical classes.

35. "Divine Service" is LCMS insider language for Sunday worship that includes preaching and celebration of the Lord's Supper. It is a way of translating the German word *Gottesdienst*, which was Martin Luther's preferred term for worship; the German can also be translated as "service of God." See Brunner, *Worship*, 21–24.

36. Interviews with Gail and George and with Ken and Phyllis.

37. As noted earlier, prior to joining St. John they were attended a large evangelical church.

Pastor Bruzek came to his interview prepared with a hand-drawn diagram illustrating how the liturgy expresses and enacts the core Protestant doctrine of justification through faith in Christ and its corollary, sanctification.[38] The diagram is a circle with the Chi Rho symbol in the center and six arrows, representing the gravitational pull emanating from the Chi Rho (the Sun of Righteousness) and pointing to named "planets." The top three arrows point to Scripture, prayer, and baptism/Eucharist, the marks of the church associated with the doctrine of justification and with worship and liturgy. Scripture, read each Sunday and interpreted through preaching, reveals to the assembly God's saving work in Christ; prayer (occurring throughout the service) that is offered in Jesus' name promises that God hears us because of Christ's saving work and models for all how and for what to pray; and in the sacraments those assembled encounter the living Christ, both in the baptismal words connected with water that ritually join us to the death and resurrection of Christ (Rom 6) and through the bread and wine that is the very body and blood of Jesus Christ.

Through the weekly liturgy of word and sacrament disciples and seekers are drawn into Christ's orbit, experiencing again and again the love of God in Christ for them and the world. Week after week, for the six months of catechetical classes, those gathered are catechized through a curriculum structured around their Sunday worship experiences. In the words of Pastor Bruzek, "The catechumenate *is* Sunday morning."

MAUNDY THURSDAY: LIMINAL RITUAL OF THE CATECHUMENATE

The initial clue to the significance of the Holy Thursday service for participants in St. John's adult catechumenate came from Keith, the first lay person I interviewed. He made a passing reference to the service early in our interview as he responded to "What led you to enter into the catechumenal process?" After commenting on Pastor Bruzek, he continued, saying, "My wife was comfortable here. We came, got hooked, met some people. We got involved in the Holy Week ceremony, Holy Thursday." Later, when asked about his experiences during Holy Week, he shared details, naming the importance of Val (the preschool director) in the preparations for the Holy Thursday liturgy. He described the services on Thursday and Friday of Holy

---

38. The classic writing by Luther on this topic is his 1521 treatise, *Freedom of a Christian*.

Week as "more thought-provoking for me," speaking of a "solemnity" that evoked "a sense of spirituality," one that "brings you closer to the Lord; it's the death he went through [that] makes you reflect on your life, the life hereafter."

As the staff person responsible for recruiting and training participants for the ritual stripping of the altar that closes the Maundy Thursday service, Val, the preschool director, provided background and detail.[39] She visits the Saturday catechetical class, explaining the structure of the Maundy Thursday service with its closing ritual of stripping the altar, and then asks, "Would you like to be a part of it?" Class participants have two weeks to sign up and commit to attending a one-hour rehearsal on Monday of Holy Week. Val begins this training with prayer before providing instructions, and then participants walk through the stripping process twice. In Val's words, this is a ritual that is "all about Jesus Christ." On Thursday evening, participants arrive early to secure an aisle seat; after the post-communion prayer and as Psalm 22 is chanted, Val and two members of the altar guild guide participants forward to receive with reverence the communion vessels, candles, and paraments from the chancel area, solemnly bearing these items to the sacristy. The last of the "General Notes" on this service interprets the ritual action: "The depth of Christ's servanthood is demonstrated as the altar is reverently stripped in preparation for the Church's observance of Jesus' death on Good Friday. On Holy Thursday, the Church and her catechumens begin the journey through the three days of Christ's Passover from death to life and from captivity to freedom."[40] The final rubric for the service states, "At the conclusion of the Stripping of the Altar, all leave the church in silence."[41]

Keith was not the only catechumen touched deeply by the power of this ritual. When prompted by me, Fritz and Dagny recalled participating in the ritual with the older of their two children. Ken, a cradle LCMS Lutheran raised in a large congregation, commented that he did not "remember Holy Week as such a big deal" in contrast to his experiences at St. John. After Phyllis noted that the Vigil was "as high as Easter [Sunday]," Ken responded that "Maundy Thursday is a big service; the catechumens are invited to help." Curt and Lucille, perhaps because it was two years from

---

39. Val Gaede, interview by Rhoda Schuler, January 19, 2019. Subsequent quotations and summaries of Val are from this interview, unless otherwise noted.

40. *Lutheran Service Book Altar Book*, 506, general note #3.

41. *Lutheran Service Book Altar Book*, 510.

the time they started visiting until the membership ritual at the Easter Vigil and because they had been welcomed at the Lord's table for much of that time, stated that early on they "were part of" the St. John community. For them, in Curt's words, the Vigil was an important moment, "but it didn't change much. We were already here." When asked if participation in the Holy Thursday service was "a sign of your new role in the congregation," both replied "yes," sharing that they had done the ritual twice—the second time because they had asked, if there was need for more people, could they help? Curt's comment sums up my overall impression from the interviews: "It's a stunning service—that's why people remember it."

Keith's interview, with his strong, christological interpretation of the Holy Thursday and Good Friday services, brings us full circle. His wife's health crisis, a recurring theme in his interview, initially brought them into contact with St. John. The love of Christ—made known through his suffering and death—in the words of Keith, "brings you closer to the Lord." Keith shared that his wife's recent losses of other family members and that her "near-death experiences" have made her more reliant on Jesus. He said, "I made a vow to take care of her," and strengthened by his relationships and the worship life at St. John, he is fulfilling his vow. Keith's story is one of sacrificial love, a narrative of his calling to love his wife "just as Christ loved the church and gave himself up for her" (Eph 5:25). His is a story of "love as the primary virtue" at St. John.

THE "FRIENDLIES": MAKING DISCIPLES STRONGER

Both Pastors Bruzek and Buchs gave as the unofficial mission statement of the congregation this pithy phrase: "Making disciples; making them stronger." If the three upper arrows on Pastor Bruzek's diagram draw people into Christ's orbit through liturgy, sacraments, and prayer, the lower three arrows on the circular diagram, with Christ at the center, point to these "planets": mercy, generosity, witness, all of which are responses to the work of justification through faith in Christ. Pastor Bruzek gave the biblical context for this "solar system" when I asked for an example of St. John living out its mission. He described the "rhythm of Christian life" as "Christ, Scripture, prayer, liturgy and Eucharist, tithing and alms, thorough mercy, and winsome witness—all from Acts." In his teaching, through the pastoral care of staff, and through the experience of the liturgy, justification naturally leads disciples into Christian living, into acts of mercy and generosity and to "a winsome witness" of God's love in Christ. Interviewing the "Friendlies," who function in an organic way as mentors or sponsors for the "catechumens," revealed the fullness of this ethos of love, best expressed in this Johannine text: "We love because he first loved us" (1 John 4:19).

Nancy explained their reason for attending the catechetical classes a second time. Some friends of theirs were attending, and she said, "I wanted them to feel loved and welcomed. I wanted them to love St. John as much as I do." For Curt and Lucille, attending the faith formation classes the second time was still for their own sake; they were still learning because, he said, "one immersed in evangelicalism has a lot to learn" about the Lutheran tradition. In part, they continue to come because they both "get so much out of it," but, as Lucille said, "Now I'm more intentional about meeting new people." Rather than sit with the same people (as they did the first time), they move around to different tables to meet others. Lucille is more confident asking questions now, modeling this practice for the sake of others who, like her during her first experience, may not feel comfortable doing so. Ken and Phyllis reported having attended every weekend for three years. The previous year they attended less frequently; one of them said, "It's not as much about me; now [we're] more selfless—meeting new people, showing support of the class, [being there] to answer questions." Lester and Nancy now also see their role more broadly; if they see someone "looking alone," they will sit with that person. Just as they did for their longtime friends, they attend because they "want people to love St. John as much as we do." By their selfless actions, Ken and Phyllis, Lester and Nancy, Curt and Lucille embody the answer to Pastor Bruzek's question: "How can [the catechumens] have an experience where they feel completely loved, welcomed?"

With "love as the primary virtue" at St. John, a major goal of making disciples "stronger" is forming them to do more than rejoice that by Christ's death and resurrection, they personally have been reconciled to God through faith. St. John's catechumenate forms and strengthens disciples who love others because God has first loved them, who embrace the Christian life as one of mercy, generosity, and a winsome witness of salvation through Christ. As Martin Luther wrote, "By faith [the inner person] is created in the image of God and . . . is joyful and glad on account of the benefits of Christ . . . Therefore, it is [that one's] sole desire to serve God joyfully without thought of gain, inspired by a love that is free and unconstrained."[42] Two couples articulated this spiritual maturity when responding with ways that the people of St. John live out the "official" mission statement.[43] Ken quoted Pastor Bruzek's language, saying that the catechumenate revolves around "Christ, Scripture, prayer, Eucharist, tithing, witness, and mercy." The mission statement, he continued "doesn't stop at salvation [and] forgiveness [as if] we're good to go; [discipleship] includes service to others." Lester expressed the same insight from the mission statement, saying "sanctification [is] there too. In the catechumenate [we learned] justification is the start but not the finish line. It's the starting line for the Christian life." When asked for the three best aspects of the catechumenal process, Lester expressed the same insight with two phrases: the catechumenate is both a "reminder of good doctrine" and "a reminder to be loving—the action part."

CONTEXTUALIZING BELIEVING, BEHAVING, AND BELONGING AT ST. JOHN

The value of *believing* at St. John—as *fides quae* (the faith that is believed)—is most evident in the length and depth of the catechumenate. Six months is necessary for one to come to know the core teachings of the Christian faith and its expression in the Lutheran tradition; knowledge of Christian doctrine, of *fides quae*, is highly valued in the LCMS denomination. The depth and complexity of the teaching also reflect the high level of education of most members. Yet the stories of Susan, for whom the most powerful teaching of Pastor Bruzek is "that I am loved," and Keith, whose cruciform spirituality resonates with the solemn Holy Thursday and Good Friday liturgies, illustrate the value at St. John of believing as the faith of the heart. That both *fides quae* and *fides qua* are held in tension reflect a statement made by Pastor Bruzek: St. John's catechumenal process attracts "the committed and the wounded."

The full "solar system of planets" at St. John speak to the twofold nature of *behavioral* expectations. That "starting line" of justification through

42. Luther, *Freedom of a Christian*, 72.

43. The home page of the congregation's website has this statement at the bottom: "St. John is a community formed by Jesus in Baptism and gathered around Scripture, Prayer, and the Eucharist. Through the Church Jesus seeks to draw all people to himself, forgiving their sins by his death on the cross and sanctifying them for a life of love for God and service to their neighbors. St. John is a member of the Lutheran Church–Missouri Synod."

faith is predicated on the presupposition that when is one drawn to Christ, staying in his orbit happens primarily through participation in the liturgy (those planets of Scripture, prayer, and sacraments). As one becomes more secure in Christ's orbit, the disciple discovers true freedom, the freedom of the Christian that comes from serving others—through acts of mercy, a winsome witness, and generosity with one's material possessions (where the median household income in the 2020 census was over $100,000). Pastor Bruzek and others used the word "tithing" as an expectation for disciples, another example of the socioeconomic context of Wheaton and of the catechumenal process attracting "the committed." But these expectations, these behaviors, are ongoing; it's part of "making disciples stronger," not a prerequisite necessary for one to "belong."

Belonging, of course, is the language of love, the "primary virtue" of St. John. In *Christianity after Religion*, Diana Butler Bass uses the Gospels to argue that belonging preceded believing in the lives of those whom Jesus encountered. "Christianity," she writes, "began with an invitation into friendship, into creating a new community, into forming relationships based on love and service."[44] Her description calls to mind Pastor Bruzek's question: "How can [the catechumens] have an experience where they feel completely loved, welcomed?"—especially those among "the wounded" in this affluent, picture-perfect suburb? As one interviewee noted, Wheaton is a community where "people need to keep up appearances." A good job, beautiful home, wonderful spouse, and well-behaved children are both signs of "worldly" success that define one's identity and are also signs implicitly understood to be the marks of a good Christian.

Katherine's story illustrates how St. John's ethos of love created a sense of belonging to one who, in her own words, "felt like an outcast" in other contexts. She had lived in the community for two years, and after getting settled, she began to look for a church because, she said, "I wanted my son to go to Sunday school like I did." Raised as a Lutheran, she Googled "Lutheran churches," discovered that St. John was nearby, and, in her words, "showed up one Sunday and never left."

Midway in our interview Katherine revealed more information that not only shed light on her comment about feeling like "an outcast" but also added a layer of complexity to the seemingly straightforward story I had heard at the beginning—a lapsed Lutheran with a Sunday school-aged child using Google to look for a nearby church. Katherine is a single

---

44. Butler Bass, *Christianity after Religion*, 205.

mother who was once engaged to and cohabitating with her child's father. After their child's birth, she realized that the relationship with her fiancé, father of her child, would not work out. Reflecting again on her first visit to St. John, she described it as "very nerve wracking." She deliberately chose to attend on a weekend when their child was with his father because, she said, she "did not want to expose him to a bad experience." What she found on that first Sunday visit was a community in which "everyone [was] very welcoming," and where, as she had said earlier, "I don't feel like an outcast." And so, she has never left. To quote Alan Kreider, "In Christianity's early centuries conversion involved changes in belonging, belief, and behavior—in the context of an experience of God that . . . for some people must have been very powerful."[45] For Katherine, the powerful experience was her first visit to St. John. The welcome given to her by these members of Christ's body, for whom love is the primary virtue, was transformational. No longer an outcast, she was drawn into the orbit of St. John and belongs to Christ and Christ's church.

---

45. Kreider, *Change of Conversion*, xv.

3

LIVING FAITH

Heart-to-Heart Combat against Sin, Death, and the Power of the Devil

"I stumbled into Living Faith Lutheran Church on Easter Sunday in 2012."[1] So says the lay catechist, whom we'll name Daniel, of his first encounter with Living Faith. There are probably many who are now members of Living Faith who stumbled in. They stumbled into this Lutheran outpost in the midst of a plethora of nondenominational and Baptist congregations in the greater Atlanta area, and specifically in Cumming, Georgia, where Living Faith is located. Many have made the circuitous journey through those other Protestant traditions in Cumming to Living Faith, including many of the catechumens I interviewed. Comparing himself to Martin Luther in his journey from the medieval church to the evangelical church, Daniel, while born and baptized into the LCMS, journeyed with his wife in the mainline Presbyterian Church (USA), and then into the churches of Charles Stanley and Andy Stanley. But frustration with free will theology led to that fateful encounter with Living Faith. Daniel bears witness to the heart-to-heart spiritual combat that Living Faith wages for the sake of the salvation of human beings in Cumming and throughout the world.

---

1. Daniel (pseudonym), interview by Kent J. Burreson, August 14, 2018. Subsequent quotations and summaries of Daniel are from this interview, unless otherwise noted.

This heart-to-heart combat begins in the context of Cumming and Forsyth County, Georgia. Originally a nearly 99 percent homogenous Caucasian county, it was all too famously the home to significant Ku Klux Klan activity throughout the history of that loosely centralized organization. Thus, Living Faith wages combat against the forces of racism and prejudice in the context of Cumming's recent past. In more recent decades, it has been able to transcend those associations and become a commuter town for metropolitan Atlanta. The pastor at Living Faith, Reverend Timothy Droegemueller, indicates that Cumming increasingly has become an upper-middle-class community with three-quarters of the residents new to the community. While racism was part of Cumming's heritage, the influx of new residents, including especially those of Asian descent, means that Cumming is increasingly cosmopolitan and urbane.[2]

Living Faith entered this increasingly ethnically pluralistic community in 2001. Assembling for worship first in a local elementary school, and then in a funeral home after Pastor Droegemueller's arrival in 2006, construction began on Living Faith's current worship space in 2013 and was completed in 2014. Foundational to Living Faith's identity is Ephesians 2:8–10, "For by grace you have been saved through faith. And this is not your own doing; it is the gift of God, not a result of works, so that no one may boast. For we are his workmanship, created in Christ Jesus for good works, which God prepared beforehand, that we should walk in them," a Scripture passage central to the Lutheran understanding of salvation by grace through faith for Christ's sake alone. From that passage Living Faith derives its mission statement and primary identity marker: "To the glory of God and the salvation of man." Salvation by grace through faith is to God's glory, as are the good works in which Christians walk as a result of being saved by grace. There is one way of the world and one way for those baptized into the body of Christ. Pastor Droegemueller intersperses the mission statement into preaching, into teaching, and into conversation. That phrase forms those who journey through Living Faith's catechumenate to be people oriented against the ways of the sinful world and toward life in Christ.

---

2. US Census Bureau. As of the 2020 US Census, Forsyth County has 163,687 Caucasian residents, 45,203 Asian residents, and 10,721 Black or African American residents. "Forsyth County, Georgia, Decennial Census, P1: Race."

Part I: Context is Everything

THE CATECHUMENATE:
FROM THE DEVIL'S PLAY TOY TO GOD'S SOLDIER

The mission of God is at the center of Living Faith's life. Pastor Droegemueller says, "Our mission is the Great Commission. Salvation to man entails understanding our vocation as a congregation to the world, especially the community around us. There is an urgency about it in our midst. This urgency means we are serious about the lasting word,"[3] which is the word of God that is preached, witnessed, and read in their midst. Central to that mission is equipping Christians at Living Faith to interpret the Scriptures well and faithfully in their daily lives. This is because it is that word to which they bear witness with those who are unbaptized in their daily lives. These opportunities are some of the ways that believers "stumble over Jesus' good works in daily life," in Pastor Droegemueller's words.[4] Their catechumenate developed in order to fulfill this mission of bringing that word to bear in the lives of those in Cumming who have not heard the saving message of God and have not been brought to the waters of baptism.

Living Faith's life as a congregation is oriented toward equipping Christians for the battle in the spirit of Ephesians:

> Be strong in the Lord and in the strength of his power; put on the whole armor of God, so that you may be able to stand against the wiles of the devil, for our struggle is not against blood and flesh but against the rulers, against the authorities, against the cosmic powers of this present darkness, against the spiritual forces of evil in the heavenly places. Therefore take up the whole armor of God, so that you may be able to withstand on the evil day and, having prevailed against everything, to stand firm. Stand, therefore, and belt your waist with truth and put on the breastplate of righteousness and lace up your sandals in preparation for the gospel of peace. With all of these, take the shield of faith, with which you will be able to quench all the flaming arrows of the evil one. Take the helmet of salvation and the sword of the Spirit, which is the word of God (Eph 6:10–20).

---

3. Pastor Timothy Droegemueller, interview by Kent J. Burreson, August 15, 2018. Subsequent quotations and summaries of Pastor Droegemueller are from this interview, unless otherwise noted.

4. As we discuss in chapter 5, for Pastor Droegemueller "stumbling over Jesus' good works in daily human life" bears witness to Jesus and his salvation and actively takes up the mantle of serving the neighbor in Christ's love in their situations of need.

Their catechumenate provides the whole armor of God through their interpretation, teaching, preaching, and application of God's word so that they can "quench the flaming arrows of the evil one." Pastor Droegemueller evokes this spirit in congregational life and Living Faith's catechumenate:

> [There is] one human race [and] there is one distinction in it: those baptized in the blood line of the Messiah and there are those the Lord wants to see baptized. That is the lens through which we see our lives. Baptism is the point of no return. We break down all false narratives, all day, every day. How do we do this best for adults? There is going to be a change of allegiance. We want to prepare people that they are going up against every demon in hell, an entire corrupt universe, and their own innate, foul, selfish self. So we want to prepare them for the battle.[5]

The reader can sense the urgency in bearing witness to the people of Cumming for Living Faith that originates in Pastor Droegemueller. The catechumenal process began to develop in 2011–2012. A year after their transition into their new worship space in 2015, he developed the current structure for the process. Drawing on a description of the early church catechumenate from Arthur Just,[6] he developed the following phases or periods of instruction: Exploration, Separation, Transition, and Incorporation. On their website they explain the stages of their catechumenate beginning with this introduction: "The Adult Catechumenate teaches people in a high paced, high stress, high tech age to abide in Jesus our Savior through every storm of life." The website then describes the process of the catechumenate in the following way:

> **Stage 1: EXPLORATION** is an investigation into the Old and New Testament Scriptures that reveal our Lord Jesus Christ. The word of God will do its work as people are led through exploration and discussion to greater understanding of the Christian faith.
>
> **Stage 2: SEPARATION** is taught by Pastor Droegemueller and focuses on the six chief parts of the Christian faith (from Luther's Small Catechism).
>
> **Stage 3: TRANSITION** helps those who desire to be baptized and/or confirmed to prepare for the challenges of life. People learn to pray, read the Bible, and understand what it means to worship God.

---

5. "Painting a Vision for Forming Lutheran Christians," panel discussion with Pastors Scott Bruzek, Timothy Droegemueller, and Dien Ashley Taylor, January 12–14, 2021.

6. Just Jr., *Heaven on Earth*, especially chapter 8, 150–79.

> **Stage 4: INCORPORATION** helps the newly baptized and confirmed members of Christ's Church to understand the patterns of living in Christ's mercy as we gather around His Word and Gifts.[7]

Pastor Droegemueller provides a more complete description of the phases in this way:

> In the Season of Pentecost (Sundays after Holy Trinity) during the exploration phase led by our Lay Catechist, we use the biblical story in the Old and New Testaments as the focus of study, sometimes with the Sunday readings as a launching point. For the most part, we simply let the Word do the work and it plays out in terms of clear teaching and conversation. In the season of Epiphany during the separation phase, we study Luther's *Small Catechism*. In the season of Lent during the transition phase, we take people into training for the Christian life who are ready to go forward to Baptism and Adult Confirmation. Everything culminates during Holy Week with Holy Thursday, Good Friday, and baptisms and confirmations at the Easter Vigil. In the Easter Season during the incorporation phase, we train people to live as part of the Body of Christ gathered around the very reality of Christ's Body and Blood for us in Holy Communion.

The congregation requires anyone who is not baptized or was baptized and/or confirmed in another Christian tradition to journey through the catechumenate. Those from Lutheran traditions, including those transferring from other LCMS congregations, are encouraged (but not required) to make the catechumenal journey in order to became familiar with the Christian life at Living Faith. Pastor Droegemueller noted that "there is not as high a level of participation in the Exploration phase (Inquiry) as we would desire. People tend to bounce in and out of that phase. Even though we emphasize it as the first phase, it tends to be viewed like a tailgating party. This is something we would like to address." The Transition phase functions as a period of discernment by which Living Faith encourages those who are not yet convinced of the truthfulness of the biblical story and witness not to continue toward baptism, confirmation, or membership.

It is critical for Living Faith that those entering the period of Transition are prepared for the spiritual battle they will enter at the moment of baptism and confirmation. Pastor Droegemueller answers the question of how they do that:

---

7. Living Faith website, bold in original.

LIVING FAITH

> We have baptized more adults than babies in the past fourteen years. How do we train these adults for this noble, valiant, amazing, countercultural life known as the Christian [life]. Because this world is going to lose them as a playmate, the devil is going to lose them as a play toy, and the flesh will no longer be the playground. We have to give them enough for this ensuing grand life, but the devil is crafty, so we want to prepare them.[8]

Living Faith's approach to their catechumenate's formation of new Christians, and Pastor Droegemueller's teaching language about and within it, finds it source in Martin Luther's language in his *Large Catechism* under the Third Petition of the Lord's Prayer:

> Therefore we who would be Christians must surely expect to have the devil with all his angels and the world as our enemies and must expect that they will inflict every possible misfortune and grief upon us. For where God's Word is preached, accepted, or believed, and bears fruit, there the holy and precious cross will also not be far behind. And let no one think that we will have peace; rather, we must sacrifice all we have on earth—possessions, honor, house and farm, spouse and children, body and life. Now, this grieves our flesh and the old creature, for it means that we must remain steadfast, suffer patiently whatever befalls us, and let go whatever is taken from us.[9]

This is the shape of heart-to-heart combat for which Living Faith seeks to prepare its catechumens.

HEART-TO-HEART COMBAT: THE WORD—THE SWORD OF THE SPIRIT

Living Faith shapes a different form of teaching and formation than is prevalent in the Christian congregations in their area and in greater Atlanta. Living Faith structures its catechumenate to reflect the journeys of those they encounter in that spiritual and cultural context. They engage in heart-to-heart combat with people who are searching for the truth through the word of God and so bring new Christians to a robust faith expressed in right belief that reflects itself in faithful Christian life within a true Christian

---

8. "Painting a Vision for Forming Lutheran Christians," panel discussion with Pastors Scott Bruzek, Timothy Droegemueller, and Dien Ashley Taylor, January 12–14, 2021.

9. Luther, *Large Catechism*, 448–49.

fellowship. Equipped in this way, they recognize when they are stumbling over Jesus' good works in their daily lives: when there are opportunities to direct people to Christ as the source of life and hope and opportunities for serving the misguided neighbor in love.

The heart-to-heart combat that is the centerpiece of their catechumenate is oriented toward discipleship in the proclaimed and written word, rooted toward a lifelong pattern. In Pastor Droegemueller's words, "We encourage people to understand that life in Christ is ongoing, lifelong catechesis! We don't really talk about other options." As the psalmist says, there are two ways: the way of the righteous and the way of the wicked (Ps 1:1–6). Living Faith forms its catechumens to walk on the scriptural way of the righteous. Walking the way of the righteous is the lifelong path of the Christian disciple:

> At the point of baptism, you are inscripted in the church militant. Your wanted poster goes up in Hell. There is going to be a switch of allegiances. You are no longer going down the lazy river of sin and damnation, but you are going up against it in the life-giving, countercultural waters of baptism. An allegiance is formed with the Triune God [and with the] two-thirds of the angels that didn't rebel with Lucifer, and there is going to be a very different life for you. We have to prepare these newly baptized for going against the flow and I'm standing with my Lord Jesus all the way through. The theology of glory is going to tell them life is going to be easier. We tell them the opposite. It's going to be tougher. Prepare for battle.[10]

It is a battle shaped by the word of God. It is a real-life, spiritual battle in the here and now. Forming that lifelong pattern for Living Faith entails "understanding their mission in terms of being sent to teach things." Throughout all the phases of their catechumenate the Sunday lectionary serves as a primary teaching foundation leading to belief and orthodox faith and away from "the cosmic powers of this present darkness" (Eph 6:12).

The catechumenal classes occur on Sunday mornings prior to worship. During the Exploration phase lay catechist Daniel describes the catechesis he leads as exploratory teaching. His primary intent is to address biblical illiteracy and expose people to the biblical story and to biblical doctrine (through a Lutheran lens). His style of instruction is lecture-oriented. He provides a narrative foundation as found especially in the Gospels and

---

10. "Painting a Vision for Forming Lutheran Christians," panel discussion with Pastors Scott Bruzek, Timothy Droegemueller, and Dien Ashley Taylor, January 12–14, 2021.

then uses particular passages to connect back to the Old Testament narrative. He aims to form them to read the Bible in its context. He then folds into that the basics of theology as they grapple with various sections of Scripture. It is both a scriptural and systematic approach. Daniel said that "people are not used to this kind of approach and so I have to ask, 'how do I draw people into it?'" Reading and interpreting the written word of God and asking significant questions becomes the primary way to draw people in. He discusses doctrinal topics that address the range of people's formation in other traditions, such as the role of the will in salvation (free versus bound), justification, and dispensational eschatology. Throughout he tries to stimulate feedback from participants, although the classes are not primarily discussion-based. He believes that the classes in the Exploration phase build on one another and so he will try to reinforce learning in subsequent classes. As Daniel says, "Living Faith is dedicated to the teaching of the word. This dedication starts with pastor and flows down from him to make sure that we get the word out rightly and faithfully."

Alongside their phase of Exploration, another example of wielding the sword of the Spirit that provides an opportunity for inquiring about the Christian faith is Living Faith's Wednesday morning service of Morning Prayer and subsequent Bible study. For the newly baptized and confirmed it is an opportunity to deepen their faith. Established members often invite newcomers to this study as an invitation into life at Living Faith. Through question-and-answer format, Pastor Droegemueller leads participants into the word of God and its implications for life in a fallen world.[11] The focus is definitively on right belief and the ways that Satan, the evil in the world, and humanity's sinfulness seek to obstruct and destroy true faith. As Pastor Droegemueller says, this pattern of instruction and intensive attention to the word of God informs Living Faith's life together in worship, the work of the parish, and opportunities for service: "We form right faith and belief by spending time in God's word." As Oscar noted about his own desire, "We didn't want to feel that we were just playing a game. How do you move people from observing doctrinal differences among Christian traditions to grappling with when those different teachings might reflect unbiblical, even idolatrous positions? We wanted to engage for ourselves how we are continually coming to God. The Lord was placing his seal on this through

---

11. He conducts lay elders' meetings following the same catechetical pattern.

his word."[12] Oscar's response reflects how formation in biblical doctrine shapes the separation from the fallen world and Satan's deception.

Catechetical formation during the Separation phase under the leadership of Pastor Droegemueller builds on the biblical foundations in Exploration but focuses on the Sunday readings in conjunction with Martin Luther's *Small Catechism*. During the Epiphany season he focuses on each of the chief parts of the catechism: Ten Commandments, Apostles' Creed, Lord's Prayer, Baptism, Confession and Absolution, and the Lord's Supper. For Pastor Droegemueller these biblical and catechetical texts are the primary building blocks of faith and of the Christian life. While teaching in the Exploration phase is much more discursive, in the Separation phase it is exploratory, Socratic, and discussion-oriented, all intended to assist the catechumen in wielding the Word of God in the spiritual battle for faith over against the sinful world. The intent is to intimately know these primary texts, especially the Creed and the Lord's Prayer, and for the catechumens to be able to recall them and their implications for their own lives of faith. One catechumen, Andy, said of his experience in the Separation phase that "the instruction on the Creeds and Lord's Prayer was most meaningful, especially during one-on-one instruction sessions with Pastor Droegemueller."[13] He affirmed the central role of catechetical instruction in Living Faith's catechumenate when he said, "The *teaching* was most beneficial! I had been taught nothing about baptism in my previous congregational experiences. Baptismal teaching, in particular, was truncated. No rationale for infant baptism was provided. So I appreciated the depth of the teaching I received."

In the Transition phase beginning on the First Sunday in Lent, Pastor Droegemueller uses the Sunday readings extensively. They emphasize particular themes within the various phases on selected Sundays. A walk-through of the liturgy usually takes place on the Third Sunday in Lent, for regular participation in Sunday worship is essential in order to "stand firm" against sin, death, and power of the devil. On the Fourth Sunday in Lent the focus is on stewardship, for one's allegiance to Christ includes recognizing that all one's earthly possessions come from God and returning a portion to God expresses the depth of that new allegiance. Equipping these disciples

---

12. Oscar (pseudonym), interview with Kent J. Burreson, August 15, 2018. Subsequent quotations and summaries of Oscar are from this interview, unless otherwise noted.

13. Andy (pseudonym), interview by Kent J. Burreson, August 14, 2018. Subsequent quotations and summaries of Andy are from this interview, unless otherwise noted.

in formation with the "whole armor of God" in all of one's life continues on the Fifth Sunday in Lent. The focus is on prayer, including the Psalms, daily patterns of prayer, and family devotions. Pastor Droegemueller says, "Here the stress is on what we do together as God's family, both in the church building and in our physical homes." Palm Sunday, the Sixth Sunday in Lent and beginning of Holy Week, focuses on Holy Communion, walking through the rite followed by a question-and-answer period and instruction as to how best to receive the Lord's Supper.

Through all of their instruction, Pastor Droegemueller and lay catechist Daniel focus on believing, especially right, orthodox belief, with belonging and behaving orbiting as constellations around the primary helix of belief. As Pastor Droegemueller indicates, "We are deliberately reacting to [what we describe] as a cultural form of Lutheranism, that dispenses with biblical and doctrinal robustness. We focus on developing a true biblical piety versus pietism. We want to steer them toward a true spirituality and away from concerns about worldly success." The teaching in the phases of the catechumenate informs the change of allegiance and the countercultural stance the catechumen is formed to take.

In Living Faith's instruction and formation there is no question that Pastor Droegemueller is the primary teacher and agent. He is intimately involved in the catechumenate, often on a very personal basis with individual catechumens, and in congregational life.[14] For example, Oscar often received personalized instruction from Pastor Droegemueller, alongside the Sunday morning catechetical classes. As Oscar observes, "I was looking for certain things. Pastor helped me to take doctrine very seriously. He would answer my questions through lengthy conversations on the phone or in person. He had the patience to lead me into all truth." Biblical doctrine serves as the sword of the Spirit to discern the devil's lies from the truth of the Triune God. Heart-to-heart combat indeed!

---

14. One might question whether too much was riding on him. As a result of their involvement in our grant project, Living Faith appointed a lay director of the catechumenate who was able to perform many of the logistical requirements for the catechumenate, relieving some of the burden from Pastor Droegemueller.

Part I: Context is Everything

HEART-TO HEART COMBAT: BAPTIZED AND FED FOR THE BATTLE

Living Faith orients the liturgical and ritual structure of its catechumenate toward the font and the altar. Their experience of baptism, confirmation, and the Lord's Supper at the Easter Vigil is the point of no return. The spiritual battle is engaged from now on. The newly baptized and confirmed now live their lives solely out of the word of God received in association with baptism and out of the fellowship of the biblical story celebrated in the Lord's Supper. While Living Faith does not have many ritual markers for the catechumenal journey, there are a few prominent ones that are meaningful. Pastor Droegemueller comments on their catechumenate's ritual structure:

> There is an ongoing continual order to what we are doing. It makes sense liturgically. Our liturgical order has become a pattern for teaching the faith. It allows an openness for dialogue. It facilitates well the relational aspects of incorporation into the body of Christ. The transitions are clearly defined. The logistics work well. It allows the congregation to spotlight the process for incorporating new members. It functions well as part of the training of the neophytes and the whole congregation. It is a part of the identity of congregational life.

The congregation builds that identity for the catechumens primarily through the Sunday eucharistic liturgy and through the Wednesday Morning Prayer service, for those who can attend the latter. Pastor Droegemueller highlights the intention of that weekly ritual formation: "Although we do not require participants to be present for the Divine Service each Sunday, they usually end up attending. We prepare them to come forward each Sunday to the altar to receive a blessing (making the sign of St. Andrew's cross) as they prepare for full Communion fellowship. Along with that sign they receive a word of prayer and blessing from me. We emphasize to them that we 'get to' go to God's house to receive his undeserved gifts! And the gifts are really, really good!!! Our entire adult catechumenate is formed around the liturgical church year and the one-year lectionary, part of the gifts they receive."[15] The weekly liturgy serves as the context for catechetical

---

15. Living Faith uses the one-year lectionary of the *Lutheran Service Book*. This lectionary appoints Gospel readings from all of the Gospels throughout the year. This lectionary was a thorough updating of the one-year lectionary of *Lutheran Worship*, the previous hymnal of The Lutheran Church–Missouri Synod. These lectionaries come out of the Saxon Lutheran tradition going back to Wittenberg and Martin Luther. The

formation and that catechesis is oriented toward participation in baptism, in the Lord's Supper, and in the liturgical life of the parish. It feeds them for the spiritual battle.

So, what are the spotlight ritual markers of this new and different life? There are no rites punctuating the Exploration phase, or that mark the transition from that phase into the Separation phase.[16] On the First Sunday in Lent when crossing the threshold into the Transition phase, the congregation presents the Elect with a copy of Luther's *Small Catechism*. Only those preparing for baptism appear before the congregation. One of the catechumens, Candice, recalled Pastor Droegemueller calling her forward to the altar. Receiving the catechism before entering this phase of more intense preparation for baptism or confirmation, and having just completed committed study of the catechism, stresses the priority the congregation places on right belief.

The catechumenate at Living Faith culminates at the baptisms, confirmations, and receptions into membership at the Easter Vigil. Of this threshold moment in the person's change of allegiance, Pastor Droegemueller comments, "What better day to be baptized than in the very powerful middle of Good Friday and Easter Sunday! We make a big deal out of remembering at the Easter Vigil that we are buried into Christ's death and raised into his resurrection in Holy Baptism. Those baptized and confirmed on this night receive the Eucharist for the first time at the Easter Vigil." Pastor Droegemueller chooses a Bible verse for each of the baptized and confirmed catechumens, a very meaningful ritual gesture for many of the candidates. Candice, reflecting on her confirmation at the Easter Vigil, said, "Knowing that I was confirming my faith in front of the body of Christ was significant and important to me."[17] Through that affirmation of belief she expressed the sense of realizing that she belonged to the Christian community in that place. Pastor Droegemueller's choosing of her verse

---

Wittenberg lectionaries were based upon the Roman lectionary tradition. Since Old Testament readings were not part of the medieval or the Saxon Lutheran tradition, the Old Testament texts were chosen in association with the Gospel readings on the basis of historic usage as preaching texts by the early, medieval, and Reformation church fathers, especially Luther.

16. There is no Rite of Acceptance into the Separation (Catechumenate) phase. So, they don't currently anoint, but they have considered initiating the practice.

17. Candice (pseudonym), interview by Kent J. Burreson, August 15, 2018. Subsequent quotations and summaries of Candice are from this interview, unless otherwise noted.

reflected that sense of belonging since he chose a verse that related to his experience with them in the catechumenate. In Candice's case, "I would always talk about being a sinner in our catechumenate classes and so my verse was from the Gospel of Matthew and reflected Jesus' dealing with sinners."

The last two ritual markers take place on the Second Sunday of Easter and at Pentecost. According to Pastor Droegemueller, there is no catechumenal ritual action on the Second Sunday of Easter but there is "a big focus on baptismal identity" in the service and in the preaching. On Pentecost they conduct a rite of vocation for the newly baptized and confirmed and for the entire assembly to renew their understanding of their vocation as baptized children of God in the world. For Pastor Droegemueller this "lets the discipleship process play itself out completely." They have fully moved from the devil's play toy to a soldier in God's kingdom that is breaking into the world in Jesus. The rite of vocation marks a return to the baptismal font as the source for their direction in living out this faith in discipleship.

HEART-TO HEART COMBAT: FIGHTING THE SPIRITUAL BATTLE TOGETHER

The common search for right faith and belief, fostered through exposure to and exploration of the word of God, creates the common belonging that characterizes Living Faith. It is life together around the living and active word. The congregation in its life of discipleship engages in heart-to-heart combat for faith by relationship-building in their gathering around the word. Relationships form in at least three contexts: relationships with Pastor Droegemueller, with members of the catechumenal cohort, and with members of the congregation.

Candice's journey through the catechumenate is representative of the experiences of others whom I interviewed. Within her catechumenal cohort of five who would be confirmed and around ten who were journeying through the catechumenate again, a community forged itself. The relationships continued to flourish even after the catechumenal experience ended. One couple moved to California but relationships with them in the cohort have endured even across that distance. Candice also formed close relationships with Pastor Droegemueller and lay catechist Daniel. "They were always available!"

Similarly, Oscar and his wife represent the search for authentic Christian community, a sense of belonging intricately intertwined with substantive believing. They "desired to be in a community who hears the word of God rightly and takes it seriously. So we journeyed through the catechumenate for the sake of the Lord's love. We were seeking this family for a long time. We sought to be absorbed in Christ." They sensed strongly the congregation's hospitality and the welcome afforded to them. The congregation identified them as members even before they had completed the catechumenate. Oscar said that through the catechumenate, "Love embraced us. People paid attention to us and the personal circumstances of our lives." It was within this community of belief that they collectively could address the "faith challenges that arise, since apostasy is real, an issue and a challenge."

A central factor in creating the sense of belonging for the catechumens was the role of the sponsors. Pastor Droegemueller chooses sponsors for each of them and presents them to the catechumens during the public enrollment into the third stage of Transition in preparation for baptism and confirmation. But there is fluidity in the appointment of sponsors and in the catechumens' engagement with their sponsors. Pastor Droegemueller embeds a lay elder into the catechumenal cohort at the start of the process. Often, that elder serves as the de facto sponsor for some in that cohort. That was the case for Andy. He built a relationship with the elders through the elder appointed to his cohort. That elder and all the elders served as his sponsors.

That was also the case with Paul. He was brought into association with Living Faith through his girlfriend at the time, who was a member of the congregation. This led to a relationship with Pastor Droegemueller and the congregation even before he journeyed through the catechumenate. It was something he said that "he needed." He needed to experience the sense of belonging to the body of Christ. Since his girlfriend served as his unofficial sponsor, he already had a sense of belonging to Living Faith. But the elder of his cohort also served as an unofficial sponsor, reinforcing his sense of belonging. Flexibility in the appointing of sponsors contributed to developing the sense of belonging among the catechumens.

Candice had a more traditional sponsor, although she chose her own sponsor. Her sponsor kept her accountable throughout the process. She joined Candice's classes as she had opportunity, and they interacted on a regular basis. This led to a mutuality of relationship in which she and her sponsor continued to hold each other accountable even after Candice's confirmation.

Part I: Context is Everything

For many, Pastor Droegemueller served as an unofficial sponsor. That was certainly the case for Oscar. He said that "the pastoral relationship was primary. I became very attached to Pastor's instruction. In a sense he was my sponsor." Likewise, for Paul, "Pastor served like a sponsor to me. I met with him once a week exploring the Word of God for two months. And following that life experience led to questions I regularly asked of him. He fed me Scripture and that prompted further study." All of this contributed to the feeling for Paul "that I had immediate relationships with everyone when I walked through the door. I felt like a member before I was confirmed."

Believing provides the foundation for and contributes to the sense of belonging that the catechumens experience at Living Faith. Andy expresses how a sense of belonging took form in his experience: "I felt excitement, relief, and love being a part of a congregation where you know everyone. It was the first time I felt that I was a part of a congregation. And of course, it was very special for me to be a part of this congregation with my fiancée. That was very special."

HEART-TO HEART COMBAT: LIVING THE COUNTERCULTURAL STREAM

Christian behavior does not receive the same emphasis as believing and belonging at Living Faith, but it is not neglected either. Pastor Droegemueller invites and encourages the newly baptized and confirmed to an experiential learning event during the phase of Incorporation after the Easter Vigil. Pastor Droegemueller notes, "This experience is intended to allow the newly initiated to participate in generating acts of mercy. They have done different things: visited shut-ins, spending a good amount of time with each one; went to a retirement center and engaged in conversation with the residents; went to the part of greater Atlanta where Chet (a hard-worn man active in service to the troubled, including prostitutes and drug-dealers) works." The latter experience was particularly formative, offering support to those in challenging financial and housing situations whose self-worth has been destroyed by drugs and the sex industry. These formative experiences shape the neophytes' understanding of Christian vocation as loving service to their neighbors and reflect their shift of allegiance from the ways of the world to the ways of God.

Andy says of his experience that they went to the home of a local family who had lost everything in a house fire. They went to encourage the family. But as Andy says, "This was just a chapter of this experience, not the end. I went back to check to see if I could offer any additional help. It felt really good to do that. We were doing our part to witness as Christians and to shine the light of Christ in dark spaces. It was very affirming." These experiences seeking to form the Christian life of faith culminate in the rite of vocation previously mentioned, which Pastor Droegemueller leads on Pentecost Sunday. This is one way in which, in Pastor Droegemueller's words, they "create the awareness for stumbling over Jesus' good works in daily life."

Even with these experiences during the stage of Incorporation (mystagogy), it was "not memorable" for Candice. Paul said, "It continued what we had been doing and I don't recall anything fundamentally different in that stage." Yet even though the period of Incorporation was not compellingly memorable, the formative value of the entire process was. Living Faith understands itself to be engaged in heart-to-heart combat for the salvation of God's human creatures through its catechumenal process. Candice certainly perceived that someone was battling for her. It wasn't just Pastor Droegemueller and the people of Living Faith. Reflecting on her experience of the catechumenate she said, "Jesus was persistent throughout. God was pursuing me!" God was waging heart-to-heart combat in Living Faith's catechumenate to claim her as God's child for life. So it is for all who walk through Living Faith's catechumenate. They change allegiances from the sinful world and Satan to the saving God and God's life. Then ensues the battle against Satan and his lies. They are prepared for the battle.

4

ST. MARY'S

Creating a Sense of Belonging

"Tell me about how you came to start an adult catechumenal process at St. Mary's," I asked Pastor M early in our interview.[1] As Pastor M recounted for me, it began with an invitation from a friend a few months into her first call as a newly ordained pastor in this small Lutheran congregation in the northeast. The friend, who was organizing continuing education opportunities for the local synod of the Evangelical Lutheran Church in America (ELCA), invited her to a training event led by Rev. Paul E. Hoffman on the adult catechumenate.[2] Hoffman, who describes his book *Faith Forming Faith* as "the story of how, through the baptismal preparation of new Christians, *we as a congregation* are formed in faith and strengthened for mission in the world, over and over again," has shared this story of faith formation at workshops throughout the ELCA.[3]

---

1. Unlike naming the congregations, pastors, and other church professionals in chapters 2, 3, and 5, "St. Mary's" and "Pastor M" are pseudonyms. We have two rationales for this decision. First, the size of the congregation makes it difficult to maintain the individuals' anonymity; second, Pastor M is no longer serving at St. Mary's, and the Voyage process is no longer part of the congregation's outreach to the community.

2. Pastor M (pseudonym), interview by Rhoda Schuler, August 7, 2018. Subsequent quotations and summaries of Pastor M are from this interview, unless otherwise noted.

3. Hoffman, *Faith Forming Faith*, 5, emphasis in original.

St. Mary's

St. Mary's, located in a bedroom community in the northeast, was the smallest of the congregations we researched, with an average Sunday attendance of seventy-two and baptized membership of roughly two hundred in 2018. The community is working class and multiethnic, drawing families to it because of affordable housing and good public schools. Founded in the early twentieth century, St. Mary's demographics are typical of many Lutheran parishes: older. The church building is modest with a typical sanctuary from that period, a fellowship hall on the lower level, and an attractive education wing added in the middle of the twentieth century. The preschool, started by the congregation in the 1970s, has a good reputation in the community, is affordable, and serves over one hundred children.

Within months of attending the training, Pastor M implemented one of Hoffman's ideas to introduce this adult faith formation process to her congregation, offering several weeks of Scripture study for the whole congregation using the method Hoffman advocated. In the fall of her first year at the parish, she and a lay catechist of the congregation, Pearl, launched Voyage, as they called the process,[4] with two small groups of members that met weekly. When I visited and conducted the first set of interviews in August 2018, the congregation was preparing for a third year of the Voyage process. This case study reveals a strong intergenerational clergy-laity leadership team, shaping a faith formation process that drew disparate individuals into the process, fostered a sense of belonging among participants, and ignited a missional spirit at St. Mary's, a small aging congregation.

LEADERSHIP TEAM:
DOUBTING THOMAS AND ZEALOUS PAUL

In her first three and one-half years, Pastor M infused the congregation with new energy, having shepherded the congregation through development of a new mission statement, restructured the church council (around key aspects of the mission statement), and implemented new worship times. Yet Pastor M described herself as the "Doubting Thomas" of the Voyage leadership team and alluded to her doubts and concerns at several points in our interview. The identification of Pearl, a retired longtime member of St. Mary's, as "zealous Paul" is implicit in many of Pearl's recorded comments, especially this one: "I want to share my faith as much as I can while I am

---

4. Pastor M's husband, a Trekkie, suggested the name, which comes from the TV series *Star Trek: Voyager* that aired from 1995 to 2001 on UPN.

on this earth."[5] The mutual respect they have for each other, combination of necessary skill sets to implement Hoffman's faith formation process, and genuine love for and interest in others coalesced into a dream team that developed and fine-tuned a "successful" adult faith formation process during Pastor M's tenure as pastor of St. Mary's.

That mutual respect Pastor M and Pearl have for one another came through in their separate interviews. Twice Pastor M referred to Pearl as her "co-minister" and spoke of her need to "let go of the reins" as pastor and allow Pearl to use her gifts in the small group discussions, which were at the core of the faith formation practice. And as Pearl noted, the presence of the pastor in these discussions was not always helpful, saying "people act differently with a pastor than with lay people." Yet Pearl valued Pastor M's leadership. When asked to name weaknesses in the congregation, Pearl replied, "People are not excited about their faith; Pastor has sure tried to change that." She also spoke in warm and supportive ways of the many changes Pastor M had introduced to the congregation.

Pastor M's comment to "let go of the reins" indicates a high level of maturity and self-assurance for a young pastor in her first call. She had earned the respect of members and seekers through strong preaching, good pastoral care, and a leadership style that empowered others (especially Pearl). Dayla, an older, cradle Lutheran who participated in the process, commented that Pastor M's "messages" were very inspiring and "hit home a lot of times."[6] Stanley, a millennial, described a theological conversation with Pastor M that transformed his understanding of the Eucharist.[7] Perhaps most revelatory of her pastoral gifts was my exchange with Betty, who said of her, "She isn't what I expected a pastor to be like." In response to my follow-up question, she continued, "She's a little non-conformist—like a regular, normal person, welcoming; she's one reason why I stay here."[8]

Two couples I interviewed commented on the warm welcome they experienced from Pastor M and Pearl. Laura and Harry were actively seeking

---

5. Pearl (pseudonym), interview by Rhoda Schuler, August 6, 2018. Subsequent quotations and summaries of Pearl are from this interview, unless otherwise noted.

6. Dayla (pseudonym), interview by Rhoda Schuler, April 20, 2019; and by phone June 2019. Subsequent quotations and summaries of Dayla are from these interviews, unless otherwise noted.

7. Stanley (pseudonym), interview by Rhoda Schuler, August 6, 2018. Subsequent quotations and summaries of Stanley are from this interview, unless otherwise noted.

8. Betty (pseudonym), interview by Rhoda Schuler, August 6, 2018. Subsequent quotations and summaries of Betty are from this interview, unless otherwise noted.

a new church home with a focus on the gospel. Harry remembered details from the first email sent by Pastor M, describing it as "light-hearted" and full of "peace and blessings" not "fire and brimstone." They also spoke highly of Pearl, commenting on her ability to "verbalize well" and to "listen."[9] Bob and Ruth, also seeking a church home, said that Pastor M had "impressed the socks off us." The welcome she gave them on her first visit made such an impact on them that "we didn't go anywhere else." When they announced they were expecting their first child, they recalled that Pearl sent them a congratulatory email.[10]

That she is a master teacher is one of the unifying themes running through my interview with Pearl. She's flexible, shaping the material used to the needs of the group. She stressed the importance of the first stage in the process (period of inquiry) because, as she said, this is where you "learn their story and then you go from there, asking what does this group need." Knowing each one's story, recognizing the unique qualities in each, is the key to her teaching: "As you get to know people, all are at different places." Elsewhere she commented, "You don't feed a baby steak." When I asked a question about resources that could reach millennials and Gen Z people, she replied, "It's not age-related, it's faith related. It's where they're at" in their faith journey that shaped Pearl's decisions about resource materials for instruction and formation. When I sat down to interview Pastor M (after interviewing Pearl the previous day), I repeated a comment someone else had said to me: "Who wouldn't want to talk to Pearl for an hour?" To which Pastor M responded, "And she's not really talking," a comment on Pearl's pastoral listening skills. The second unifying theme in Pearl's interview is the motivation for her teaching, which is her missional zeal to share her faith with others, exemplified by her comments about Pastor M trying to get people "excited about their faith" and these words: "If you *want* to share your faith, it gets contagious."

From the confluence of Pastor M's youth and energy and of Pearl's wisdom and skilled teaching flowed a leadership team willing to experiment, adjust, and fashion a successful faith formation process. Pastor M's "doubting Thomas" syndrome was tempered by Pearl's missionary zeal and

---

9. Laura and Harry (pseudonyms), interview by Rhoda Schuler, August 7, 2018. Subsequent quotations and summaries of Laura and Harry are from this interview, unless otherwise noted.

10. Bob and Ruth (pseudonyms), interview by Rhoda Schuler, April 19, 2019; and by phone June 11, 2019. Subsequent quotations and summaries of Bob and Ruth are from these interviews, unless otherwise noted.

natural skills as a teacher and facilitator.[11] Their shared compassion and genuine love for others gave birth to a faith formation process that first and foremost created a sense of belonging among the participants.

ENGAGEMENT WITH THE WORD: FORMING COMMUNITY AND BELONGING AMONG SEEKERS

The adult catechumenate at St. Mary's was modeled on that developed by Paul Hoffman. It, like other adult catechumenates, draws inspiration from the early church and follows the fourfold pattern discussed in the introduction: periods of inquiry, catechesis, enlightenment (baptismal preparation), and mystagogy.[12] By the third year, according to Pastor M, she and Pearl opted for a streamlined pattern for smaller congregations suggested by Hoffman in his workshop, which combined the periods of catechesis and enlightenment and compressed the whole process by several months. The "inquirers" or seekers—those who had visited and expressed interest in St. Mary's—were invited to weekly gatherings of Scripture study led by Pearl, preceded by a meal or light refreshments. Serving a meal was one of the practices about which Pastor M, "doubting Thomas," had initial reservations; but she later recognized its value for building community and a sense of belonging.

Betty aptly described the Scripture study: "We didn't ask questions; we answered them." As Pearl explained, she would read the appointed Gospel text for the Sunday three times. First, the participants were instructed to listen for a word or phrase that caught their attention. After sharing their thoughts with the group, they heard the reading a second time as they reflected on this question: How is God speaking to you in this story? Each would then share their thoughts in a phrase or sentence. For the third reading, the group was given a question specific to the text that had been prepared by Pearl and Pastor M. *Faith Forming Faith* suggests this example for the lectionary reading of John 9, the man born blind: "Out of what darkness and into what light is God calling you?"[13] As Betty said, the group answered

---

11. Pearl has all the qualities described in *Welcome to Christ: Catechetical Guide*: "What are the qualities of a catechist?," 32–41.

12. Hoffman, *Faith Forming Faith*, 7. The term "enlightenment" is language used in patristic sources and in the Roman Catholic RCIA documents.

13. Hoffman, *Faith Forming Faith*, 13.

rather than asked questions, and through the sharing of individual answers to a common question, a bond was formed within the group.

As recommended by the Hoffman-led workshop, the gatherings closed with the participants praying for one another, of which Pastor M said, "I'm again the chief doubter—even for Pearl this was a new practice." As Pearl explained, the group would stand in a circle, hold hands, and was instructed to pray for the person on their right or left, as determined by Pearl, who would begin and end the prayer time. Not everyone participated initially, and one person at first experienced it as "intimidating," while another expressed discomfort when others prayed on that one's behalf. Yet Pearl reported that by the end of the period of catechesis/enlightenment, most did so willingly, although there was an occasional surprise: "And when [one usually quiet person] prayed out loud, I nearly fell on the floor."

These simple practices, reading and meditating on lectionary Gospel readings and praying for one another, touch on all three of the BEs, believing, belonging, and behaving, in the "conversion process" discussed by Diana Butler Bass and Alan Kreider in the Introduction to Part I. When asked what the most meaningful aspects of the Voyage process at St. Mary's were, nearly all named the small group discussion first. When asked why, the answers varied. Some commented on the connections they drew between the discussions and hearing the text in Sunday worship; as Harry said, the reflection and discussion "changed my take" on the Scripture readings. From these responses one sees how the practice of hearing and meditating on the word strengthened their *belief* in Christ. Several named the prayer time as that which made the gathering meaningful, alluding to the way in which these gatherings shaped their *behavior* by teaching them to pray for others.

Yet what stands out in their collective responses is the sense of community and *belonging* that was created over the weeks of their gatherings. Stanley's interview unfolded the way he gradually experienced a sense of acceptance, first from Pastor M and Pearl, and later from others in the group. Victoria recalled the gatherings as a time to hear "what others thought and had been through."[14] Betty's response was similar, saying that "you learned a lot about other people but also . . . about yourself." And Laura commented that "at prayer time by the end [of the gatherings] we felt like St. Mary's was a family." As Paul Hoffman wrote, the purpose is "faith formation, not

---

14. Victoria, (pseudonym), Facetime interview by Rhoda Schuler, October 13, 2018. Subsequent quotations and summaries of Victoria are from this interview, unless otherwise noted.

PART I: CONTEXT IS EVERYTHING

faith *information*."[15] At St. Mary's, as the study of Scripture formed each Voyager's faith, the process itself also created a sense of belonging among the participants. Faith formation happens in community, not in isolation, and authentic faith formation also forms individuals into community.

RITUALS: DRAWING CATECHUMENS INTO THE LIFE OF THE CHURCH AND CREATING SPACE FOR A MISSIONAL ETHOS

Pastor M and Pearl settled into a pattern and rhythm for the adult catechumenate at St. Mary's that began in early January with the weekly meetings of the Voyagers; during Lent the "coaches" (their word for sponsors) joined the weekly meeting of Scripture study and prayer, thus expanding the community of Voyagers to include members of the congregation. The whole congregation participated in the catechumenal process through the many rituals that marked the stages in the process. These included a rite of welcome on the first Sunday in Lent, rites on subsequent Sundays in Lent that included a blessing and gift (Bible, hymnal, catechism, etc.), and the affirmation of baptism at the Easter Vigil. The rituals accomplished the dual purpose of drawing the catechumens into the life of the congregation and of creating space for a missional ethos to develop and mature within the congregation's membership.

Pastor M had confessed in our interview that the many rituals suggested in Hoffman's workshop and book brought out her Doubting Thomas syndrome; at first she had said, "No one wants to stand up in front of a congregation . . ." The experiences of the Voyagers indicate the power of ritual. Commenting on the weekly rituals during Lent, Ruth said that these "cemented our identity in the church." Dayla had vivid memories of the blessing with laying on of hands at the Vigil, saying "I got a warm, very good feeling . . . In some respects [it was like] how Jesus would lay his hands on people, and they were healed." Bob made some profound theological statements based on his experience of the rituals; he spoke of "water as a symbol of life" and of being "born again in Christ" through the sprinkling ritual and affirmation of baptism. He also remembered that at the enrollment rite "the congregation [was] going to pray for you in the next step of this voyage." These rituals—enrollment at the beginning, the weekly rituals

---

15. Hoffman, *Faith Forming Faith*, 10, emphasis in original.

during Lent, and the affirmation of baptism at the Easter Vigil—profoundly drew Ruth, Dayla, and Bob into a deeper relationship with Christ and his body, the church.

Dayla also described "feeling at home" on the Sunday of the rite of enrollment; from that point on the manner in which people of the congregation greeted her on Sundays made a deep impression on her. Betty made a similar comment about the rite of enrollment: "I was taking a step forward and others were seeing that and welcoming me." Stanley also recalled the affirmation he felt at the Vigil when the whole congregation was "praying openly" for all the Voyagers. One can conclude from these comments that the public rituals fostered a missional ethos in the congregation. From a practical perspective, active members of St. Mary's could be sure that these particular folks were in the Voyage process (and not some longtime member who would expect to be known), and thus they could approach them in the narthex and converse. From a ritual perspective, the practice of praying weekly for the Voyagers formed them as people of God who supported those preparing for baptismal affirmation and committing themselves to living out their baptism in this community of faith. To welcome the Voyagers and pray for them created space both physical and spiritual for the people of St. Mary's to be missional in word and deed.

MYSTAGOGY: FORMING THE BELIEFS OF NEOPHYTES

The Voyage process concluded with a period of mystagogy during the fifty days of Easter. In the early church, this period focused on instruction in the sacraments, or *mystērion*, to use the Greek word, following the baptism and first reception of the Eucharist by the adult neophytes. The Voyagers continued to meet weekly for similar instruction, including review of Luther's *Small Catechism* and the history of the congregation. What they had seen, heard, and experienced ritually was now laid out for them in a systematic, instructional format. Many found it beneficial.

Betty, who had said that her initial desire when she joined the Voyage process was "to know more," said of the resource on the catechism used at St. Mary's,[16] "that was what I was looking for." Ruth, for whom belief was important, had said early in the interview, "To be honest, the process is backwards; first you should learn what a church believes—then go to Bible study to grow together." For Ruth, what was most meaningful and beneficial

---

16. Erlander, *Baptized, We Live*.

in the period of mystagogy was the resource on the catechism, which she described as a "booklet with easy language, good for discussion. For me, it was a refresher of confirmation." Bob, her husband, agreed, saying she had "hit it on the head—confirmation refresher." Dayla, the octogenarian cradle Lutheran, said, "I feel I learned more about the background of my religion."

With the phrase, "the process is backwards," Ruth articulated what is most radical about the catechumenal model used at St. Mary's, especially for Lutherans, whose sixteenth-century origins are steeped in controversies about what Lutherans believed vis-à-vis other Protestants and Roman Catholics. Yet the experiences of Voyagers support the scholarly work of Diana Butler Bass, who claim that for many on the path to conversion a sense of "belonging" precedes "believing." According to Bass, "Belonging is an issue of identity" and "is intimately related to being."[17] Her research, rooted in the postmodern North American context, uncovers these core questions: Who I am? And where do I belong? As a Christian, she finds that the journeys narrated in Scripture have "one grounding point: God. And who is God? I am (Exod 3:14)."[18] For Bass, that grounding point, the I am, transforms the existential questions of today into Whose am I?[19] This is the question addressed in the periods of inquiry and catechesis at St. Mary's, as Voyagers explore whose they are in relation to the Sunday Gospel readings. The third question to which they respond asks in one form or another how they see themselves in relation to the story of Jesus. Once they have found their identity in God and this community of faith, the questions of believing are addressed in the period of mystagogy.

"LIKE HERE TO HERE": A LIFE-CHANGING PROCESS

When I asked Pearl to "give me an example of one way you see your congregation living out its mission statement," she replied, using air quotes: "We're trying to 'make disciples.'" I responded, "Give me one story of making a disciple," to which Pearl responded as she gestured, "Like here [holding up the palm of her hand toward me] to here [turning her hand 180 degrees]." She then recounted the experience of a Voyager, whom she described as "very cautious, thoughtful, and curious" but who rarely spoke through much of the process. By the end the person had become so fully engaged that, Pearl

---

17. Butler Bass, *Christianity after Religion*, 171.
18. Butler Bass, *Christianity after Religion*, 180.
19. Butler Bass, *Christianity after Religion*, 180–90.

said, "we couldn't shut that one up." To illustrate this "like-here-to-here" faith formation are four narratives of Voyagers. The Scripture passage at the headings encapsulates each one's faith journey, further illustrating the differences among the Voyagers. Taken together, these narratives demonstrate the power of this pattern for Christian faith formation to be effective across generational boundaries, transforming a disparate group of individuals into a community.

For now we see in a mirror, dimly, but then we will see face to face. Now I know only in part; then I will know fully, even as I have been fully known. (1 Cor 13:12)

Betty, a middle-aged boomer, visited St. Mary's in the midst of a personal crisis; despite an overwhelmingly positive first experience worshiping there, Betty was not quite ready to plunge into membership at the parish. As she said, "I wanted to get to know more about the congregation and the people," and she "needed to know more" about what they believed. When she signed up for Voyage, she "was hesitant; I didn't know what to expect." But the period of inquiry, which requires no commitment to attend, drew her in, because she "had so many questions." Her description of initial experiences with the small group discussions and prayer time expressed her ambivalence; she was "nervous" and "uncomfortable." Even though she had been assured there were no wrong answers, she worried, "Am I saying the wrong thing?" Because she is "shy" in front of groups, the prayer time at the end was "intimidating at first."

She came with her many questions, but much to her surprise, "We didn't ask questions; we answered them!" Her desire "to know more" was gradually supplanted by being known—to herself and by others—as the group formed a sense of community. As she expressed it, through the small group discussions and shared prayers, "you learned a lot about other people but also [it's] how you learned about yourself." At one point she contrasted St. Mary's with other churches she had attended; the small size of St. Mary's was "a plus" because it was easy to get to know people. At other parishes she had felt "isolated" and "intimidated." When she expressed concern about the negative effects of social media that many experience, such as isolation, she spoke also of the community she discovered at St. Mary's, seeing the genuine, face-to-face interactions with people connected to a worshiping community as an antidote to the isolation and other problems caused by social media.

Part I: Context is Everything

One can chart Betty's move from ambivalence to assurance through her reactions to the rituals. At the rite of enrollment, she felt "a nervous excitement," and the presence of her coach made her more comfortable with the experience. Reflecting more on this ritual, she said, "I was becoming one of them." She saw that the series of "blessings" on the Sundays in Lent were "building up to the big event" of the Easter Vigil. When asked about the Vigil, she was short on the ritual details but effusive about the overall experience, saying, "It was incredible, beyond my expectations! How can I tell you? The people were cheering at the end." Betty came seeking answers to many questions and a "need to know more." Through the Voyage process, Betty discovered the joy of being fully known by God in a community of believers. One of her most poignant statements summarizes her experience: "I think St. Mary's found me. I don't think I found St. Mary's."

Lord, do not trouble yourself, for I am not worthy . . . ; therefore I did not presume to come to you. (Luke 7:6b–7a)

Stanley's faith journey fits the "profile" of millennials, a much-studied demographic by those concerned about the exodus of this generation from the church.[20] One study identified these primary reasons why many had left: millennials saw the church as "a creativity killer," especially in reimagining what the church might be for their generation; as "shallow" and "boring," with "easy platitudes"; as "repressive" and "exclusive" in a culture with the opposite values; as "antiscience" and a place which does not allow them "to express doubts" about their faith.[21]

When he started the Voyage process, Stanley described how he felt leading up to the rite of enrollment: "impatient; bored and tired." Although he found value in the small group format, he said early in our interview that "I feel like I made people angry." He was acutely aware of generational differences, describing himself as one with "a gray view of the world" in contrast to some in the group with a black/white perspective. The openness of Pastor M and Pearl, who were "very understanding" of his different point of view "even if they didn't agree with me," kept him in the process.

The interview questions, following the sequence of the faith formation process, mirrored Stanley's gradual shift in thinking about St. Mary's, the

---

20. According to Gallup News, membership in a church, synagogue, or mosque dipped below 50 percent in 2020.

21. Kinnaman, *You Lost Me*, 91–93.

Voyage process, and himself. Asked about how he felt in the weeks leading to the Easter Vigil, Stanley replied, "Pretty good. People seemed happier to have me as a part of the community. My point of view changed a little bit. I felt more part of the community at that point, more able to express questions about the reality of God and what I was really feeling."

Stanley's struggles also reflect negative experiences growing up in the Catholic Church. He was taught that the Eucharist was "a privilege," and "If you weren't clean, you didn't go." It was "weird that anyone could go without feeling bad and guilt." He felt unworthy during the group prayer time when Voyagers prayed for one another, saying, "What did I do that was so special that God should do something for me?" A pivotal point for him was a conversation with Pastor M that reoriented his theological understanding of the Eucharist; from that point on he received the sacrament at St. Mary's.

Stanley's journey not only highlights ways in which this pattern of faith formation can "work" for millennials; his story also underscores a reality the church must face: any successful efforts to draw this demographic back into the church will bring about major changes in the church. Although Stanley completed the Voyage process, he is likely to continue carrying with him doubts about his faith and the existence of God; his faith community will need to see the value of "solidarity in not having solidarity" about such core matters of the Christian faith.

Then they told what had happened on the road, and how he had been made known to them in the breaking of the bread. (Luke 24:34)

One might ask whether Dayla, a life-long Lutheran and member of the "greatest generation," needed to attend a lengthy catechumenal process. Why wasn't a letter of transfer enough to get her officially on the membership roll and issue her a box of contribution envelopes? To quote Dayla, "I feel super blessed to go through this. . . . I've never experienced anything like this."[22] The most striking theme emerging from Dayla's interview was that the holistic nature of the process—the various stages and the rituals—all deepened her faith life. The interview questions, specific to the different stages and rituals, seemed to prompt Dayla to speak in broad, general terms about the entire process.

---

22. Dayla often used indefinite pronouns such as "this" and "it," which are best interpreted as references to the entire catechumenal process.

Part I: Context is Everything

For Dayla, believing, rooted in word and sacrament, was a second central theme. She discussed in very specific detail the small group discussions on the Gospel readings, commenting on the multiple readings of the text and times of meditation, and articulating what she found meaningful in the process: "Being able to open up, share what the text meant to me." When asked about Pastor M, she specifically referenced her preaching: "She's fantastic; very inspiring. Her messages hit home a lot of times." Responding to prompts about the weekly blessings during Lent, she named the laying on of hands by her sponsors, recalling "how Jesus would lay his hands on people, and they were healed." Her response demonstrates the power of ritual action to evoke biblical narratives and deepen faith. A question on baptism led her to ruminate on the Eucharist, saying, "I do feel that I'm a little closer to God in my heart and my soul. It [the Voyage process] opened up everything for me."

Dayla's experience mirrors that of the disciples on the road to Emmaus. The Scriptures were opened to her through the weekly text study group and Pastor M's preaching, and in the Eucharist she encountered the risen Christ in a deeper way. As Dayla put it, "I would recommend [Voyage] to other people—even if you are a long-time confirmed and baptized member." "Why?" I asked. Because, she replied, "It gave me a whole different and deeper understanding and reaffirmed everything." Although the process was profoundly personal for her, it was at the same time communal. Commenting on the response of the congregation at the Easter Vigil, she said, "They kind of took to the road with me."

I therefore . . . beg you to lead a life worthy of the calling to which you have been called. (Eph 4:1)

In response to the first prompt, "Tell me how you got connected to St. Mary's," Laura and Harry revealed that both were divorced and that when their relationship became serious, they began the search for a new church home. Harry was anxious to find a church without "the old fire and brimstone," perhaps fearing judgment by the pastor because this middle-aged couple was living together before they married. Their interview illustrates two transformations.

First, as they went through the transformation into a blended family while in Voyage, they became part of "the family" of St. Mary's. Familial language and images occurred frequently as they spoke of their experiences with the congregation. Laura commented that "at the prayer time by the end [of the catechumenal process], we felt like St. Mary's was a family." Harry noted that the shared meal allowed them to get to know people. They were anxious to find a safe space for Laura's son and raved about the ways the people in the congregation "treated him like gold." In their coaches they found a married couple who accepted their not-yet-marital status, whose actions built community, and who helped them find a new home to purchase within a good school district for "their" (Harry's word) son. They delighted in sharing details of their wedding at St. Mary's with Pastor M presiding.

Second, although Laura and Harry's initial goal was to join a church, the Voyage process transformed that goal by transforming their faith, by making disciples of them, disciples of Jesus called to serve in the church and world. Both used the word "proud" to describe how they felt at the rite of enrollment. After verbalizing it, Laura first wondered if it was a sin to feel proud, but then noted that her pride was in "fulfilling a desire for my family." Her life is whole with a loving husband who is committed to her and her son, and who shares her Lutheran faith with a firm commitment. She said, "I have a sense of peace after every Sunday." Harry was proud that he was "keeping a commitment to myself and my family." The period of mystagogy transformed their faith. Laura, raised in the Lutheran tradition, was told as a child, "This is what you need to know—but [I was] never taught why." During the mystagogy sessions, she said she learned what it means to be "a real Lutheran," and "now we know how we want to live as Christians." They had already taken leading roles in VBS, expressed their desire to serve as coaches, and wanted to serve in other ways. As Harry said, "I don't have keys—yet." As "real Lutherans," they were resting secure in their salvation through faith in Christ and were excited "to lead a life worthy" of their calling from Jesus.[23]

MISSIONAL ETHOS AND LIFE PASSAGES: OPPORTUNITIES FOR A MINISTRY OF PRESENCE

As Dr. Scott Bruzek, pastor of St. John's Lutheran Church, said, "When a visitor steps over our threshold, it's a miracle." Connecting those seekers

---

23. By 2021, Laura was president of the congregation; phone conversation with the current pastor of St. Mary's, September 28, 2021. No doubt the household now has keys to the church.

Part I: Context is Everything

to others in the congregation is a vital step toward drawing adults into a congregation's faith formation process. That the Voyage process fostered a missional ethos at St. Mary's was expressed consistently by the participants, who universally spoke of the welcome and sense of belonging they experienced from the whole congregation, primarily through interactions during and following worship. The coaches, carefully chosen by Pastor M and Pearl, are the bridge between those two leaders and congregational members. The regular rituals not only help the membership identify the Voyagers but also ritually link them to the whole catechumenal process in a way that a pastor's "new member class," conducted in isolation from the worshiping community, can never do.

Victoria's story is one of those miracles of a visitor crossing the threshold: "After the first service I knew this was where I needed to be," she said, and then went into more detail. She "was very scared" to go the first time but sat next to a "welcoming woman" who took her downstairs for coffee after the service. Her words illustrate the power of a seemingly small act of welcome. If she knew the welcoming woman's name, Victoria did not mention it, so there is no way to hear the story from the perspective of this nameless woman; but perhaps she might find herself in the company of those on Christ's right hand saying, "Lord, ... when was it that we saw you a stranger and welcomed you?" (Matt 25:38).

Pastor M and Pearl, as a respected lay leader in the congregation, acted as the welcoming gateway for many. More than one Voyager commented on the welcoming emails Pastor M sent, and Bob and Ruth were particularly touched by the congratulatory email from Pearl when they announced they were expecting their first child. Being present with Voyagers during life transitions was not limited to the Voyage leaders, Pastor M and Pearl. Stanley reached out to his coach when he was experiencing a major life crisis, who then offered helpful guidance. Betty, whose mother had died shortly before our interview, said that her coach came to the visitation and other members attended the funeral at the Catholic parish, a gesture that she "wasn't expecting." Laura and Harry noted that people from the congregation had attended their wedding, which Harry described as "a headlining act" for St. Mary's. The presence of several people from the congregation at their wedding had clearly cemented for Laura and Harry that they were part of this "family" of faith. Voyagers' sense of belonging was intensified when congregational members showed up for these major rituals associated with life transitions. Such ways of connecting with new disciples can be encouraged and fostered by the leadership until it becomes a *habitus* of the people of God.

FINAL WORDS OF CAUTION AND HOPE

To end this idyllic picture of a successful catechumenal process, I conclude with some caveats. A significant finding of our research is the importance of a long pastorate for the process to be developed contextually and to take root in the whole congregation. Shortly after I concluded my research, Pastor M left St. Mary's. Then the pandemic hit, and St. Mary's was unable to continue the Voyage process. In fall 2021 I spoke by phone with the current pastor of St. Mary's, who did not seem inclined to resume the Voyage process. Each pastor brings a specific set of gifts and priorities to a parish, and I sensed that this pastor had her own vision for outreach.

Whether St. Mary's could have maintained its adult faith formation over the long haul had Pastor M stayed is an open question. Both she and Pearl articulated a primary weakness of the model, namely, that it was solely dependent on the leadership of four people: Pastor M, Pearl, and their spouses, who prepared and served the meals for the Voyagers from early January through Lent. Pearl commented on the difficulty they had cajoling members to prepare a dessert or salad for the meals, and Pastor M spoke of the sheer exhaustion the four of them felt after Easter Sunday. Without doubt, introducing and implementing this kind of labor-intensive process in a small congregation is risky because it requires significant resources of time, talent, and treasure in the short and long term.

Nevertheless, by weaving together many interviews into this narrative, the transformative power of this faith formation process for the individuals and the congregation was unmistakable. The church is called to preach, teach, and baptize, making disciples of all peoples. St. Mary's did so effectively through a welcoming spirit that created a sense of belonging and modeled Christian behavior, through rituals that supported Voyagers and connected them to the worshiping community, and by communicating the beliefs of the church in a way that created and deepened the faith of participants.

5

REDEEMER

Receiving, Teaching, Celebrating, and Sharing Christ Jesus

I have a picture from the time that I spent at Redeemer researching their catechumenate during Holy Week in 2019.[1] All of the newly baptized and confirmed—along with Pastor Dien Ashley Taylor, Deaconess Raquel A. Rojas, and me, graciously invited into their family picture—are gathered in their white robes with the baptismal font in the foreground. They are holding their Redeemer crosses, a gift from the assembly. In that picture, one can see the impact of the catechumenate upon those received into Redeemer's life as Pastor Taylor describes it: "Glowing, happy people who were just birthed into the body of Christ at Redeemer."[2] The change is palpable. These newly baptized and confirmed are different than they were before they made the journey through Redeemer's catechumenate. They are among the "glowing, happy people" that are Redeemer Evangelical Lutheran

---

1. I visited Redeemer three times during the course of our research-funded grant: October 2–4, 2018; March 8–11, 2019; and April 18–22, 2019. Throughout the course of those visits I interviewed Pastor Dien Ashley Taylor, Deaconess Raquel A. Rojas, church secretary Sandy (pseudonym), and members (pseudonyms) Peter, Maura, Preston, Stewart, Julie, Mark, Lydia, Bertrand, Holly, Delilah, Millie, Leanne, Amy, Lily, and David.

2. Rev. Dr. Dien Ashley Taylor, interview by Kent J. Burreson, October 3, 2018. Subsequent quotations and summaries of Pastor Taylor are from this interview, unless otherwise noted.

Church, the Bronx, New York. The change that the catechumenate effects at Redeemer is apparent. Reflecting the beginning of Redeemer's mission statement, "By God's grace," one participant indicated, "I did something amazing."[3] The catechumenal journey culminating in baptism truly has renewed and regenerated them. They *are* different.

The changes in the catechumens' lives resulting from Redeemer's catechumenate are part of the fabric of this community's life. The catechumenate is inseparable from Redeemer's communal life, and the congregation's communal life is inseparable from their catechumenate. There is an integrated dance taking place between their catechumenate and congregational life. This has been the case since Pastor Dien Ashley Taylor arrived at Redeemer in May 2001, having served first as the associate pastor of Trinity Evangelical Lutheran Church in the Bronx. He developed the catechumenate shortly after that as the means for evangelizing and incorporating new and de-churched Christians into Redeemer's life. Growing up in Queens, another New York City borough, meant that as a participant in the cultural milieu that is the Big Apple, he arrived at Redeemer with street credibility in the Bronx. He was convinced that the ancient catechumenate—as exemplified in the Roman Catholic Rite of Christian Initiation of Adults and in the Lutheran *Welcome to Christ* materials—could be adapted to the cultural context that is the Bronx. He also believed that the catechumenate flowed out of Redeemer's history and could be shaped to find a central place in the congregation's culture. In many ways, Redeemer always had done church differently than surrounding congregations.

The catechumenate would be another way for Redeemer to be specifically Lutheran in being church, as it is surrounded by other Christian denominations and other religious institutions within walking distance. Yet, there was hope that Redeemer's catechumenate could become a model for other congregations as a way of living as a community that regularly births and nurtures new Christians in their walk together as the body of Christ. And so it has. Encouraging other congregations—even in greater New York and in the Atlantic region—that the catechumenate can be a great blessing to congregational identity and life has not always been easy. Nonetheless, Pastor Taylor, Deaconess Rojas (who joined the congregation as a deaconess intern in 2009 and then as a called deaconess in 2010), and

---

3. Lily (pseudonym), interview by Kent J. Burreson, March 9–10, 2019. Subsequent quotations and summaries of Lily are from this interview, unless otherwise noted.

the congregation itself have made every effort to "light a fire"[4] in other congregations to embrace the benefits of the catechumenate's faith formation practices.

The results are apparent. The number and viability of LCMS congregations are shrinking in every area of the country, and New York and the Bronx are no exception.[5] But, as Pastor Taylor says, "Redeemer is still standing."[6] Redeemer has grown both numerically and spiritually. They are known both in the neighborhood and in New York City. And those who make the journey through their catechumenate generally stay. The congregation's retention rate over the years of the catechumenate is over 90 percent. This includes those who remain a part of Redeemer's local life and others who become active in other congregations when they move away from the Bronx. As Deaconess Rojas says, "Look at what God is doing at Redeemer!"

REDEEMER: A PRAYING COMMUNITY OF SERVICE

What Redeemer is doing springs from its mission statement: "Redeemer Evangelical Lutheran Church, by God's grace, is a praying community of service that receives, teaches, celebrates and shares Christ Jesus."[7] This mission statement is more than just a formality. It is a living expression of the congregation. At every worship service at Redeemer the congregation speaks their mission at least once, if not numerous times, as led by Pastor Taylor. The congregation not only owns the words by memory, the people also know how to express it through hand motions. To witness the congregation's speaking and signing of its mission is a spiritually uplifting experience. The energy, joy, and conviction is tangible. Their mission

---

4. Deaconess Raquel A. Rojas, interview by Kent J. Burreson, October 3, 2018. Subsequent quotations and summaries of Deaconess Rojas are from this interview, unless otherwise noted.

5. According to the LCMS website, membership has fallen from a peak of 2.6 million baptized in 1969 to "nearly 2 million baptized" (1.96 million) in 2018, the most recent information available on the denomination's website. As with many US denominations, the membership is aging, and congregations are shrinking in size, although not as dramatically as some.

6. Pastor Taylor reports that the number of Lutheran (LCMS and ELCA) congregations in the Bronx has shrunk from nearly thirty to eleven in the past forty years.

7. Redeemer Evangelical Lutheran Church, the Bronx, website.

statement expresses who they are. They embody it in their life together in all its aspects, but no less so through their catechumenate.

BY GOD'S GRACE: A BRIEF HISTORY OF REDEEMER

This praying community of service was founded in the Wakefield area of the Bronx as an outreach by St. Mark's Evangelical Lutheran Church in nearby Yonkers. The first worship service occurred on Easter Sunday, April 15, 1928, in a rented storefront. The fledgling congregation purchased property at the corner of Boyd Avenue and Barnes Avenue, where the current church building and adjacent parish house still reside. While the Wakefield neighborhood has experienced significant change since 1928, the pastoral office has been a point of continuity in the congregation's life. As it approaches its one-hundred-year anniversary, Redeemer has had only five pastors. The two longest serving pastors have been the two most recent, Rev. Theodore Wittrock (1969–2000) and Rev. Dr. Dien Ashley Taylor (2001–present).[8] This pastoral continuity and stability is one of the primary factors in the vitality of congregational life and in the congregation's grounding in the pattern of the catechumenate. Pastor Taylor knows the city well and is able to negotiate interpersonally through the governmental, societal, cultural, economic, and ecclesial and spiritual realities that constitute New York City and the Bronx in particular.

Redeemer has also benefited from the ministry of others within congregational life and the catechumenate. From 2002 until her death in 2011, Rosa Cruz Molina served as Redeemer's educated lay catechist, assisting Pastor Taylor in the formation of adults into faith and life. In 2010, following her internship at Redeemer (and a neighboring congregation) Raquel A. Rojas was called to serve as a full-time deaconess. She continues to play a primary role alongside Pastor Taylor in the implementation of the catechumenate. Lastly, religious educator and parish office administrator Sandy has also played a vital role in the catechumenate and in church life. Born in the South Bronx, when she was two years old, her family moved to the Wakefield section of the Bronx and joined Redeemer. She began teaching Sunday school at Redeemer when she was sixteen and has been a faithful member for over half a century. Having served as an early childhood educator and then devoted her time to raising her children, she eventually became the parish office administrator while also serving as the volunteer

---

8. He has a PhD in religious education.

director of religious education. She calls herself an "outspoken advocate for the catechumenate," a position from which she says she will never be swayed.[9] She invests herself in the catechumenate, assisting with organizational details, serving every year as a sponsor, often for multiple people, and trumpeting the process to the catechumens, the congregation, and the community. Strong pastoral and lay commitment to and leadership of the catechumenate is critical to its success at Redeemer.

REDEEMER: A PLACE "WHERE GOD'S PEOPLE PRAY"

To visit Redeemer and to enter their catechumenal process is to witness the congregation's life in action.[10] Sandy describes Redeemer as a congregation that is "Spirit-filled, open, and real in their life together," with a catechumenate that reflects that. In the catechumenate, one sees that they are a community that receives, teaches, celebrates, and shares Christ Jesus. Sandy believes that this is grounded on former Pastor Theodore Wittrock's legacy of love. He was committed to the congregation and the constantly changing neighborhood around it. Pastor Taylor has carried that legacy into the present. Following Pastor Taylor's installation, worship attendance initially doubled and has grown increasingly since then. This has happened in the midst of declines in membership and attendance at LCMS churches and in other churches in Wakefield and in the Bronx. As a result of their growth and vibrancy as a congregation, they have been a beacon for other congregations in the area and an aid to struggling congregations. A leading

---

9. Sandy (pseudonym), interview by Kent J. Burreson, October 2, 2018. Subsequent quotations and summaries of Sandy are from this interview, unless otherwise noted.

10. Redeemer's catechumenate as formation in the parish's life parallels the argument that Diana Macalintal makes in her book *Your Parish Is the Curriculum*. She argues that faith formation is an apprenticeship toward discipleship. As such, faith formation *is* the responsibility of the entire parish. The members of the parish do what they normally do as Christians but recognize that they are witnessing at all times to the catechumens and neophytes. They are asked to give attention to how they live as Christians so as to best model a life of faith that flows from the gospel. In this sense, as Macalintal notes, the catechumenate is not a program, but a family. Catechumens are becoming part of this family. The church, by conducting a faith formation apprenticeship, is incorporating them into this way of conversion and faith. They learn to love Jesus through the love of Jesus' family and learn to love Jesus' family from the love of Jesus that they experience. Through the congregation God is drawing the catechumens into a community of love and forgiveness (38). The entire Christian parish apprentices catechumens, the newly baptized and confirmed, and one another into being disciples of the Lord Jesus.

LCMS pastor in the area refers to Redeemer as a "model congregation." This places pressure on them, but it is born from embracing the responsibility and the possibilities that come from their energetic and spiritually fulfilling life together.

The opportunities in the Bronx and in New York City are abundant. All one has to do is walk the block, as Redeemer often does, and one will see the opportunities. The world is at Redeemer's doorstep. Originally the home to Irish- and Italian-American populations, it is now home to sizable Caribbean (especially Jamaican), Guyanese, Hispanic, and African American populations. The areas around Wakefield, both in the Bronx and near it—Woodlawn, Mt. Vernon, Yonkers—are equally as diverse. African Americans, Caucasians, West Indians, Asians, Hispanics, and others populate many of these areas in significant percentages. A working, middle-class population, Wakefield continues to grow and diversify.

Historically this demographic shift has been a struggle for Lutheran congregations of German or Scandinavian heritage. Yet, Redeemer, out of its legacy of love, embraced this reality with joy and vigor. Following the lead of Pastors Wittrock and Taylor, leaders in the congregation were able to identify with and welcome the move to a non-German, diverse racial makeup. They have taken to heart being able to embrace their community and to live fully within it. Their property, especially the front lawn, is a community gathering place. The congregation itself often gathers there and invites those passing by and who live in the neighborhood to join them. They actively engage in community outreach—to taxi drivers, those living in the prostitution industry, and to those learning to speak English as a second language. The congregation maintains an active online presence through their website, including numerous videos and pictures that manifest their life together.

One of the primary ways that they connect with people in the Bronx is through their website's prayer submission portal. They truly aim to be a place where "God's People pray." Their mission is to engage as many people as they can with the good news of Christ. As Deaconess Raquel says, "We cannot be afraid. One of our goals is to work so that more people—children, youth, and adults—will know Jesus." This does not mean there are not challenges and weaknesses in Redeemer's life. Sandy cited the lack of parking (they have no parking lot), the ongoing need for financial resources, and staffing needs. Pastor Taylor and Deaconess Rojas carry a significant burden in nurturing congregational life. Although, they would not call it a burden. It is a call that they cherish. And that is because it leads to renewed life in the congregation and the community. As one catechumen expressed it, "Redeemer is authentic. . . . This was the type of life I wanted. It felt good and I felt alive here."[11]

SHARING . . . CHRIST JESUS

Authenticity is characteristic of Redeemer's life because it is characteristic of the catechumenate there. Redeemer's adult catechumenal process structurally looks very similar to the RCIA and to the ancient catechumenate. The four periods of the catechumenate—Inquiry, Catechumenate, Enlightenment, and Post-Baptismal Mystagogy—are all included. The ritual transitions also follow those ancient and RCIA patterns: Acceptance into the Catechumenate, Enrollment for Initiation, and the Rites of Initiation on Holy Saturday. Normally the Inquiry period begins in September and Mystagogy ends at the beginning of June.[12] Pastor Taylor uses many of the texts from the rites of the RCIA, supplementing and adapting them toward Lutheran sensibilities where necessary with the rites found in *Welcome to Christ*, the inter-Lutheran catechumenal resource published in the early 1990s.

The first period of the catechumenate, Inquiry, is truly a fluid venture. The Bronx, and the Wakefield area within it, are no exception to this fluidity, as very transient communities. People come and go. That transient nature applies to the catechumenate as well. People are often coming and going from the catechumenate. And that is all right. Redeemer's catechumenate, especially the period of Inquiry, needs to be flexible, with the pathways into and out porous in order to pastorally serve those who are inquiring. It is not uncommon for people to enter the catechumenate and then take a hiatus before it ends, only to return in a subsequent year. Some have entered and exited the catechumenate three times or more. But once someone has entered, Pastor Taylor considers that person to have come under his pastoral guidance. If the person leaves the catechumenate, he will continue to pastorally minister to them. He will call to check up on them on a periodic basis. He will encourage the person to continue to attend worship and to re-enter

---

11. Maura (pseudonym), interview by Kent J. Burreson, October 2, 2018. Subsequent quotations and summaries of Maura are from this interview, unless otherwise noted.

12. Over the years they have occasionally run two cohorts at the same time. The second cohort would be structured around summer and fall feast days, culminating with the Rites of Initiation on All Saints' Day.

the catechumenate at the time that is best for them, all while understanding the dynamics of human life and reasons why a person might opt to leave, only to begin again later. While the catechumenate is a group-oriented experience at Redeemer, each catechumen walks within that group as an individual. It is not a one-size-fits-all approach. Redeemer nurtures the individual experience within the context of the corporate experience.

Corporately, the period of inquiry is word-centered. Throughout the catechumenate the Sunday readings serve as the focal point for instruction. Deaconess Rojas and Pastor Taylor supplement the focus on the proclaimed word with reflection on Martin Luther's *Small Catechism*, *Large Catechism*, hymnody, and other classic texts from the Christian tradition, both ancient and modern. The pedagogical approach in this period includes both mini-lecture and extensive discussion. As Julie notes, "There were always activities to work on together. And that didn't mean couples were always working together. Couples didn't always sit together. Everybody was together and so paired up as they were seated."[13] Always at the center is the word. Stewart noted that "the word of God was always read and discussed from the different perspectives of those in the room."[14]

RECEIVING . . . CHRIST JESUS, THE SACRAMENTAL WATER AND FIRE

"The catechumenate is like snorkeling in the water. You are always in the water," says Sandy, the parish office administrator. That water is the sacramental life of the congregation centered in the word. The faith formation process at Redeemer is an invitation to enter this sacramental way of life. The congregation would resonate with the words of Revelation 22:17: "The Spirit and the Bride say, 'Come.' And let the one who hears say, 'Come.' And let the one who is thirsty come; let the one who desires take the water of life without price." Redeemer desires the same thing for those whom they invite into their catechumenate: Come and take the water of life.

Calling the Eucharist a sacramental fire at Redeemer also would not be an understatement. The Lord's Supper is at the center of and permeates

---

13. Julie (pseudonym), interview by Kent J. Burreson, October 4, 2018. Subsequent quotations and summaries of Julie are from this interview, unless otherwise noted.

14. As *Go Make Disciples* notes, "Welcome happens [in Inquiry] when the scriptures are broken open and read. As Inquirers read and hear God's word, they tell stories, ask questions, and begin forming relationships in a Christian community" (77).

Part I: Context is Everything

all that Redeemer does. The Divine Service is celebrated at least five times a week: on Saturdays at 5:30 PM, on Sundays at 8:00 AM and 11:00 AM, and on Wednesdays at noon and 6:30 PM. In addition, the Eucharist is celebrated on any feast day during the week. It is not unusual in any given week to have as many as six to seven eucharistic services. As Sandy says, "We celebrate around the altar. All the saints gather together around it. And through it we say, 'We are with you!'" Through the centrality of the Lord's Supper (and baptism too) as the catechumenate demonstrates, the congregation seeks to promote a "sacramental awareness" to itself and to the congregations that are watching Redeemer. Sandy hopes that Redeemer will be a light to other congregations and inspire them where they are serving.

Redeemer's eucharistically centered worship is what might best be described as evangelical-catholic. What does that mean? It is worship that is focused on the gospel of justification by grace through faith in Jesus Christ. But it is worship that flows out of the catholic practice of the church through all times and places and that is contoured to fit the cultural surroundings of the Bronx in the present. The Eucharist follows the Western outline of the Mass as included in the LCMS *Lutheran Service Book*. But Pastor Taylor borrows resources from far and wide. As I experienced, there might be a hymn set to a tune by Mendelssohn juxtaposed to an African American spiritual followed by a modern Jamaican hymn. Pastor Taylor uses the eucharistic prayer tradition of the early church as expressed in contemporary eucharistic prayers. This is coupled with an intentional use of traditional ceremony, such as the elevation of the host and cup. Yet, there is a significant degree of informality, especially in the conversations and calls to response with which Pastor Taylor engages the congregation. The congregation's songs and praises are exuberant. There is no holding back. They understand worship to be a holistic endeavor. Every part of their being, not only their mouths and ears and eyes, but also their hands, arms, legs, and torsos are a part of the expression of praise and thanksgiving for what Christ has done. The catechumenate shapes and calls forth such a holistic, bodily response through the practices and rites that are part of it.

Flowing from that sacramental awareness and rich worship experience, Redeemer is in mission as well: To invite as many as possible to "receive, teach, celebrate, and share Christ Jesus." As Sandy says, the sacrament "equips us to go out the door sharing. Everyone is sent. They know the mission." It is also a reason that teaching is central to the congregation's life. Through their investment in teaching, they form the congregational ethos depicted here. As Sandy says, they are "obsessed with teaching—of all ages, levels, and abilities." The entire community participates in grafting new Christians into the assembly of God's people that is Redeemer. Each parish auxiliary (named with acronyms of body parts) grafts new people into this part of Redeemer's life, underscoring how all are part of the body of Christ and all are engaged in service.

CELEBRATING ... CHRIST JESUS

Redeemer welcomes inquirers and catechumens to a celebration—weekly, yearly, lifelong. It is a worship celebration that embraces the whole person. The various worship rites of Redeemer's catechumenate aim toward holistic formation. The rites attend to the transition of the whole person into a new life in Christ: body, spirit, mind, and heart. It draws forth a rich emotional response from those who make the journey, a response reflective of each catechumen's emotional makeup. As Sandy said, "We [the congregation and the catechumens] live experientially in the catechumenate." The congregation finds in the ritual of the catechumenate a centering identity, the expression of their life together. The catechumenate and its rituals reveal their life as an assembly and form them, repeatedly, to be Redeemer, the place that "receives, teaches, celebrates, and shares Christ Jesus."

The living out of their life together through the rites means that the catechumenate is very public. The catechumens are before the assembly; they are known to all. In fact, Pastor Taylor leads the rites at all of Redeemer's weekend services so that there can be no obstacle for any of the catechumens' attending. Redeemer believes that its life as church is public so that salvation in Christ Jesus is proclaimed in the Wakefield neighborhood, the Bronx, New York City, and beyond. The rites that incorporate people into Redeemer's life should be no less public. This is manifest in the very tangible nature of the rites with their physical gestures and contact.

This also means that the congregation takes ownership of the catechumenate and of its rites. Birthing new Christians is the congregation's responsibility, not just that of the deaconess or the pastor. One of the ways that Pastor Taylor forms this perception in the congregation is through the use of elements in the rites that stretch throughout that year's catechumenate. For example, he chooses a song that accompanies the central actions of the rites. It can be a gospel refrain, a hymn verse, or some other piece that is sturdy enough to be sung repetitively. It fits the themes of the catechumenate that year, does not include "Alleluia" (since many of the rites occur during Lent), and is sufficiently celebrative and christological in nature to be used in five different seasons of the church year.[15] It is a primary ritual marker of the catechumenal journey for the congregation and the catechumens.

The catechumens are making a journey toward conversion to baptism. They are walking on the way that is Jesus. This journey has a teleology: heaven, the kingdom of God. The catechumens (and the assembly) ask and are asked, "Why delay longer? This is the best day to follow Jesus." The catechumens who walk this road to its culmination at the rites of initiation will answer that question affirmatively then: Now *is* the best day! The assembly sings the chosen song for each catechumen at each of the rites. By singing this song for each catechumen, the assembly treats each of them as God's work of salvation and indicates its intention and willingness to foster their conversion and accompany their walk in the life of Christ at Redeemer.

The Stage of Inquiry

The Redeemer assembly understands themselves as God's agents for fostering the conversion of the catechumens. As a result, the catechumens are never alone throughout the process. The congregation surrounds and supports them in a myriad of ways. That sense of being surrounded and being in community begins with the cohort of catechumens themselves. As Sandy noted, one of the congregation's primary concerns is that they are being bound together. Building personal relationships within the cohort of catechumens is seen as a primary task. Formation during inquiry provides the first opportunity to do so. Deaconess Rojas often gives them activities to work on together and provides a common objective for them to aim toward. Then, through the time of inquiry and into the catechumenate, they are able to hear one another's questions. As Stewart realized, "I am not the only one who has these questions."[16] There is a common shared outlook

---

15. In the year that I visited, the chosen refrain was "To Go to Heaven," in *This Far by Faith*, #181. The text reads:
> "To go to heaven my heart is longing. / How shall I get there without prolonging? Chorus: The way is Jesus. He changes never. / The Savior wants you with him forever." After two additional verses, the final verse reads: "*Why delay longer? This is the best day / To follow Jesus, who is the true way.*"

16. Stewart (pseudonym), interview by Kent J. Burreson, October 4, 2018. Subsequent quotations and summaries of Stewart are from this interview, unless otherwise noted.

on inquiring into the Christian life and that common outlook shapes an awareness of community within the group.

The intention is to incorporate them into the broader community that is Redeemer. That is why it is, as Deaconess Rojas observed, an "all-in catechumenate." Anyone who is new to Redeemer walks through the catechumenate in order to participate in Redeemer's life together as a community. Obviously, those who are unbaptized will make the journey. Also, those who are baptized, confirmed, and even coming from other congregations in The Lutheran Church–Missouri Synod or other traditions participate appropriately in the journey and growth as well. With that diversity, then, some coming from other traditions already receive the Lord's Supper and others do not. The latter receive the Lord's Supper after confirmation and reception into membership at the Vigil of Easter. The point here is that everyone makes the journey to Jesus. If one wants to understand Redeemer's life as a praying community of service and what it means to live as a part of this community then the journey through the catechumenate will form one to enter into this community and live in it. This is one of the reasons why the catechumens are known to the Redeemer community and why they are always prominent in the worship services of Redeemer. In this way, as Sandy says, the "catechumens and candidates feel that they are in the center of the action of the body of Christ." They are treasured and valued by Redeemer. They are at the center of Redeemer's life.

The Stage of the Catechumenate

After the period of Inquiry, those who want to explore the Christian faith at Redeemer more intentionally transition into the period of the catechumenate. They do so through the Rite of Acceptance in worship on the first Sunday in Advent. Then they are officially considered catechumens. This rite is centered in the act of anointing and prayer. It recognizes the new life being formed in the catechumens throughout the catechumenate when Pastor Taylor says: "Receive the sign of your new life as catechumens."[17] As the sponsors place their right hands on the shoulders of the catechumens, Pastor Taylor anoints them with the sign of the cross on their foreheads, ears, eyes, lips, heart, shoulders, hands, and feet. As each part of the body is anointed, people are directed to how each body part is involved in discipleship, with shoulders that bear the yoke of Christ, eyes that behold the glory

---

17. Text adapted from *Rite of Christian Initiation of Adults*, 25.

of God, ears that listen to the word of God, and feet that walk in the way of the Lord. Usually at Redeemer each catechumen has more than one sponsor who surrounds them and stretches out their hand either directly on or over the catechumen's shoulder. It is a demonstration of the entire community's support and of the Holy Spirit's presence in the life of the church, now poured out on these catechumens.

The period of the catechumenate intensively deepens the experience of faith for the catechumens at Redeemer. Lasting from the First Sunday of Advent to the First Sunday in Lent, catechumenal sessions continue to focus on the Sunday readings, especially the Gospels and the implications of those readings for the catechumens' faith. These discussions deliver a greater familiarity with the Triune God's revelation of his kingdom through his crucified and risen Son and in the power of the Spirit.

The Stage of Enlightenment

The Rite of Election marks the transition from the period of the Catechumenate into the period of Enlightenment. This is the primary threshold crossing rite at Redeemer. At this point the catechumens indicate their desire to be baptized and the candidates indicate their desire to be confirmed. All express their desire intentionally to embrace the life of discipleship within the family of God at Redeemer. An address to the congregation voices this desire for the catechumens, "Now they ask that, after the scrutinies of Lent, they be allowed to partake of the sacraments of Holy Baptism and the Holy Eucharist, fully participating in the body of Christ."[18] The Rite of Election takes place on the First Sunday in Lent following the creed and preceding the Prayer of the Church in the eucharistic liturgy. Their election for participation in the life of the body of Christ belongs to the sponsors and the congregation. Pastor Taylor announces their election: "I announce to you here that our community has decided to call them to the sacraments. Therefore, I ask their sponsors to state their opinions once again, so that you may all hear. Sponsors, do you consider these candidates worthy to be admitted to the sacraments of Christian initiation? If so, please answer by saying, 'Yes, we do.'"[19] The sponsors bear witness that the congregation is electing them to become a part of this community and calls them to live in conformity to the congregation's life in Christ. The center

18. Text adapted from *Rite of Christian Initiation of Adults*, 67.
19. Text adapted from *Rite of Christian Initiation of Adults*, 68.

of this rite is the signing of the Book of the Elect by the catechumens. With their sponsors surrounding them, and all of the congregation extending their hands over them, each catechumen solemnly signs the book indicating their desire "to enter fully into the life of the Church."[20] Pastor Taylor then declares the catechumens to be members of the Elect who will be initiated into the sacred mysteries (Rites of Initiation) at the Easter Vigil.

The Elect now transition into the period of Enlightenment. This period stretches from the First Sunday in Lent to the Rites of Initiation at the Easter Vigil. It intensifies the formation that has taken place in the previous periods, focusing it toward the Rites of Initiation at the Easter Vigil. Formation through the Sunday readings—supplemented by Luther's *Small Catechism*, the liturgies and hymnody—doesn't fundamentally change. But the opportunity for reflection on the word's significance for living as disciples of the Lord Jesus Christ intensifies. As Maura said of this period, "There was more reflection and preparation. It was more intense but not in a negative way. I understood better the what and the why of Christian faith. . . . We also were more sparing in the kind and amount of food that we ate in association with our gatherings. All of this deepened my sense of commitment throughout this period."

The period of Enlightenment is punctuated by the five Sundays in Lent and the Sunday of the passion with the palm procession. Three of these Sundays especially prepare the Elect for initiation into life in Christ. These are the Sundays of the scrutinies—the third, fourth, and fifth Sundays in Lent. The title "scrutinies" is unfortunately misleading. It appeals back to fourth-century practice when the Christian community closely examined the conduct of the Elect's lives and the seriousness of their commitment toward becoming disciples of the Lord Jesus and their seriousness to engage in spiritual warfare against sin and evil. But the scrutinies in the RCIA are not primarily such intensive examinations of the Elect's lives. The orientation and purpose of the scrutinies in the modern RCIA is for the Elect to "renounce sin and evil and profess faith in the Triune God at their baptism."[21] These scrutinies help people learn about sin—especially their own—and the Holy Spirit elicits in them the desire to be delivered from sin and evil. This is certainly true of the scrutinies at Redeemer.

The scrutinies also allow for the handing over to the Elect of primary catechetical texts: the Apostles' Creed, the Lord's Prayer, and the Ten

---

20. Text adapted from *Rite of Christian Initiation of Adults*, 70.

21. Tufano, Turner, and Williamson, *Guide for Celebrating Christian Initiation with Adults*, 58.

Commandments on each of the successive Sundays. Not only do the Elect hear these primary texts, but Redeemer gives them permanent, physical copies of these formative texts that could be framed and prominently displayed. Through these presentations, the assembly is handing on the faith to those who will soon be initiated into baptismal life. The Elect are asked to make these texts their own and to live the Christian life in light of them.

At Redeemer, the last Scrutiny on the Fifth Sunday in Lent leads into Holy Week: Passion Sunday with its palm procession; Maundy Thursday with the washing of feet; Good Friday with the enactment of the passion narrative; the Easter Vigil with the Rites of Initiation; and Easter Sunday with the newly baptized and confirmed manifesting the new birth in Christ. On Passion Sunday the assembly invites the catechumens to join them in manifesting the presence of Christ by processing with those assembled for worship through their Bronx neighborhood. Their experience intensifies on Maundy Thursday with the rite of the washing of feet. Pastor Taylor washes the feet of all the Elect. This is a deliberate and emotionally heightened experience as the pastor, who has led the Elect throughout the experience of the catechumenate, kneels at their feet and silently washes them. With water in a basin, he caringly cleanses both feet, dries them, and then applies lotion to their feet (a modern inculturation of an ancient practice). Lydia reacted to the powerful gesture in this way, "Pastor washed our feet! In that act, my whole body was taken, a new body was created." So the footwashing serves as a potent expression of the nature of baptism.[22]

The Vigil of Easter

There are no particular rites associated with the catechumenate on Good Friday at Redeemer, although the Elect are encouraged to attend and witness the dramatic visual reenactment of the passion from the Gospel of St. John. The drama of the passion leads into Holy Saturday and the celebration of the Easter Vigil. The journey of the Elect culminates in this night of nights at Redeemer.[23]

Redeemer does not spare anything ritually or symbolically in their practice of the Easter Vigil. They invest fully in each part of it with a

22. See Ambrose of Milan's discussion of the foot washing at baptism in his Mystagogical Catechesis 3.4–7 in Yarnold, *Awe-Inspiring Rites*, 121–23.

23. Redeemer structures their Easter Vigil following the pattern in the *LSB Altar Book* and paralleling the practice of the Roman Catholic Church and other traditions throughout Christianity.

three-hour-plus service (without a significant erosion in attendance). It begins with the outdoor Service of Light and the procession into the church led by the paschal candle. The Elect sit in their own section at the front of the nave, with those being confirmed clothed in their white vestments and those who are to be baptized waiting to receive that vestment during the liturgy. Everyone in the assembly knows that this is the night when the Elect will be incorporated into the parish and the life of the church. As Lily observed, "I didn't realize the magnitude of what was happening at the start of the Vigil. It started with the bonfire and then we placed the pink papers with our sins listed on them into the fire.[24] There were struggles with lighting the [paschal] candle. This elevated for me the stress to trust Jesus, as he says in his own words, 'Believe in me.' From that moment on and throughout the service, all five senses were awakened. We went from dark to light and I knew I had support. I felt supported." Vividly, the body of Christ grows and everyone is engaged.

The rites of initiation have three parts at Redeemer: baptism, confirmation, and participation in the celebration of the Lord's Supper. In the baptismal rite the candidates for baptism gather around the font along with all of their sponsors. The font stands immediately in front of the pews so that the congregation can witness the baptisms. Pastor Taylor anoints the Elect for baptism[25] with the oil of catechumens (an act ritualizing the casting out of sin, evil, and Satan). Following a prayer over the baptismal water, Pastor Taylor asks the Elect to renounce evil, the devil, and the devil's empty promises, and to confess their faith through the words of the Apostles' Creed (which had been delivered to them during the scrutinies). He then baptizes each of them, using an abundance of water over their heads that splashes out of and around the space of the font. As Mark said of his baptism, "The most striking part of the experience was while I was leaning over the font. I can't explain it or put it into words. In the midst of the abundant water—much more than I expected—pouring over me at the font, I felt cleansed and that a burden had been lifted." Pastor Taylor then vests them in their white baptismal gowns and presents them with a candle lit from the paschal candle, symbolic of letting their light, as those baptized into Jesus, shine before people. He then gives a kiss of peace to each on their heads.

---

24. Redeemer allows people to write particular prayers and the like that are placed into the great fire.

25. In 2019 there were three catechumens/elect for baptism.

PART I: CONTEXT IS EVERYTHING

The baptized then return to their seats and join those being confirmed.[26] All the Elect then reject evil and Satan, profess the faith of the Apostles' Creed, and make their vows to live as Christians and remain true to this confession of faith. Pastor Taylor then invites each candidate to the altar rail. He lays his hand on each candidate's head and anoints each candidate with chrism oil. He then passes the oil decanter under their noses so that they can smell the sweet-smelling chrism.[27] Of the signing, Julie said, "I received a visual sign that I have been marked by God. Even now years later I can see and perceive that visual mark God placed upon me through the anointing in the shape of the cross." Amy spoke of the confirmation in very emotional terms: "I didn't expect a ton of the anointing. But I felt the presence. I got emotional with all the others. It very personally touched all of us. Even on Easter Sunday we could all still smell the oil. The oil and the anointing were a physical manifestation of the blessing of God. It heightened the experience of our senses."[28]

The pastor then gives each of them their confirmation verse from Holy Scripture. While all of this is taking place, the candidates are surrounded by their sponsors and others from the congregation who come forward, laying their hands on the candidates' shoulders and extending their hands over them. It is not unusual for each candidate to have five or more people surrounding them at the rail. Following the baptisms and confirmations, the assembly will signal their approval and welcome through thunderous applause. This continues as the congregation gives thanks to God for Holy Baptism and the "Alleluia" returns with the ringing of bells and the singing of the Gloria.

The culminating act of the rites of initiation at Redeemer is fellowship with the entire assembly in the Holy Eucharist. Following the eucharistic liturgy, Pastor Taylor invites the newly baptized, confirmed, and those making profession of their faith and joining the congregation's life, and their sponsors, to receive the Lord's Supper, many for the first time.[29] Joining in the feast brings to fulfillment their journey through the catechumenate. It is a time of great joy and celebration for the newly baptized and confirmed and for the assembly, that now fully receives them into their life together.

26. In 2019 there were eight confirmed in addition to the three who were baptized.

27. The liturgical scholar Aidan Kavanagh referred to the chrism as "God's grace olfactorally [sic] incarnate." Cited in Huck, *Three Days*, 171–75.

28. Amy (pseudonym), interview by Kent J. Burreson, March 9–10, 2019. Subsequent quotations and summaries of Amy are from this interview, unless otherwise noted.

29. Seven people in 2019.

Following the worship service, all are invited to a celebratory reception. Maura, commenting on her own experience of the initiation rites, says,

> It was a beautiful ceremony—from the moment of robing, to holding the candles, to seeing the congregation's support, to walking in procession. It was *magical*. These rites allowed me to understand everything I had experienced to that point. It brought it all together. I participated fully. Deaconess had taught us how to partake of the Lord's Supper. I received my own Bible verse in joining the congregation. I went forward to receive the Lord's Supper—I'm once again in Christ. Through my sponsors and everyone who extended their hands out over me, I felt loved and a part of the community of Christ.[30]

The joy of the Easter Vigil extends into the three services of Easter Sunday punctuated by a breakfast meal throughout the morning. At the breakfast the newly baptized and confirmed are once again recognized and honored.

The Stage of Post-Baptismal Mystagogy

Throughout the final period of mystagogy the neophytes will reflect on what happened to them at their baptisms and confirmations and the significance of these experiences for their lives of faith in the saving God. Maura's keen insight into the mystagogy period shows the formative power of adult faith formation: "After you're done, you're not really done. The mystagogy period was very beneficial." Pastor Taylor observed of this period, "The newly baptized and confirmed are glowing, happy people just as though they just gave birth or were given birth! Their countenance and expression changes. They wonder why it has to end." Of course, they can and do reinvest in church activities, serving as sponsors, and as witnesses in their community. It isn't the end of course, but only the beginning. As one of those interviewed in the documentary video about the catechumenate, *This is the Night*, says, "These people are very aware that once they are initiated into this church that is when the whole thing starts. The catechumenate was the appetizers and this is the main course. And it is a fabulous feast!"[31]

The catechumens have made the journey and are now themselves fully part of the community that receives, teaches, celebrates, and shares Christ

---

30. I hear Maura using the word "magical" to mean "transcendent"—not a word that would be in her vocabulary. She experienced God active in the moment.

31. *This is the Night* (VHS).

Jesus. As Mark summarized his experience, "I thought it would be routine. But it was like jumping out of an airplane. Here it is, it is going down. I was actually nervous, even scared. But the whole community is there. There is a parachute. It is the body of Christ, visible here at Redeemer."[32]

The words of Paul summarize Mark's experience well, "But you were washed, you were sanctified, you were justified in the name of the Lord Jesus Christ and in the Spirit of our God" (1 Cor 6:11).

TEACHING . . . CHRIST JESUS

At the center of the catechetical formation that seeks to shape the catechumens' lives are Deaconess Rojas and Pastor Taylor, who are both deeply involved in the catechumenate. Deaconess Rojas primarily has responsibility for teaching the adult catechumens on Sunday morning[33] while Pastor Taylor is leading worship.[34] The catechumens experience Pastor Taylor's formative impact through the rites connected to the catechumenate and through his preaching. The congregation considers this a mommy/daddy model, with Deaconess Rojas as the mom and Pastor Taylor as the dad. Members of the congregation and participants in the catechumenate understand both of their roles in this way spiritually and fondly refer to them as spiritual mom and dad.[35] This conceptualization of the relationship between the catechumens and the two of them reflects Paul's words, "And you became imitators of us and of the Lord, for in spite of persecution you received the word with joy from the Holy Spirit, so that you became an example to all the believers in Macedonia and in Achaia" (1 Thess 1:6-7). They are primary examples of what lives of faith look like and how the newly initiated are to live within this community of service. In many ways, by joining the catechumenate, the catechumens were inviting Pastor Taylor and Deaconess Rojas into their lives in fairly intimate ways, to walk with them and give shape to their lives as a mom and a dad would do. As Peter indicated, Pastor Taylor's counsel was invaluable. When he entered the

---

32. Mark (pseudonym), interview by Kent J. Burreson, April 21, 2019. Subsequent quotations and summaries of Mark are from this interview, unless otherwise noted.

33. Classes last about an hour.

34. He is primarily responsible for the instruction and formation in their youth catechumenate.

35. Interview with Pastor Taylor; Lydia (pseudonym), interview by Kent J. Burreson, March 9–10, 2019. Subsequent quotations and summaries of Lydia are from this interview, unless otherwise noted.

catechumenate he was not 100 percent committed to becoming a disciple of the Lord Jesus. He became aware of the nature of that commitment and the path he needed to follow to develop it through Pastor Taylor's guidance. As he said, Pastor Taylor showed him "what changes I need to make and the growth I need in daily life."[36]

Redeemer invests heavily both in ritual practices and in building personal relationships and integrating neophytes into community. However, that does not mean Redeemer neglects the more formal methods of catechesis in the classroom environment. Each class is different, often due to the varying backgrounds of the participants. Some come with no prior religious background. Others have been LCMS their entire lives. The diversity of the cohort directs the pattern of the teaching. While the Bible, liturgy, hymns, and Luther's *Small Catechism* all serve as connection points for Christian faith, Deaconess Rojas and Pastor Taylor often use Martin Luther's *Large Catechism* extensively as a basis for instruction.[37]

Each year a theme is developed (which unites the adult and the youth catechumenate), often from elements very familiar in contemporary culture that give direction to the catechumenate.[38] In addition, they are very eclectic in their pedagogical approaches, adapting the pedagogy to the learning styles of the catechumens involved. From the beginning, both Pastor Taylor and Deaconess Rojas have utilized elements such as these to accommodate different learning styles, including conversations within the cohort, whether two-on-two, or three-on-three, or other formats; discussion in a group where one person repeats back the essential elements of the discussion for all; hand motions associated with parts of the catechism or key phrases to reinforce learning; constructing things such as mock dramas or videos; centering prayer to be conscious of the power of the word; praying with a candle, an icon, or a cross in hand; journaling; examination and discussion of hymns; lecture; memorization (especially of the liturgy so that they know everything by heart).

Through all of these methods, as Deaconess Rojas, indicates: "The focus is on experiential learning to expose the catechumens to congregational life and to strengthen, through the catechumens, the vitality of congregational life. This exposure to congregational life deepens in mystagogy when

---

36. Peter (pseudonym), interview by Kent J. Burreson, October 2, 2018. Subsequent quotations and summaries of Peter are from this interview, unless otherwise noted.

37. Interview with Deaconess Rojas.

38. Past themes have included: "Return to Sender," "Fast and Furious," "Salt and Light."

the trustees, various officers, and the auxiliary groups in the congregation come and talk to the neophytes about life at Redeemer." It is a holistic formation.

Yet, there is also an authentic and intentional doctrinal content to what is taught. Redeemer understands itself to be forming Christians, and, in particular, Lutheran Christians.[39] As Lily said, "The education was thorough for understanding what it means to be Lutheran." Deaconess Rojas and Pastor Taylor are intentional about communicating the faith in ways that are easy to understand and that stick with the catechumens. Julie said, "They have the ability to present information in a basic form that you can understand, that you can know what they are talking about. They are very good at breaking things down clearly. Our three-year-old can get it." Or as Stewart said, "It wasn't above my head." The structure of the catechetical sessions led by Deaconess Rojas were conducive to active engagement in the context of the catechumens' lives. Maura summarizes the experience in this way:

> She would begin in a reflective mode by asking questions of us. A period of review, through mini-lecture and discussion, of the Sunday readings and the sermon would elicit the meaning of those texts. They taught the Creeds and the Lord's Prayer and explained the meaning of both texts. She asked questions and we were encouraged to ask questions.... I never felt pushed—it was our spiritual journey, but certain things were expected. Focusing on parts of Luther's *Small Catechism* every week led to lots of discussion. In those discussions, she would often probe deeply, seeking to elicit how we would respond.

This is a formation that is meant to take hold.

To facilitate the formation taking hold they would often intersect what the catechumens had experienced in worship with the biblical and catechetical texts. They regularly connect ritual and teaching. Lily said of this liturgically connected teaching, "They explained why we make the sign of the cross. And we were able to ask questions. They explained what is going on in the worship services. This made it easier to pay attention. They

---

39. Pastor Taylor noted in his comments on the draft of this chapter that "the study of the Confessions of the Evangelical Lutheran Church is something done at Redeemer in an ongoing way, and neophytes are invited to join in those continued opportunities for growth and learning." Quoted in an attachment (Word document containing comments on the draft of this chapter), email from Dien Ashley Taylor to Kent Burreson and Rhoda Schuler, May 27, 2024. Redeemer is clear about its identity as a Lutheran congregation.

encouraged us to focus and meditate on the word and so think about what we received. And they taught us to learn the meaning of the symbols used in worship." There was also deliberate formation in how to pray, since Redeemer is a place "Where God's people pray." Peter said, "Deaconess taught us how to be able to pray. She broke down a structure for prayer. We learned that prayer simply was asking something of someone else. By doing so, we learned to put things into the hands of the Lord." Learning to pray (like learning the classic collect form, for example) was a formative part of their education in the faith.

Sponsors play a crucial role at Redeemer in training the catechumens how to pray, especially by witnessing to their own prayer life and how they pray. Even more than that, sponsors play a central role in developing in the catechumens a sense of belonging at Redeemer. As Sandy indicates, "Much discernment went into pairing up sponsors and neophytes." Often Pastor Taylor and Deaconess Rojas know the interpersonal connections of the catechumens with people in the congregation, whether family or friends. With this knowledge, they deliberately choose sponsors for the catechumens. Yet, that doesn't preclude others serving as unofficial sponsors as well, a role that the congregation has no misgivings about assuming to themselves. One sees the readiness the congregation has to assume this role when all the sponsors gather around the candidates during the Rite of Election or at Confirmation at the Easter Vigil.

Part of the sponsors role is, in Sandy's words, "To serve as a mentor in the pews, explaining what we are doing in worship and helping them to participate and 'do' the liturgy. Afterward, we can converse, touch and hug, as appropriate. And we can indicate that we are present for questions at all times—phone, internet, etc. I regularly ask [those I sponsor], how are things going in class and in your life?" One of the catechumens, Millie, said of her experience with her sponsor, "Everyone was supportive. If there was anything I needed they were happy to provide. That took a load off of me. My daughter is my sponsor. She called me to check on me. With the sponsors, there is a community, and we are held accountable. Love and community are at the center of that experience."[40] Embracing the sense of belonging at Redeemer is at the heart of the catechumenate, and the sponsors play a critical role in developing that sense.

---

40. Millie (pseudonym), interview by Kent J. Burreson, April 21, 2019. Subsequent quotations and summaries of Millie are from this interview, unless otherwise noted.

Part I: Context is Everything

Without question, Redeemer's catechumenate is ritually oriented. The rites and rituals of the catechumenate do the heavy lifting for the experience, forming and shaping new Christians for life as part of this community of Christ. But foundational and pedagogically innovative catechetical instruction leads to clarity of belief. The relationships of the congregation members to the catechumens, especially through the sponsors, develops a clear sense of belonging in the catechumens. As Amy said about her confirmation anointing, "This is the right place.... God led the way on the path. Through the path God confirmed that." That path, the catechumenate at Redeemer, leads to new life, renewed life. As Maura said about her experience, "There was a clear connection in my life. For the first time I understood what it meant to be a Christian. I felt overwhelming joy. Everything is very authentic at Redeemer . . . [and this] was the type of life I wanted to have. And now it felt good to be—alive!"

That is the goal for Redeemer's catechumenate: By God's grace, living in Christ and in the body of Christ at Redeemer. Redeemer shapes its catechumens to live as those who receive, teach, celebrate, and share Christ Jesus and new life in him. A profound transformation is the result of journeying through their catechumenate. Amy reflects on the transformational impact of the journey:

> [The services over the Three Days] connected everything; made it all complete. The connection to my baptism was there. All the readings over the last couple of days connected everything. It all brought it all together. All the services: Good Friday, my first time. The overall connection? It was an affirmation of all the years [leading to this]. Individual study reached a culmination in the rite. It brought everything together. Including all of the Bible—it all goes back to the word. There was clarity in terms of connection. I received the oil of exorcism. I was struggling professionally, all the mistakes I had made. I believed things would get better. But I did not fully understand until we entered Lent. What age did Jesus know he was going to die? Jesus could handle it. I was able to ponder my faith more deeply, more purposefully, more intentionally.

Amy could handle it too, because she was now a part of the body of Christ at Redeemer, a place that, by God's grace, receives, teaches, celebrates, and shares Christ Jesus as the way, the truth, and the life. Redeemer's catechumenate: where the end is just the beginning.

INTRODUCTION TO PART II

Common Themes across Uncommon Contexts

Redeemer Evangelical Lutheran Church in the Bronx is a long way from Living Faith Lutheran Church in Cumming, Georgia, not only geographically but also contextually. Redeemer's context is decidedly urban, very racially diverse, low income, and the congregation, founded in 1928, has a long history in the Bronx. In contrast, Cumming, Georgia, in which Living Faith is located, has morphed in the last twenty years from a small town in a rural county to a suburban, bedroom community for Atlanta. The county where Cumming is located is much less racially diverse and more distinctly middle class than the Bronx,[1] and Living Faith, constituted officially as a congregation in 2001, is a mere youth when compared to Redeemer. A similar case could be made for St. Mary's and St. John—they are separated by significant differences in context (size, age demographics, and membership's socioeconomic status) just as they are separated by a significant number of miles. Yet our research reveals some striking commonalities among the four congregations, which the three chapters in part II highlight.

---

1. See "QuickFacts: Forsyth County, Georgia; Bronx County, New York; United States." A comparison of US Census Bureau figures from Forsyth County, Georgia, and Bronx County, New York illustrates these differences. White alone, not Hispanic or Latino: Forsyth: 63.9 percent; Bronx: 8.7 percent. Black or African American alone: Forsyth: 4.9 percent; Bronx: 43.6 percent. Median household income (in 2022 dollars), 2018–2022: Forsyth: $131,660; Bronx: $47,000. Population estimates, July 1, 2023: Forsyth: 272,887; Bronx: 1,356,476. Population per square mile, 2020: Forsyth: 1,118.7; Bronx: 34,920.2.

Introduction to Part II: Common Themes

Our conversation partner in chapter 6, "Fostering a Missional *Habitus*," is Alan Hirsch, author, adjunct faculty in the area of missions, and who, according to his website, is "known for his innovative approach to mission . . . [and is] widely considered to be a thought leader and key mission strategist for churches across the Western world."[2] His book *The Forgotten Ways* unlocks the code of "missional-DNA," describing various "essential elements" that are characteristic of congregations with a missional focus. In our opinion, Hirsch's critique of his own evangelical tradition's missional strategies from the 1980s and nineties gives credibility to his current thinking about and reflection on missional strategies. Chapter 6 summarizes his "elements of mDNA" and attempts to show correlation between these characteristics and common features that surfaced from our interviews at St. John, Living Faith, St. Mary's, and Redeemer congregations. We propose that the adult catechumenate of these four congregations has been a major catalyst that has initiated the missional *habitus* in each congregation.

Chapter 7, "The Path of Conversion: Belonging, Believing, Behaving," unfolds in greater detail the themes we have drawn from Diana Butler Bass and Alan Kreider (named in the introduction to part I) and covered briefly in the chapters on the congregations. Kreider's analysis of the shifting weight and order of the three BEs in the early centuries of the church and Bass's critique that the post-Reformation era pattern (believing, behaving, then belonging) has failed to address the changing cultural milieu of our times provide the foundation for exploring these categories within the faith formation process of our four research congregations. Here we have found congruence between Bass's reordering of the three BEs and our research findings; namely, that participants in the adult catechumenate from three of the four congregations consistently verbalized language of belonging in their narratives of how and why they were drawn into the pattern of discipleship. We suggest that this dominant theme of belonging occurs alongside of a formation process that also shapes believing and behaving, and this simultaneity opens up creative possibilities to other pastors, church professionals, and lay leaders in congregations desiring to address the spiritual needs of both seekers and lifelong Christians.

Chapter 8, "Ritual: Enacting and Rehearsing the Christian Story," is a topic we have approached "with fear and trembling" yet with hope—hope that we can overcome the bifurcation among church professionals who, in our experience, perceive a great chasm between two "camps"—those who

---

2. Alan Hirsch (website).

Introduction to Part II: Common Themes

are "missionally minded" and those who are "liturgical geeks/scholars." To begin the process of closing this chasm, we present examples of the power of ritual from history, daily life, and all four of our research congregations—even those with less ritual experiences tied to the catechumenate.

For the second half of chapter 8, our primary conversation partner is James K. A. Smith, Christian philosopher, whose website states that he is an "award-winning author and a widely traveled speaker, [who] has emerged as a thought leader with a unique gift of translation, building bridges between the academy, society, and the church."[3] As a devout Christian, Smith's scholarly work in philosophy informs his faith in thoughtful, rich ways. His recent publications bring together current trends in philosophy and Christian ritual that address the malaise of contemporary culture, offering a way of understanding ritual as a means to form Christians—particularly through regular Sunday worship—that we find compelling and consonant for bearing witness to Jesus Christ in our post-Christendom context. As he says, "It is in such [ritual] practices that our love is trained, disciplined, shaped, and formed."[4]

If our readers were inspired by the stories told by participants in and leaders of the adult catechumenal processes in part I, with part II our goal is to move our readers from inspiration to action. Thus, each of these three chapters concludes with a series of questions for reflection and discussion. As we wrote at the start of this book, "We tell these inspiring individual stories of faith formation and present the missional mindset of congregations in the hope that the creative power of the Spirit will spark imaginative thinking among pastors, other church professionals, and lay leaders."

---

3. James K. A. Smith (website), "About."
4. Smith, *Imagining the Kingdom*, 13.

6

FOSTERING A MISSIONAL *HABITUS*

As stated in the introduction, we are convinced that an adult faith formation process "has the potential not only to form adults into active disciples of Christ but also to bring forth a missional mindset within the congregation." To demonstrate how the adult catechumenate fosters a missional ethos within our four model congregations, we use the language and categories of Alan Hirsch, author and mission strategist, as a framework. Hirsch coins the term "Apostolic Genius" and defines it as "the built-in life force . . . of God's people."[1] This life force, further defined by Hirsch as "the primal missional potencies of the gospel and of God's people," is present in the church and individual Christians but "lies dormant in you, me, and every local church that seeks to follow Jesus faithfully in any time."[2] At the center of Hirsch's diagram of "The Structure of Apostolic Genius" is a starburst bearing the words "Jesus is Lord."[3] For Hirsch, the source of power for the missional impulse of Jesus' first followers is encapsulated in this New Testament confession of faith, and its power is in its simplicity: "The desperate, prayer-soaked human clinging to Jesus, the reliance on his Spirit, and the distillation of the gospel message into the simple, uncluttered message of Jesus as Lord and Savior is what catalyzed the missional potencies inherent in the people of God."[4]

1. Hirsch, *Forgotten Ways*, 18.
2. Hirsch, *Forgotten Ways*, 22.
3. Hirsch, *Forgotten Ways*, 25.
4. Hirsch, *Forgotten Ways*, 86.

Part II: Common Themes across Uncommon Contexts

Surrounding the "Jesus is Lord" starburst are five circles connected to one another by a single line between them, forming a hexagon around the starburst that permeates these five "living components or elements" that are constitutive of Apostolic Genius. To extend the analogy of Apostolic Genius as an organic "life force," Hirsch calls these five "living components" missional DNA (shortened to mDNA),[5] describing them as interrelated "elements of mDNA, forming a complex and living structure," and labeling these five elements as disciple making, missional-incarnational impulse, apostolic environment, organic systems, and "*communitas*, not community."[6]

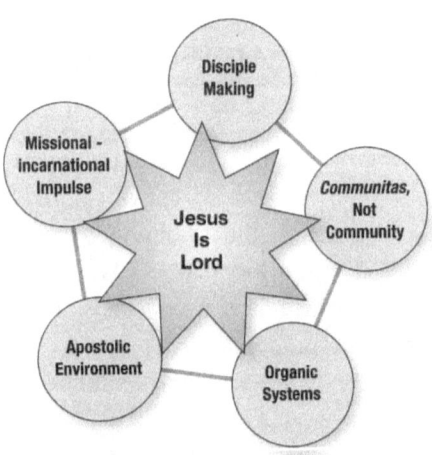

The key here is that Apostolic Genius (characterized by mDNA) is embedded in the church's life and, Hirsch says, "is coded into each and every community through latent mDNA; only for most of us it lies buried and forgotten."[7] In the congregations whose catechumenates we researched, this Apostolic Genius has been reawakened or sustained by their catechumenates. Apostolic Genius is the church living out its identity as God's mission to the world, and an active, purposeful catechumenate forms that Apostolic Genius in the people of God. Pastor Droegemueller's description of Living Faith's catechumenal process illustrates how it shapes their mission as a congregation:

---

5. Hirsch, *Forgotten Ways*, 18.

6. Hirsch, *Forgotten Ways*, 24–25. He devotes a full chapter of the book to each of the five elements and to the epicenter, "Jesus is Lord."

7. Hirsch, *Forgotten Ways*, 78.

Our mission is the Great Commission (Matt 28:16–20). Salvation to humanity entails the people of God in this place understanding their vocation. We facilitate their understanding of their vocations by [examining] the variegated moments in the lives of the members of Living Faith in relationship to and in submission to the word of God. We try to create awareness for them in their daily life so that they can perceive when they stumble over the epiphanies of the gospel. We want to bear witness to and practice the freeing reality and experience of the gospel in our daily vocations and relationships.[8]

Pastor Droegemueller describes a vision of "mentoring in the pews"[9]—the transformation of a congregation toward a missional identity through the faith formation process oriented toward and grounded in baptism. The source of this missional *habitus*[10] is the justification of the sinner in Christ, but the modeling of the transformation comes through the life of the congregation. Diana Macalintal, Roman Catholic expert on the catechumenate, posits the RCIA in similar language, saying, "your parish is the curriculum."[11] Within such a construct, faith formation conceives of God's mission in the congregation through the lens of an apprenticeship model rather than an information download model. In the words of Paul Hoffman, "The WAY offers people an apprenticeship into faith in Christ."[12] Sponsors at Redeemer, Living Faith, and St. Mary's serve as mentors toward this apprenticeship. As Pastor Droegemueller at Living Faith says, the sponsors "provide Christian friendship, giving the catechumens someone

---

8. Pastor Timothy Droegemueller, interview by Kent J. Burreson, August 15, 2018. Subsequent quotations and summaries of Pastor Droegemueller are from this interview, unless otherwise noted. For Pastor Droegemueller, "the epiphanies of the gospel" are the opportunities in daily human life to bear witness to Jesus and his salvation and to serve the neighbor in Christ's love in their situations of need.

9. Sandy (pseudonym), interview by Kent J. Burreson, October 3, 2018. The phrase was used by this member at Redeemer Evangelical Lutheran Church. Subsequent quotations and summaries of Sandy are from this interview, unless otherwise noted.

10. *Habitus* is a term from the discipline of sociology made popular by Pierre Bourdieu. It describes the way a person understands and responds to the social world that the person inhabits; how one responds to that world evokes the person's character, skills, and habits. In faith formation, the person's "social world" may be radically altered by entering the world of the Christians; a new *habitus* or way of responding to the world is formed through the catechumenate.

11. Macalintal, *Your Parish Is the Curriculum*, 13.

12. Hoffman, *Faith Forming Faith*, 6. "The WAY" is his congregation's name for their catechumenal process.

to talk to. It provides the catechumens with accountability and lets them know that they are not alone in this journey." The entire body of Christ makes this journey through the catechumenate together—people with real lives, schedules, and experiences—all trying to walk together immersed in Scripture and the life in Christ. Faith formation profoundly embeds this common life in the Christian community.

The formation of a missional identity like those reflected in the congregations we researched begins with the candidates for baptism and those renewing their baptisms.[13] The process leading to and from baptism, where they are joined to the crucified and risen Christ as their Lord and Savior (the New Testament confession of faith at the center of Hirsch's diagram), creates a new identity for them, a missional identity. As one candidate from Redeemer congregation said: "I truly feel a member of the church. There is a commitment I have undertaken. I have an understanding of the mission of the church, of the mission of God. I integrate it all into my life. I pray all the time. I am a Christian *all the time.*"[14] The congregation's investment in the formation of these candidates for baptism reshapes the congregation's own self-understanding and through these candidates places the church's mission at the center of the congregation's spirit and life. Stories from our four research congregations framed through Hirsch's five constitutive mDNA elements, living and active, illustrate the catechumenate's role as a catalyst that awakens the Apostolic Genius and plants a missional mindset into the center of congregational life.

DISCIPLE-MAKING IN FAITH FORMATION

Of the five elements of mDNA, Alan Hirsch first discusses disciple-making because, based on his experience and observations, "*this* element . . . is perhaps the most critical element in the mDNA mix."[15] He identifies three causes for the lost "art of disciple-making": the reduction of the teaching of the faith to an intellectual transmission of ideas, the pervasiveness of "cultural Christianity," and our consumer culture that "pushes against a true

---

13. Renewal of baptism would encompass traditional confirmation, reaffirmation of faith, and transfer of membership.

14. Maura (pseudonym), interview by Kent J. Burreson, October 2, 2018. Subsequent quotations and summaries of Maura are from this interview, unless otherwise noted.

15. Hirsch, *Forgotten Ways*, 102, emphasis in original.

following of Jesus."[16] He critiques his own evangelical tradition, citing the prevalence of "seeker friendly" worship as an erosion of disciple-making[17] as well as the adoption of market principles popularized by church growth proponents, concluding that under their "influence . . . consumerism has actually become the driving ideology of the church's ministry."[18] Pastor Bruzek's comment that "we don't need any more members; but we definitely need more disciples"[19] echoes Hirsch's claim that "*this* element" is the "most critical," and much of Bruzek's reflections on the subject resonant with Hirsch's advocacy for recovery of the "lost art" of making disciples.

As one trained in marketing and advertising, Hirsch also sees consumerism as a serious threat to the Christian faith. "If," he writes, "the role of religion is to offer a sense of identity, purpose, meaning, and community, then it can be said that consumerism fulfills all these criteria."[20] Bertrand's story illustrates how the catechumenate can reclaim the church's mission to offer "identity, purpose, meaning, and community" through its witness to Jesus Christ.

Bertrand, a native of Jamaica, was vacationing in New York City. A friend told him they were going to church at Redeemer. Bertrand examined the congregation with a very critical eye. Did they bear witness to what they professed? He came again, asking whether there was authenticity in their life together. He found that their life under Jesus was transparent and true. So, he decided he wanted to know more about this congregation, about the church, about Christ. Bertrand started participating in their weekly formation classes leading toward baptism. Through Skype he continued his instruction after returning to Jamaica. At last, Easter was approaching. Bertrand decided he could not miss becoming a child of God at Redeemer. So, he flew from Jamaica in the days preceding Passion Sunday. Obstacles reared their ugly heads. Immigration and Customs Enforcement detained Bertrand for over eleven hours, refusing to believe he was returning to the United States to be baptized, even though he had a letter from the pastor. Through the intercessions of the pastor and the witness of members of the

---

16. Hirsch, *Forgotten Ways*, 104.
17. Hirsch, *Forgotten Ways*, 104.
18. Hirsch, *Forgotten Ways*, 110.

19. Pastor Scott Bruzek, interview by Rhoda Schuler, August 8, 2018. Subsequent quotations and summaries of Pastor Bruzek are from this interview, unless otherwise noted.

20. Hirsch, *Forgotten Ways*, 107.

congregation, US Immigration and Customs Enforcement released him in time for the Holy Week services. On Maundy Thursday he had his feet washed, and at the Easter Vigil he was baptized and anointed, sealed as a child of God. The obstacles notwithstanding, Bertrand called it a fabulous journey into a new family filled with love. Through Redeemer's formation process, Bertrand's questions were answered by a hospitable assembly bearing witness to the unrelenting love of God in Jesus, and he journeyed with them on the road to discipleship. Bertrand and Redeemer together were transformed through the death and resurrection encountered in the catechumenal journey. Here was a disciple-in-the-making. One can sense Bertrand's awareness of becoming a disciple in his own words:

> The journey to baptism and being baptized has changed my life. It has also impacted my family and my work and where my priorities lie. I used to worry about everything. Life is now simpler. Things are not as important to me that were important. I loved cars and had an expensive car. I sold that car. It was no longer important. A meeting with Pastor in which we went through the rite of confession, and I confessed my misplaced priorities, was a turning point. That made me feel lighter. After that, and throughout this process, I am now steppin' differently.[21]

Bertrand's *identity* was now in Christ. His *purpose* for living was the mission of the Lord. The *meaning* of things was oriented toward life in Christ. And his new *community* was the Christian community, which included now his wife and his children. Redeemer's witness had birthed a new disciple in Bertrand.

With an adult catechumenate at the center of congregational life, our research congregations counter a "low bar" approach to membership and exemplify "this most critical element" of Hirsch's mDNA—disciple-making—with a catechumenal process that requires time and commitment from the congregation and catechumens and that leads to authentic discipleship. Authenticity of congregational life was something Bertrand discerned about Redeemer and was a reason that he entered their catechumenate. As he said,

> I did an assessment from the first day. I learned something from the first time I visited. I saw consistency in the church. After that, I gave it three times of coming back to see if this was true. It was.

21. Bertrand (pseudonym), interview by Kent J. Burreson, March 9–10, 2019. Subsequent quotations and summaries of Bertrand are from this interview, unless otherwise noted.

> The church was very authentic. In the times that I have been back [Bertrand has since moved to a different part of New York state], I realize how much I miss the welcome of Redeemer. That hospitality and authenticity drew me here. It is still like the first time that I came. Redeemer is vibrant. There is a difference here. Nothing changes. I will miss that.[22]

Authenticity is embedded in the formation of disciples. It is manifested in the congregation's time and commitment toward the task that draws disciples into each one's true, authentic identity through baptism into Christ.

According to Hirsch, discipleship is "following Jesus and becoming increasingly like him (Christlikeness)."[23] In the Lutheran tradition that "Christlikeness," or patterning one's life on the life of Jesus, is rooted in baptism from a decidedly Pauline perspective, who says of himself, "it is no longer I who live but Christ who lives in me" (Gal 2:20), and who asks rhetorically, "Do you not know that all of us who have been baptized into Christ Jesus were baptized into his death?" (Rom 6:3). Drawing on this Pauline imagery, Martin Luther declared that "the power and effect of baptism . . . is nothing else than the slaying of the old Adam and the resurrection of the new creature, both of which must continue in us our whole life long. Thus a Christian life is nothing else than a daily baptism, begun once and continuing ever after."[24]

In the Lutheran tradition, discipleship is not an upward trajectory of becoming a "better and better" person; on the contrary, to be more Christlike is to become "deader and deader"[25] through the daily "slaying of the old Adam" rooted in baptism. As Luther wrote, "Therefore let all Christians regard their baptism as the daily garment that they are to wear all the time. Every day they should be found in faith and with its fruits, suppressing the old creature and growing up in the new. If we want to be Christians, we must practice the work that makes us Christians."[26] Because the adult catechumenate is anchored in baptism, our research congregations awakened and ignited an authentic process of disciple-making; that is, a process in

---

22. Bertrand (pseudonym) from group interview, interview by Kent J. Burreson, April 21, 2019.

23. Hirsch, *Forgotten Ways*, 41.

24. Luther, *Large Catechism*, 465.

25. Gerhard O. Forde, class lecture, "Theology of the Sacraments," Luther Seminary, St. Paul, Minnesota, Spring 1996.

26. Luther, *Large Catechism*, 466.

Part II: Common Themes across Uncommon Contexts

which daily living "in faith and with its fruits" is constitutive to discipleship, as Bertrand's story illustrates.

Based on our research, the path toward transformation into disciples occurs primarily through two means: 1) by encountering Christ in the proclamation and study of God's word and 2) through initiation into the community. Dayla, a "cradle Lutheran" in her eighties who participated in the Voyage process at St. Mary's, said, "I feel super blessed to go through this. . . . I've never experienced anything like this."[27] "This"—the whole catechumenal process—transformed her faith life. That she encountered Christ through the word was revealed by the specific details she recalled from the small group discussions on the Gospel readings, commenting on the multiple readings of the text and times of meditation, and articulating what she found meaningful in the process: "Being able to open up, share what the text meant to me." Encountering Christ in preaching was also part of her catechumenal experience, as she said of Pastor M, "She's fantastic; very inspiring. Her messages hit home a lot of times." A question on baptism led her to ruminate on the Eucharist, saying, "I do feel that I'm a little closer to God in my heart and my soul. It [the Voyage process] opened up everything for me."

Mark, one of the newly baptized at Redeemer, speaks of his experience of initiation into the community at the Vigil as a transforming encounter with Christ: "It will sink in. It's all so fresh. This morning . . . I was expectant. I thought I'd be ready to go, because the whole past week [Holy Week] brought everything full circle. For example, the light of the church breaks forth after everything had been covered. In the same way, I feel like a new person. I could do anything through Christ. He has my back."[28] In his experience of the Easter Vigil baptismal liturgy, Mark had become a new person, an experience heightened by the response of the Redeemer community. Commenting on the congregation's welcome after his baptism, both in the service and after it, he said: "It was overwhelming. Before I came to the church I was fairly closed to strangers. I need to warm up. They are way too nice. I am overwhelmed. Coming from the font they are congratulating me. It is a personal victory I can share with all. I feel more connected." There

---

27. Dayla (pseudonym), interview by Rhoda Schuler, March 19, 2019; and by phone June 2019. She often used indefinite pronouns such as "this" and "it," which are best interpreted as references to the entire catechumenal process. Subsequent quotations and summaries of Dayla are from this interview, unless otherwise noted.

28. Mark (pseudonym) from group interview, interviewed by Kent J. Burreson, April 21, 2019.

is an authentic character to faith formation. It not only expects a lifelong commitment as a disciple of Christ Jesus, but it also creates the conditions for a commitment that constantly seeks to incorporate others into a community of authentic relationships.

Mark's experience points to another feature of a disciple-making congregation, one in which contagious relationships are built and nurtured.[29] As Mark said, those contagious relationships hold "as long as I'm always in the faith." Pearl, the lay catechist from St. Mary's, as one who built and nurtured relationships with those in the catechumenal process, echoed a similar sentiment, saying, "If you want to share your faith it gets contagious."[30] Dagny from St. John, drawn into the congregation through the witness of Audrey, put it this way: "There's something really special about this church; I want to be that way too."[31] Alongside Pearl's deep desire "to share my faith as much as I can while I am on this earth" is her ability to create and nurture relationships. The emphasis on building community and nurturing relationships that is integral to the catechumenal process parallels the next of Hirch's mDNA components.

MISSIONAL-INCARNATIONAL IMPULSE

Hirsch contrasts a missional-incarnational impulse with the primary impulse toward mission that holds in most First World settings, the evangelistic-attractional impulse. He defines the latter as a missionally oriented approach that attracts people to become part of a church/community/institution in order to grow the church (increase its numbers) and strengthen the life of the institution.[32] In contrast to this fundamental impulse of attraction is the missional-incarnational impulse of *sending* the people of God into the world, a movement that mirrors the Father's sending of his Son into this world. As Hirsch says, it is "the practical outworking of the mission of God (the *Missio Dei*) and of the Incarnation. It is thus rooted in the very way that God has redeemed the world, and in how God revealed

---

29. Hirsch, *Forgotten Ways*, 105–6.

30. Pearl (pseudonym), interview by Rhoda Schuler, August 6, 2018. Subsequent quotations and summaries of Pearl are from this interview, unless otherwise noted.

31. Fritz and Dagny (pseudonyms), interview by Rhoda Schuler, August 8, 2018. Subsequent quotations and summaries of Fritz and Dagny are from this interview, unless otherwise noted.

32. Hirsch, *Forgotten Ways*, 128–31.

himself to us."³³ In other words, God instantiates his mission to renew his creation when his Son becomes incarnate, takes on human flesh, and moves into our human neighborhood (John 1:14). As Hirsch points out, through the incarnation God in his Son identifies with all that it means to be God's human creatures. The Son reveals the image of God in human flesh. Thus, the Son discloses for us what we become as human creatures of God joined to him.³⁴ Hirsch expands on this implication of the missional-incarnational impulse, saying,

> The Incarnation not only qualifies God's acts in the world, but must also qualify ours. If God's central way of reaching his world was to incarnate himself in Jesus, then our way of reaching the world should likewise be *incarnational*. To act incarnationally therefore will mean in part that in our mission to those outside of the faith we will need to exercise a genuine identification and affinity with those we are attempting to reach. . . . But the basic motive of incarnational ministry is also *revelatory*—that they may come to know God through Jesus.³⁵

This missional-incarnational impulse was instantiated in the congregations we studied. They were deeply embedded in their contexts and understood their life as a witness to those around them. A prime example of the incarnational side, that "genuine identification and affinity," comes from Betty, who works at a local library in St. Mary's neighborhood.³⁶ One day, she notarized a document for Theresa, a member of St. Mary's. Shortly after that encounter, Theresa invited Betty to make a presentation at a book club of folks from St. Mary's hosted at Theresa's home. Betty reported that the presentation went well, and that she was not attending church at that time. A year or more after the book presentation, she was actively looking for a church when a crisis happened (she lost her cat), and Betty said, "the next day I took myself to church" at St. Mary's. The Spirit was at work through a shared love of books, this natural affinity between Betty and Theresa, who embodied what Hirsch calls the missional-incarnational impulse. The two connected in and through Betty's world of books. Betty's experience in the

---

33. Hirsch, *Forgotten Ways*, 128.
34. Hirsch, *Forgotten Ways*, 132.
35. Hirsch, *Forgotten Ways*, 133, emphasis in original.
36. Betty (pseudonym), interview by Rhoda Schuler, August 6, 2018. Subsequent quotations and summaries of Betty are from this interview, unless otherwise noted.

adult catechumenate, where she came to "know God through Jesus," was the revelatory side of this impulse.

In this book's Introduction we wrote about Audrey, a disciple from St. John, who is another exemplar of the missional-incarnational impulse. She, like Theresa at St. Mary's, was a "real and abiding presence"[37] in her neighborhood, welcoming Fritz and Dagny into their shared world of a suburban, middle-class life. Because they experienced her friendship as authentic, when she invited them to the Advent dinners at St. John, it was a natural extension of their shared life as neighbors. As God sent his Word to become flesh and dwell among humanity and make known the Father, so Audrey was also dwelling in the world and by her words and deeds making God known to Fritz and Dagny.

Leaving the suburban worlds of St. John and St. Mary, further examples of the missional-incarnational impulse are drawn from the disciples of Redeemer Lutheran in the Bronx. The first uses a surprising (for us) resource, *Portals of Prayer*, a quarterly publication of daily devotions.[38] Deaconess Rojas from Redeemer used the phrase "a hot item" to describe the popularity of *Portals of Prayer* among the people of Redeemer.[39] Because the devotions are "short, quick, and [the booklet is] compact," Redeemer disciples carry the booklets with them and read the devotions as they are "waiting for the bus, on the train, or going up the elevator." Since they are engaged in this spiritual practice in public places, others "look, see, and talk" about and to the Redeemer disciples. The public act of reading a daily devotion (with Scripture, a meditation on that word of God, and a brief prayer), done first of all as a means to increase and deepen their personal faith in Christ, becomes a missional-incarnational impulse, a way to make God known to others in Christ.

Portals of Prayer are delivered in bulk quantities to LCMS congregations four times a year. Deaconess Rojas said that when a new issue arrives, some people

> are taking handfuls—three or four—one for themselves, one for those they are traveling with, or to give to those in their other cubicles [at work], or [for] those that are at the dry cleaners because

---

37. Hirsch, *Forgotten Ways*, 133.

38. *Portals of Prayer* booklets have been published by the LCMS since Lent 1937 and are ubiquitous in LCMS congregations. It's a devotional resource we associate with our Midwestern parents and grandparents, hence our surprise at this story.

39. Rojas and Schuler, "Called in Christ for Witness and Service."

that's what [their neighbors] are looking for—that *good word*. And it doesn't just stop there. Sometimes we've even heard that if it was such a good word, or they've been talking with a co-worker, they've actually ripped out one of [the pages], and handed that specific devotion to them and said, "read this, learn this, hear this" and that becomes a tool and a witness for teaching and sharing Christ Jesus in a very unique way.[40]

The sharing of *Portals of Prayer* reflects the embedding of a missional mindset at Redeemer. A similar embedding of the missional-incarnation impulse is reflected in the activity and witness of Stewart and Julie. Even before coming to Redeemer, they had started a non-profit organization that offers social, recreational, and educational trips for high school youth to travel to places they would not otherwise be able to visit. They run this organization "on the side" of their regular vocational lives and activities. Because of the expense, the time, and the commitment, their friends and acquaintances had often wondered why they do this. But Stewart and Julie realized why as soon as they walked through the catechumenate at Redeemer. It was a no-brainer. This effort was their embodiment of the incarnational life of Redeemer. Often youth who participate in the program hear of and experience Christ on these trips. Stewart and Julie's friends, who had been baffled by their dedication and self-giving, understood why when they visited Redeemer. Their friends could sense that Stewart and Julie's organization is the very expression of the missional-incarnational life of Redeemer.

As Hirsch indicates, the missional-incarnational impulse is a sending impulse (as opposed to attractional). The church as the people of God is sent into the world as seeds of God's renewing work in Jesus. The catechumenates at St. Mary's, Redeemer, St. John, and Living Faith shape that self-understanding of being sent in the congregations, offering an incarnational presence in their immediate world. Key to fostering a missional-incarnational impulse is the next of Hirsch's mDNA elements.

APOSTOLIC ENVIRONMENT

Based on his consideration of the New Testament and missional movements throughout church history, Hirsch describes an apostolic environment as one focused on "the extension of Christianity," where the leadership draws

---

40. Rojas and Schuler, "Called in Christ for Witness and Service."

Fostering a Missional *Habitus*

"the church to its essential calling" and guides "it into its destiny as a missionary people with a transformative message for the world."[41] Hirsch uses the terms "apostolic leadership," "apostolic person," and "apostolic ministry" because a certain type of leadership is the key ingredient that creates an "apostolic environment." He writes, "There is no substantial word for this catalytic social power [where Apostolic Genius is unleashed] other than, to reinvoke biblical language, *apostolic*."[42] Hirsch unpacks the qualities of apostolic leadership both negatively and positively. It is not, he says, "the predominant, top-down CEO concept of leadership" nor "transactional leadership." The latter, based on "an exchange of value" is the most common in the church and problematic because its source of authority has a secular rather than biblical basis; the former, also common in the church, "tends to disempower others"[43] rather than "equip the saints for the work of ministry" (Eph 4:12).

In contrast, leadership that creates an apostolic environment "embodies, symbolizes, and *re*-presents the apostolic mission" to the congregation, and the pastor "provides the personal reference point as well as the spiritual context for the other ministries of God's people."[44] The leaders in an apostolic environment envision the mission of the church as the mission of God the Father through his crucified and resurrected Son by the power of the Spirit toward the renewal and restoration of all humanity and the entire cosmos.

An apostolic environment is one that perceives the entire world as the canvas for the mission of God. Pastor Taylor embodies that mission in his attitude toward what constitutes his parish. It is not restricted to Redeemer and the area of Wakefield that surrounds it. All of the Bronx and the entirety of New York City is not too large to be considered the canvas on which God is at work in his ministry. Both Pastor Taylor and one of the catechumens Kent interviewed, Holly, tell her story of coming into relationship with Redeemer. It is a story that represents the breadth of that apostolic environment. One weekday Pastor Taylor was pumping gas at a station in the Bronx. As is typical of his approach to ministry in the city, he was wearing his clergy attire and collar. A woman who was pumping gas nearby came to him in the grips of sorrow. She asked if he would pray for

---

41. Hirsch, *Forgotten Ways*, 152.
42. Hirsch, *Forgotten Ways*, 150–51, emphasis in the original.
43. Hirsch, *Forgotten Ways*, 160, 163.
44. Hirsch, *Forgotten Ways*, 152, 154.

and with her. He said he would gladly do so but wanted to know what the source of her sorrow was. She recounted the story of the sudden death of her twenty-year-old son in a tragic accident. After praying with her at the gas pump, he asked when and where the funeral would take place. Pastor Taylor showed up at the funeral, even though Holly was not a member of Redeemer. He was asked to bring some words to the funeral assembly, which he did. Of the words that he spoke Holly said, "He brought the only thing relevant, the comfort of the gospel. I cried and cried. And he said that all of Redeemer was praying for me and my family."[45] The gas station encounter and Pastor Taylor's words at her son's funeral led Holly to want to investigate Redeemer's life. So, she visited Redeemer a few times and realized that what she experienced from Pastor Taylor was the very shape of the congregation's life. They were a congregation in mission, whose teaching was reflected in a renewed life in mission toward the world. After her experience of walking through the catechumenate, Holly said, "I'm not going anywhere. I'm happy I did it. Best commitment I ever made. I felt strengthened in my place. Overflowing joy [was] in my heart—God was within me." Pastor Taylor's pastoral care for Holly demonstrated apostolic ministry, his own personal missional *habitus*, and the missional identity of Redeemer.[46]

Hirsch names "three primary functions of apostolic ministry," the first two of which bring together the "dual elements of pioneer missionary and working theologian."[47] This language resonates closely with the missional *habitus* of our research congregations, formed through the adult catechumenate, which integrates the outward mission of the church to the world with apostolic doctrine and teaching. A strong emphasis on doctrine and church teaching, a hallmark of the LCMS, was most evident in the adult catechumenate of two congregations, St. John and Living Faith.[48]

---

45. Holly (pseudonym), interview by Kent J. Burreson, March 9–10, 2019. Subsequent quotations and summaries of Holly are from this interview, unless otherwise noted.

46. Pastor Taylor has relayed this story on numerous occasions, most recently in a Zoom presentation to Kent J. Burreson's class, "Adult Catechumenate and Faith Formation," on May 6, 2024.

47. Hirsch, *Forgotten Ways*, 154–56. The two functions are "To embed mDNA through pioneering new ground for the gospel and church" and "To guard mDNA through the application and integration of apostolic theology."

48. That Redeemer is not included in this section in no way implies that Redeemer is unfaithful to the Lutheran confession of faith and the foundational teaching that undergirds that confession. Our goal was to provide a variety of examples from all four congregations to demonstrate that all are engaged in fostering a missional *habitus*.

Chapter 2 paints the image of Pastor Bruzek at St. John as a "master teacher" whose "style of teaching . . . is lecture-based, polished, engaging, and content-rich in Lutheran theology" and who "encourages questions and uses a vast array of resources . . . to illustrate his teaching"—that is, the teaching of the church as confessed in the creeds of the church and articulated through a Lutheran lens. The novice participating in the catechumenate at St. John may not realize that there is an established curriculum intent on embedding doctrine in the mind along with fanning the flames of a living faith in Christ Jesus in the heart, but Pastor Bruzek is clear about this dual goal and the means. The curriculum is Lutheran theology unfolded through the framework of the Divine Service, the Sunday liturgy of word and sacrament.

That St. John's catechumenate often includes Christians who come both from American evangelicalism and the Roman Catholic traditions calls for some careful teaching that presents the differences clearly yet in a way that does not alienate. As one couple noted, "He doesn't bash other denominations," but makes "clear distinctions" about "why we believe what we believe."[49] Thus, Pastor Bruzek embodies the missionary/theologian character of an "apostolic leader," one who—to use his words—gives a "winsome witness" centered in the person and work of Jesus Christ yet framed in apostolic teaching to safeguard the message of the gospel.

Those completing the adult catechumenate are received as members of St. John at the Easter Vigil through an official ritual of the LCMS, the rite "For candidates for confirmation and reception of membership."[50] Pastor Bruzek's commitment to sound doctrine, intrinsic in his teaching, comes through explicitly in the ritual; his commitment to apostolic teaching is strong but subtle while the missional focus of his "apostolic leadership" is always at the forefront.

In ways similar to Pastor Bruzek, Pastor Droegemueller at Living Faith is committed to apostolic teaching with a stress on a missional ethos in the congregation. In his own reflection Pastor Droegemueller says that "we stress law/gospel preaching and the sacraments in the life of the

49. Curt and Lucille (pseudonyms), interview by Rhoda Schuler, August 8, 2018. Subsequent quotations and summaries of Curt and Lucille are from this interview, unless otherwise noted.

50. *Lutheran Service Book Altar Book*, 542–46. The usage was confirmed by Pastor Bruzek, email to Rhoda Schuler, December 1, 2023. In this rite, participants are questioned about their fidelity to the Triune God through the baptismal creedal questions; and they also affirm their commitment to Scripture as "the inspired Word of God" and Lutheran doctrine as "faithful and true."

congregation."⁵¹ From a Lutheran perspective these emphases would represent apostolic teaching. But it is an apostolic teaching proclaimed and expressed through a ministry that he says "aims to show genuine love and concern and to mentally observe where concerns of faith are present in people's lives." Apostolic leadership flourishes in active pastoral care for people through genuine and truthful apostolic teaching. His decision to use the one-year lectionary, as opposed to the more prevalent three-year lectionary, demonstrates this apostolic leadership. He and the congregation believe that many entering their catechumenate are essentially biblically illiterate. Knowledge of the written word of God is limited; one of the strengths of the one-year lectionary is its repetition. He believes that repetition is helpful in grounding catechumens and the congregation more firmly in the word. In his words, "It amounts to one big sermon on the life of Christ." The decision to use the one-year lectionary was an exercise in apostolic leadership, guiding the congregation into a practice that led them into apostolic truth, yet made in a spirit of genuine pastoral concern. Candice would affirm the wisdom of this decision. When she entered the catechumenate at Living Faith she desired deep doctrinal knowledge. Her experience of the catechumenate was that they "engaged the word of God seriously and I was firmly grounded in the word. In fact, the members of my cohort experienced a shared knowledge of the word through both the teaching of the lay catechist and Pastor Droegemueller."⁵²

The catechumenate has the effect of embedding an apostolic environment in a congregation. In the congregations we studied, the pastoral and lay leaders of the congregation lead out of the crucible of the catechumenate. Through the catechumenate each pastor "embodies, symbolizes, and *re*-presents the apostolic mission to the missional community."⁵³ By its structure, the catechumenate intertwines apostolic teaching and doctrine and the external mission of the church. As Hirsch concludes, "Apostolic influence awakens the church to its true calling and identity."⁵⁴ Since the catechumenate is oriented toward the birthing of new

---

51. In the Lutheran tradition, a law/gospel hermeneutic is the key to scriptural interpretation.

52. Candice (pseudonym), interview by Kent J. Burreson, August 15, 2018. Subsequent quotations and summaries of Candice are from this interview, unless otherwise noted.

53. Hirsch, *Forgotten Ways*, 152.

54. Hirsch, *Forgotten Ways*, 177.

Christians—especially adults but youth and children as well—it embeds the vision that the congregation is constantly in mission to the world.

ORGANIC SYSTEMS

The fourth primary element of mDNA in a congregation is that it functions as an organic system rather than as an institution. Hirsch's critique derives from his personal experience in ministry, saying "that as we grew and began to operate in the classic church growth mode it became increasingly harder to find God in the midst of the progressively more machinelike apparatus required to 'run a church.'"[55] He writes against institutionalism, which happens when the necessary "structural support" becomes "centralized governance."[56] The church's life, according to Hirsh, should not be mechanistic, but organic, flowing from faith and feeding the community's life together. Of this element Hirsch contends, "The church in its most phenomenal form . . . organizes itself as a living organism that reflects more how God has structured life itself, as opposed to a machine, which is the artificial, inorganic alternative to a living system."[57] The congregations we researched functioned as living networks where Christ was unabashedly at the center and shared beliefs, principles, interests, and goals permeated all the strands of the network. The catechumenate mirrors the dynamic networks of congregational life as a hub of activity with various groups of people and individuals as nodes in the network.[58]

At St. John, one can find the hint of such a living network in a phrase that some members picked up from frequent usage by Pastor Bruzek: "Find your spot; work your spot."[59] Participants in adult faith formation do not complete a "spiritual gifts" survey and then get matched up with the appropriate committee on which to serve. The "finding" happens organically, through informal networks and chance encounters. Keith is an example of the latter. That chance encounter, according to Keith, happened when his wife was hospitalized, and Pastor Bruzek visited her. Afterward, as he and

---

55. Hirsch, *Forgotten Ways*, 182.
56. Hirsch, *Forgotten Ways*, 187.
57. Hirsch, *Forgotten Ways*, 180.
58. Hirsch, *Forgotten Ways*, 200–205.
59. Lucille and Curt (pseudonyms) and Ken and Phyllis (pseudonyms) interviews by Rhoda Schuler, August 8, 2018. Subsequent quotations and summaries of Ken and Phyllis are from this interview, unless otherwise noted.

Part II: Common Themes across Uncommon Contexts

Pastor Bruzek were having coffee together, Keith recalled Pastor Bruzek telling him about the group of retired members who meet weekly and tend to facility maintenance needs. "Listen," Keith reported the pastor saying, "I could really use you here." Keith, having found "his spot," has been a regular member of the group since.[60]

In contrast to the deliberate, carefully planned pairing of sponsors with candidates/catechumens practiced at St. Mary's and Living Faith are the "Friendlies" of St. John, described in detail in chapter 2. These folks exemplify an organic model; they continued to attend the catechumenate classes after their initial experience because they wanted to learn more. Over time and through an organic, internal process, they came to realize that their presence among those first-time participants was an opportunity to build relationships, to model mature discipleship, and to embody St. John's ethos of love within the weekly catechumenal gatherings.

At Redeemer Lutheran in the Bronx, the pandemic was the catalyst that reversed an organic network of service—those who first had been served became those who did the serving. The "grandmothers" of the congregation (i.e., wise, seasoned, and established members) readily took up the task of assisting parents with and then mentoring and guiding the young children into full participation in worship. When the pandemic struck and vulnerable populations sheltered in place for months, some of those same children, now youth and young adults, cared for needs of their Redeemer "grandmothers."

Like the various parts of the human body, many are involved in advancing the mission of the church in society through the birthing and nurturing of new disciples by means of the catechumenate. Members of all the congregations knew they had a role to play and would readily engage in the formation process at the points where they could and desired to do so. The wisdom of Paul Hoffman, author of *Faith Forming Faith*, affirms Hirsch's insistence on an organic rather than "institutional" approach when developing an adult catechumenate. Serving as a consultant during our first grant, Hoffman offered some final sagacious words, with these as his most memorable to the leaders from the mentored congregations: "Whatever you do when you get home, *don't* form a committee!"[61]

---

60. Keith (pseudonym), interview by Rhoda Schuler, August 8, 2018. Subsequent quotations and summaries of Keith are from this interview, unless otherwise noted.

61. Calvin Grant Capstone Event for Leaders, Concordia Seminary, St. Louis, June 6–8, 2019.

COMMUNITAS, NOT COMMUNITY

The final mDNA element of a missional church is the formation of *communitas* in a congregation. Hirsch distinguishes this from "community," which he identifies as a quality of an established institution. Its goal is merely to sustain and maintain its life. *Communitas*, rather, is a people living under a missionally liminal situation, which he describes as "that situation where people find themselves in an in-between, marginal state in relation to the surrounding society, a place that could involve significant danger and disorientation, but not necessarily so."[62] Hirsch says that the people of God

> form themselves around a common mission that calls them into a dangerous journey to unknown places—a mission that calls the church to shake off its collective securities and to plunge into the world of action, where its members will experience disorientation and marginalization but also *where they encounter God and one another in a new way*. *Communitas* is therefore always linked with the experience of liminality. It involves adventure and movement, and it describes that unique experience of *togetherness*.[63]

To Hirsch's list of ordeal, disorientation, danger, and marginality as the defining characteristics of *communitas*, we add imagination, particularly as it relates to the catechumenate. The biblical narrative, especially the story of Jesus in the Gospels used widely in the adult faith formation of some congregations, can open the imagination of catechumens and candidates to new ways of understanding discipleship, baptismal living, and the totality of congregational life.

Pastor Bruzek, as a master teacher in the adult catechumenate at St. John, developed his curriculum around the liturgy of the church. He breaks open the words on a printed page of a hymnal (experienced by some laity as boring, archaic, or empty, ritualistic words—especially when rattled off in a perfunctory manner by pastors) through a teaching process that sparks the imagination of participants in the catechumenate. The teaching is reinforced on Sunday mornings with a slow and deliberate liturgical presiding that invites personal reflection. Three people in their interviews recounted the use of a cartoon of roadkill with the caption "Get well soon." This, they said, was used to make the point that people are "dead" in their sins, unable

---

62. Hirsch, *Forgotten Ways*, 220.

63. Hirsch, *Forgotten Ways*, 221. Phrase "where . . . new way": emphasis added; "togetherness": emphasis in original.

PART II: Common Themes across Uncommon Contexts

to revive and heal themselves.[64] With their imaginations sparked by this humor, they could enter into the opening section of the Divine Service, the confession of sins, confessing that they are "by nature sinful and unclean," and understand its full import for their spiritual lives.

Hirsch's language of ordeal, disorientation, and danger reflect the reality of living in a missional state where people "encounter God and one another in a new way." St. John's missional *habitus* was unleashed during a time of crisis, one which shook the congregation's well-established "institutional" thinking.[65] Founded in 1867, the congregation's elementary school was a strong part of its identity.[66] Chronic financial difficulties present for decades escalated to a crisis level during the economic downturn in 2008–2009, impacting households with job losses and home foreclosures. Some families with children in the school were unable to pay tuition bills, and the school was, in the words of Val (who was serving as school principal at the time), in "terrible trouble." When a plan to downsize the school in order to keep the doors open failed to receive the support of school families, St. John was forced to close it, a decision very unpopular with some members and one that thrust the congregation into a liminal state of uncertainty.

During this time of disorientation within the congregation, Pastor Bruzek, as senior pastor, took the brunt of the criticism for the school closure; although he had the support of the elected leaders of the congregation, who were fully informed and understood that the school could not recover financial viability, a significant number of families left the congregation. Such an exodus is not uncommon when parishes face such a crisis, and the fallout can sometimes have a crippling effect. But as Hirsch points out, it is just such a time "that calls [the people of God] into a dangerous journey to unknown places . . . that calls the church to shake off its collective securities and to plunge into the world of action, where its members will . . . encounter God and one another in a new way," experiencing *communitas*.[67]

---

64. Susan (pseudonym), interview by Rhoda Schuler, August 7, 2018; and Lester and Nancy (pseudonyms), interview by Rhoda Schuler, July 24, 2018. Subsequent quotations and summaries of Susan and of Lester and Nancy are from this interview, unless otherwise noted.

65. This account is based on interviews by Rhoda Schuler with Pastor Scott Bruzek, August 8, 2018, and with Val Gaede, preschool director, January 19, 2019.

66. Many LCMS congregations founded in the nineteenth century had the church and school model; the LCMS is the second largest parochial school system in the US, surpassed only by the Roman Catholic system. By the time of the crisis, enrollment in the school had dropped from a peak of 350 to 150.

67. Hirsch, *Forgotten Ways*, 221.

That "new way" for St. John was described in these words by Pastor Bruzek: "Those who stayed are intent on being kind and loving others." The congregation's size is smaller but the commitment of the members—better, of its *disciples*—is greater, and the ethos of the congregation, "turbo-charged by the catechumenate," has moved away from the goal of institutional maintenance to missional *habitus* grounded in God's love for the world and expressed through "loving others."[68]

The story of St. Mary's is less dramatic than that of St. John, but one that illustrates well the opportunity to effect change at the start of a new pastorate, when a congregation is in that liminal space. Having passed through the "dangerous journey" of a pastoral vacancy, the people of St. Mary's were ready for new ventures and change.[69] In discussing the strengths and weaknesses of the congregation, Pastor M described liminality and its disorienting aspect. She named as a weakness "fear" that led to "acting out of a sense of scarcity—of time, money, people—rather than abundance." Paradoxically, when naming strengths, she spoke of the "willingness [of people] to take risks." Pastor M credited her predecessor, the first female pastor of the congregation, for laying the foundation upon which Pastor M could build, and she challenged them to take risks and make significant changes.

In addition to introducing the adult catechumenate to the congregation, in her first three years Pastor M had led the congregation through the process of writing a new mission statement; restructuring the church council positions around that new mission statement; and implementing new worship times. At the time of our interview, she was preparing to restructure the children's education program. She freely admitted that these changes were successful because those from whom she might have faced resistance had either moved out of the community or had died. During those first three years of ministry, she buried twenty-two members. Yet, that many deaths in a small congregation may also have kept St. Mary's in a state of liminality, one that ultimately created an openness on the part of the people to new ventures. After two years of declining membership, St. Mary's was on an upward track at the time of our interview.

---

68. Pastor Bruzek stated that when he arrived at the congregation, there were 1,800 members "on the books" but weekly attendance was 600. At the time of our interview (pre-pandemic), membership was 950 with 700 in attendance weekly.

69. Pearl (pseudonym); and Pastor M, interview by Rhoda Schuler, August 7, 2018. Subsequent quotations and summaries of Pastor M are from this interview, unless otherwise noted.

Part II: Common Themes across Uncommon Contexts

The new mission statement, "At St. Mary's we are a worshipping, welcoming, growing, and giving community," informed the structuring of their constitution, reducing the number of committees from fifteen to four, each of which relates to one of the verbs in the mission statement. The adult catechumenate clearly falls under the category of "growing," which for Pastor M was not only numerical growth but also, and as important, a deepened "spirituality, relationship with Jesus Christ." Indeed, the Voyager process embraces the entire mission statement. By virtue of the public, ritual component, Voyager formed the whole worshiping community into a missional *habitus*, as they publicly prayed for the catechumens. The rite of welcome, which brought the catechumens before the congregation, enabled and empowered members with no formal connections to the Voyager process to welcome newcomers both ritually during the service and personally afterwards, drawing the newcomers more fully into the life of the congregation; and the assignment of "coaches" or sponsors, mature disciples who served as mentors, modeled for the newcomers a giving ethos, described by Pastor M as "a strong part of the congregation's identity." With its Apostolic Genius reawakened through risky, community-transforming changes, the Voyager process was a catalyst that renewed a missional ethos within the congregation.

JESUS AS LORD: RETURNING TO THE CENTER

In the Lutheran tradition the baptismal paradigm of dying and rising (Rom 6) is central to the mission of the faith formation process.[70] As Pastor Droegemueller at Living Faith said of theirs, "We make a big deal out of remembering at the Easter Vigil that we are buried into Christ's death in baptism, and raised into his resurrection in holy baptism."[71] Planting newcomers at the center of congregational life embeds the dying and rising pattern as the central way of understanding the shape of a congregation's life and its missional *habitus*. This process is about congregational transformation, not some program for welcoming new members. As Deaconess Rojas at Redeemer affirms, "It transforms our way of life and impacts our daily

---

70. By highlighting our own tradition and roots, we hope that others might see the biblical roots of this language, and if it resonates with the reader, we hope they might appropriate it for their contexts.

71. Quote by Pastor Droegemueller from his response to the survey instrument we used to determine which congregations would participate in our grant research, July 6, 2018.

living." As a catechumen at Redeemer said, "It changed my very life."[72] This transformation flows from the watershed baptismal event because the people of God in Christ are never *not* in formation until baptism is completed in death. In these congregations, through their rituals and formation, the catechumens and the congregations are constantly putting to death their sinful, selfish selves and being raised with Christ as a new creation, eager to be engaged in the mission of God at all times.[73] Since this is God's mission in his Son—to make us into the true, faithful humans God intended—as Hirsch says, "We never move from being a disciple on the way."[74]

The catechumenate shapes a community that reflects Hirsch's definition of a missional church: "A community of God's people that defines itself, and organizes its life around, its real purpose of being an agent of God's mission to the world."[75] In a missional church the intent is that mDNA flows through every believer and the entire community of faith. Embedding mDNA in this way seeks to transform the life and identity of a congregation and permeate the catechumenate such that it forms a missional mindset. As Alan Hirsch observes at the end of his book,

> We need to hit the road again. We are the people of the Way, and our path lies before us, inviting us into a new future in which we are permitted to shape and participate. In trying to rearticulate the nature of authentic Christian community, that of a *communitas* formed around a mission . . . we evoke that yearning and that willingness to undertake an adventurous journey of rediscovery of that ancient force called Apostolic Genius.[76]

In faith formation the church hits the road as a community in missional movement. As one catechumen put it, "This is a forever walk."[77]

---

72. Stewart (pseudonym), interview by Kent J. Burreson, October 3, 2018. Subsequent quotations and summaries of Stewart are from this interview, unless otherwise noted.

73. Often in congregations this missional mindset is true theologically, but not practically. The catechumenate helps congregations to be aware of this disconnect by holding up publicly the catechumens as central to the congregation's identity. The absence of catechumens in front of the congregation ought to be a sign to the congregation that they are not engaged in the mission of God.

74. Hirsch, *Forgotten Ways*, 103.

75. Hirsch, *Forgotten Ways*, 82.

76. Hirsch, *Forgotten Ways*, 241.

77. Julie (pseudonym), interviewed by Kent J. Burreson, October 4, 2018.

Part II: Common Themes across Uncommon Contexts

For Reflection and Discussion

1. Is there a story in this chapter that opens up your imagination toward renewal of faith formation practices in your congregation? In what way is your imagination sparked?

2. What elements of mDNA reveal themselves in your congregation's life together? How can you capitalize on the elements you see in your congregation in developing faith formation practices? How might you activate the "dormant" mDNA elements through stronger faith formation practices in your congregation?

3. How might you structure and develop practices to form and make disciples in your context? How might faith formation practices or an adult catechumenate contribute to making disciples in your context?

4. How do your current ways of instructing adult members reflect the intellectualization of such practices within the church? How might you retain an emphasis on doctrinal content while also opening up your instructional methods to more experiential learning?

5. In what ways are your outreach efforts based on an attractional model? How might you rethink them toward an incarnational model?

6. What are the barriers for you as a pastor or for the pastoral leadership in your congregation that are preventing the creation of an apostolic environment? How might those barriers be overcome so that your congregation might embrace a richer faith formation process?

7. How does your congregation focus primarily on maintaining its institutional life? How does it operate as a living organism where new ideas and new practices are embraced so as to engage in mission to the world?

8. When has your congregation been in an in-between, marginal state? What might it look like now for your congregation to inhabit such a state in your context? How might the catechumenate help you to arrive at such a marginal state?

9. Reflect on these words of wisdom from Paul Hoffman: "Whatever you do, don't form a committee!" What alternative ways to introduce a catechumenate might your congregation embrace?

7

THE PATH OF CONVERSION

Belonging, Believing, Behaving

We return to the three BEs—behaving, believing, belonging—in order to highlight the flexibility of the adult catechumenate and examine commonalities in the process among the disparate congregations of our research. As we noted in the introduction to part I, early church historian Alan Kreider and historian of American Christianity Diana Butler Bass, who have both written about the conversion process through the lens of these B-words, have informed the analysis of our research. Although we might not second all of their assumptions and conclusions, their insights into the conversion process and the changing pattern of conversion throughout history have provided a useful interpretive lens for our research.

Kreider's examination of conversion stories from the second to the sixth century contrasts the conversions of the second and third centuries that "took place amidst risk and high adventure," decisions made freely after counting the cost, with those of the fourth through sixth centuries, marked by "a belonging . . . now associated with compulsion" that asked the convert "to ratify a social order . . . to swim in the mainstream, not in a crosscurrent. . . . [For] the mainstream was now Christian."[1] He challenges the church to find lessons applicable to our times from those earliest centuries and points out mistakes to avoid. Bass lays out statistics similar

---

1. Kreider, *Change of Conversion*, 70.

to those we cited in the Introduction but considers them not "grim" but hopeful. She sees signs of an "awakening," which she describes as "a Great Returning to ancient understandings of the human quest for the divine.... [of] reclaiming a faith where belief is not quite the same thing as an answer, where behavior is not following a list of dos and don'ts, and where belonging... is less like joining an exclusive club and more of a relationship with God and others."[2] These core insights from both authors correlate with the lively faith communities we researched.

Both authors describe shifts in emphasis and priority of the three BEs throughout Christian history and generalize about the order of the three in the conversion process. In the early church, Kreider argues, the behavior of Christians was not only that which first attracted others to Christianity; in the catechumenal process itself, training in right behavior was also *prior* to teaching the faith, and belonging began with baptism, neatly fitting each B-word into the catechumenal pattern. Once candidates received approval from church leaders, they were "admitted... to Stage 2—the catechumenate," during which the "teaching seems to have concentrated on a reshaping of the converts' *behavior*." Once candidates' behavior met necessary benchmarks, they were "admitted to Stage 3—enlightenment—which concentrated upon *belief*." Finally, at baptism "they experienced *belonging*."[3] Perhaps it was so, but it seems to us a bit too "neat" and regimented.[4] Nevertheless, Kreider's conclusion that the priority and predominance of Christian behavior in the earliest centuries of the catechumenate shifted by the fourth and fifth centuries to the priority and predominance of Christian belief is plausible, as is his assertion that the stress on behavior diminished with the rise of Christendom.[5]

Bass asserts that, at least since the Reformation, Western Christianity has followed this sequence: belief, then behavior, "and finally belonging,... [a] pattern [that Protestants and Catholics] turned into rituals of catechism,

---

2. Butler Bass, *Christianity after Religion*, 99.

3. Kreider, *Change of Conversion*, 22, emphasis in original.

4. Research by liturgical scholars on the main source material for Kreider's neat, linear progression, the so-called *Apostolic Tradition of Hippolytus*, cautions against drawing definitive conclusions from this and other early church orders, saying that the authors/editors of early church orders "may have been indulging in an idealizing dream... imagining what the organization and liturgy of their community would be like if they were allowed to have their own way and impose their idiosyncratic ideas on the rest of the congregation." Bradshaw, *Search for the Origins*, 95.

5. Kreider, *Change of Conversion*, 102; see also Ferguson, "Catechesis and Initiation."

The Path of Conversion

character formation, and Confirmation."[6] Her assessment rings true to us, based on the historical evidence and on our personal experiences as "cradle Lutherans" in the LCMS, where full membership was attained through the rite of confirmation, which was also the gateway to the Lord's Supper (when one truly "belonged") and the point at which the newly confirmed received contribution envelopes.[7] Based on our research, we find compelling Bass's assessment that our contemporary context calls for a reshuffling of the BEs, one that moves belonging to earlier stages of the process,[8] for in three of our four case studies belonging is the dominant theme in participant interviews.

Worth repeating here is the wisdom of Pastor Bruzek: "When I was young, we used to ask people what they thought [or perhaps, believed]; now people ask, 'How do you feel?'" In answer to that question, people today respond that they feel "empty, lost, broken, listless, betrayed, miserable, angry, loveless, afraid, victimized, alienated, oppressed, in despair"—all of which can be compressed into the statement "I feel alone and unloved."[9] Participants in St. John's catechumenate spoke of the love of Christ made real to them; of the pastors embodying "love with a capital L"; and of wanting friends going through the catechumenate "to feel loved and welcomed" as they had felt. In response to the cries of those who feel lonely and unloved, St. John's has become a place where "love is the primary virtue." Pastor Bruzek's diagnosis of American society's spiritual malady—feeling lonely and unloved—is supported by the US Surgeon General's 2023 Advisory, "Our Epidemic of Loneliness and Isolation," which outlines the many health risks associated with "social disconnection" and cites the finding that "about one-in-two adults in America reported experiencing loneliness."[10] That so many of those interviewed in our research used language of

---

6. Butler Bass, *Christianity after Religion*, 201.

7. Since the 1970s there has been a decoupling of youth's first communion from the Rite of Confirmation in American Lutheranism. Most ELCA congregations now offer first communion by the fifth grade or earlier; a significant number of LCMS congregations have a similar practice for fifth graders, but the current Rite of Confirmation has wording that recognizes the divergent practices. One of the "General Notes" reads: "Confirmation is a custom of the Church ... [that] links the catechumens to their Baptism, celebrates the reception of the Lord's Word among them, and in cases where the candidates have not yet communed, welcomes them to the Lord's Table." *Lutheran Service Book Agenda*, 28.

8. Butler Bass, *Christianity after Religion*, 201–9.

9. "Painting a Vision for Forming Lutheran Christians," panel discussion with Pastors Scott Bruzek, Timothy Droegemueller, and Dien Ashley Taylor, October 20–22, 2020.

10. "Our Epidemic of Loneliness and Isolation," 4.

belonging persuades us that social disconnection and loneliness are the spiritual crises of today that the church is called to address. Each research congregation is an example of an adult catechumenal process as an effective means of connecting people who are yearning for identity and belonging to claim their identity in Christ and to discover the freedom and joy of belonging within the communion of saints.

Our research reveals a predominance of "belonging" language from those interviewed at St. Mary's, Redeemer, and St. John; at Living Faith, "believing" was the dominant theme. A deeper analysis of the data uncovers the presence of all three BEs in all four congregations in varying degrees and emphases. But rather than a clear succession of formation and incorporation into the life of the church one B-word at a time, the interviews disclose a simultaneity of belonging, believing, and behaving within the stages of the formation process. By exploring this simultaneity along with the "dominant" BE-language in each congregation, we hope to awaken readers to the creative possibilities inherent in an adult faith formation process in their contexts.

ST. JOHN: ENCIRCLED WITH PASTORAL CARE, ENTICED BY LOVE

The language of love, "the primary virtue" at St. John, is language of intimacy and belonging. Pastor Bruzek's diagnosis of our society's malady—that people "feel alone and unloved"—is as true today as when we first talked face to face at St. John's in August 2018.[11] As narrated in chapter 2, the congregation's ethos of love revolves around the exceptional pastoral care that is planned, practiced, and deliberate (with the database "tracking" system), yet also genuine. The database follows Sunday attendance, flagging households when there is a succession of absences. The pastoral staff, recognizing that this behavior can be a sign of some kind of crisis, reaches out to these flagged households. One could easily imagine that hearing from one's pastor after several weeks of being AWOL from worship might be perceived as heavy-handed and a cause for guilt or shame. Yet the experience of Gail

---

11. Full disclosure: Scott Bruzek and Rhoda Schuler first met in the 1980s, when he was a seminary field worker assigned to serve at the congregation in the St. Louis area where she was member. They had not kept in touch, but when Kent and Rhoda were soliciting congregations to be part of their research, that prior connection was a factor in his decision to respond to (and not delete) the initial email request.

and George, who have a child with a chronic health problem that can keep them from Sunday liturgy, was quite the opposite. Speaking of the pastoral staff, George commented, "it's about love with a capital L," to which Gail immediately added, "They always notice when we're not here" because of their child's health issue; the juxtaposition of the comments clearly shows that the pastoral outreach is interpreted as an act of love and care.[12]

Chapter 2 describes the catechumenal process at St. John as "liminal moments of pastoral care," setting forth the low-key, individual encounters of participants with members of the pastoral team that unobtrusively moved participants through each "stage." Stepping back from the individual interviews brings into focus the collective mosaic. Encircling their stories of the catechumenate is the love of Christ, embodied for them by Pastors Bruzek, Buchs, and Nelson, strong and gentle shepherds, leading Christ's flock to still waters and preparing a table for them each Sunday to feast on Christ. Pastor Bruzek's question is rhetorical: "How can [the catechumens] have an experience where they feel completely loved, welcomed?" The love, the sense of belonging, encircles the participants in the catechumenate throughout the process. As at St. Mary's and Redeemer, that sense of belonging grows stronger as participants' beliefs and behaviors are simultaneously being formed through the Sunday liturgy and weekly catechesis sessions.

Pastor Bruzek's hand-drawn illustration visualizes how, throughout the catechumenal process, the faith of the church is taught and Christian behavior is modeled and habituated in the participants. Encircled by St. John's ethos of love is the Chi Rho with the marks of the discipleship emanating from that central symbol of Christ. Above the circle of love is the word "liturgy" with an arrow pointing downward to the circle. The structure for the weekly catechetical instruction is the Sunday liturgy of word and sacrament; on one level, the instruction helps those unfamiliar with this classic shape of worship to understand it and thus participate in it more fully. But the liturgy also informs the content of the teaching. For example, the service begins with confession and absolution, at which the people confess that they "are by nature sinful and unclean," opening up a teaching opportunity for the doctrine of original sin and humanity's need for forgiveness and the grace of God. Without question, the Saturday

---

12. Gail and George (pseudonyms), interview by Rhoda Schuler, January 20, 2019. Subsequent quotations and summaries of Gail and George are from this interview, unless otherwise noted.

morning catechesis at St. John has a strong emphasis on the *fides quae*; it is about what the church believes, as many of those interviewed said.[13] Yet structuring the doctrinal teaching according to the liturgy also forms and nurtures the *fides qua*, the faith of the heart that responds to the call of the Holy Spirit, a personal faith that is deepened by encountering Christ in the word preached and in the sacraments of baptism and Eucharist. Those new to church life, who enter the six-month catechumenate with its expectation of regular church attendance, are formed and become habituated in this core spiritual practice.

The arrow below the word "liturgy" is pointing to the three marks of discipleship in the upper half of the circle, those that form and strengthen the faith of disciples—Scripture, sacraments, and prayer. The marks that are the disciples' response to God's grace and unconditional love—mercy, generosity, and witness—focus on living as disciples of Jesus in the world, as indicated by the arrows moving from these marks of discipleship beyond the encircling ethos of love.

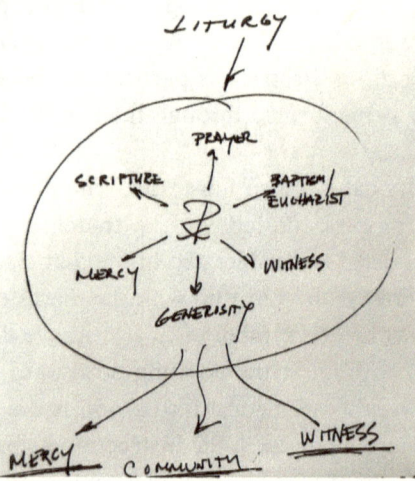

One of the "Friendlies," Ken, recited these marks of discipleship, an indication that these terms are recurring themes in the catechetical sessions, and others used similar words (tithing, acts of mercy, the action part) in their interviews. Within the catechumenal process at St. John is a simultaneity of

---

13. George spoke of his appreciation for "the law/gospel balance" at St. John. Curt said, "I came for the sacramental theology and discovered side benefits I can't imagine living without." Lester summed up their experience as a "reminder of good doctrine [and] a reminder to be loving."

formation in both belief and behavior. The most striking language of this simultaneity came from two of the "Friendlies," commenting on the congregation's mission statement. After quoting the marks of discipleship, Ken said that the mission statement "doesn't stop at salvation [and] forgiveness [as if] we're good to go; [discipleship] includes service to others."[14] Lester stated it this way: "sanctification [is] there too. In the catechumenate [we learned] justification is the start but not the finish line. It's the starting line for the Christian life."[15]

The language of the catechumenal process (Scripture, sacraments, and prayer; mercy, generosity, and witness) permeates the totality of the worship life as well as the teaching and service activities across generational lines. Enveloped in the ethos of love at St. John, the baptized of the congregation are continuously being formed into disciples who believe with their hearts and minds the truth of Jesus Christ and whose behavior centers in lives of service and witness to the world. Descriptions of regular activities in the Sunday worship folder illustrate the common language of discipleship.[16] The Sunday morning Adult Bible Study announcement proclaims that the "*Scriptures and the Sacraments* assure us that our Lord is near, and more, that He is always for us and never against us." The Sunday morning High School Catechumenate is considering what "*God's Word*" has to say on "topics that matter to the lives of young adults. How can we be *faithful to Christ* and His church *while interacting with the world* around us?" Confirmation for youth is more than instruction: "We'll be emphasizing *how our faith is lived out* and not simply learned. This means *praying more than learning information about prayer*, and worshiping rather than learning information about liturgy." A weekday Men's Bible Study is titled "How Martin Luther's view on monasticism can *renew our life of prayer*." Members are invited to a training session in order "to join the Lutheran Early Response Team (LERT) [and serve as] volunteers when asked to help after a disaster ... This basic training will prepare team members and focus on Christian care in

14. Ken and Phyllis (pseudonyms), interview by Rhoda Schuler, August 9, 2018. Subsequent quotations and summaries of Ken and Phyllis are from this interview, unless otherwise noted.

15. Lester and Nancy (pseudonyms), interview by Rhoda Schuler, August 8, 2018. Subsequent quotations and summaries of Lester and Nancy are from this interview, unless otherwise noted. The terms "justification" and "sanctification" are not words that are ordinarily on the lips of laity—another indication of the strong doctrinal focus of the teaching.

16. St. John Lutheran Church, Wheaton, Illinois, worship folder, February 25, 2024, 21–23. Emphasis added in all quotations.

times of a disaster—*Christ's mercy is the basis for everything we say and do."* At the Confirmation Servant Event participants "will help inspect, sort, and package *food that will be distributed to hungry neighbors."*

Enveloped in the love of Christ, secure in their sense of belonging, Jesus' disciples at St. John Lutheran Church across generations are daily formed as people who trust in God's promises revealed in and through Jesus' life, death, and resurrection and who joyfully live lives of mercy, generosity, and witness to the world.

LIVING FAITH: THE GRAVITATIONAL PULL OF RIGHT BELIEF

As the chapter on Living Faith chronicled, their catechumenate focuses on heart-to-heart combat in the spiritual battle for true faith and right belief. Believing is a primary feature of their catechumenate. As Pastor Droegemueller indicated in a panel discussion in one of our online conferences: "The truth is the truth. It's the law of gravity. You can't run from it. Catechesis is life-long. We can't play games. We need a shift in how we understand catechesis and life. God's word changes us. It absolutely obliterates the power of sin. It raises the dead. This is what we are trying to recapture in the catechumenate. The training is an invasion of the created order. We need to train people over and over and over."[17] The spiritual battle is one for belief that God establishes God's kingdom (invasion of the created order) of truth and mercy in Christ Jesus. Belief is centered in the word of God. For Living Faith that word of God changes those whom it encounters; they move from allegiance to Satan to allegiance to God through faith. Training to confront the powers of evil is a lifelong endeavor that begins in the catechumenate at Living Faith.

As we observed in chapter 3, through their catechumenate Living Faith responds to a cultural form of Christianity and Lutheranism that downplays matters of belief. At Living Faith serious study of biblical doctrine shapes both what these disciples believe and fosters a robust life of faith that lives out of the gospel. Thus, while believing is primary at Living Faith, belonging and behavior flow from formation in that belief. Oscar's description of his own change of allegiance reflects the centrality of believing, but also the importance of belonging to the true Christian community

---

17. "Painting a Vision for Forming Lutheran Christians," panel discussion with Pastors Scott Bruzek, Timothy Droegemueller and Dien Ashley Taylor, January 12–14, 2021.

The Path of Conversion

and to behaving in ways appropriate to that teaching.[18] Oscar was initially hesitant to enter and complete Living Faith's catechumenate. He grew up a Methodist minister's son. As a teenager he embraced a cultural Christianity. It was a form of Christianity that "never discussed doctrine and never heard the gospel." This included a symbolic understanding of the Lord's Supper, that the bread and wine were merely signs of the Lord's grace and love. Feeling a deep absence in his life, he "cried out to God for help." He listened to radio preachers and joined various nondenominational, free-will theology, biblically grounded congregations. But he was burdened by the demands of doing good and not knowing how much was enough. This led him to dig intensely into Scripture to compare what he was hearing on the radio and in those congregations with the written word of God. After briefly joining a Reformed Baptist Church, he started listening to Lutheran teachers online. He increasingly became convinced of the truthfulness of Lutheran doctrine. That eventually led him to Living Faith.

Oscar recognized the biblical foundation and truthfulness of Living Faith's teaching. However, due to his Methodist and nondenominational background he struggled with the sacraments as physical, earthly encounters with God's grace and their performative nature, in which, from a Lutheran perspective, God is active in them bringing forgiveness, life, and salvation. As a result of that struggle, he went through the catechumenate three times, attending fewer and fewer classes each time, but honing in on the issues that were problematic for him. This increasingly included lengthy phone and in-person catechetical conversations with Pastor Droegemueller. The third time was the charm. He crossed the threshold of belief regarding the effective sacramental nature of baptism and the Lord's Supper and then belonged to the fellowship at Living Faith. The sacraments became for him "a sign of correct belief and belonging." After the Easter Vigil service Oscar and his wife didn't make it to the congregational reception. Instead, they "stood at the font and talked for half an hour about what had just happened at the font. We shared in the joy of the event." Proper biblical believing grounded the very belonging they had been seeking.

This concern with biblical doctrine was not unique to Oscar. Paul had Pastor Droegemueller programmed to speed dial on his phone. While the catechumenate classes were formative and helpful, he had deeper questions

---

18. Oscar (pseudonym), interview with Kent J. Burreson, August 15, 2018. Subsequent quotations and summaries of Oscar are from this interview, unless otherwise noted.

PART II: COMMON THEMES ACROSS UNCOMMON CONTEXTS

that he did not ask in class. He would call Pastor Droegemueller regularly to explore these questions and get answers. These questions reflected his desire to dig deeper into knowledge of biblical teaching, how to convey it in the arenas in which he lives, and its implications for life in the world. As Oscar's and Paul's stories demonstrate, believing is the central factor in the catechumenate that constitutes belonging and behaving at Living Faith. As Pastor Droegemueller says, "The truth is the truth. It's the law of gravity." In that law of gravity catechumens at Living Faith find their footing again.

ST. MARY'S: A TAPESTRY OF BELONGING

The sense of belonging created by the Voyager process at St. Mary's is like the warp of a woven tapestry, running from the from top to bottom, from beginning to end, providing strength for the fabric woven with each stage of the process. During the informal, fluid stage of inquiry the word "welcome" was central, initiating a sense of belonging in seekers. Victoria, who described herself as "not someone who likes a lot of attention," was very scared the first time she walked in the door, but the woman seated next to her made her feel "very welcomed." And, she added, "After the first service I knew this was where I needed to be."[19] Pastor M's diligence and warmth, commented on by several interviewees, fostered a sense of welcome. Bob and Ruth said the welcome they received from Pastor M at their first visit "knocked our socks off." New to the area and searching for a home church, their first church-shopping visit was to St. Mary's, and they "didn't go anywhere else."[20] Betty, moved to attend church by the crisis of her missing cat, remembered Pastor M empathically saying, "I know what it's like; I'm an animal lover too." Betty was "comfortable" around Pastor M and "always found her very welcoming."[21]

---

19. Victoria (pseudonym), interview by Rhoda Schuler, October 13, 2018. Subsequent quotations and summaries of Victoria are from this interview, unless otherwise noted.

20. Bob and Ruth (pseudonym), interview by Rhoda Schuler, April 19, 2019. Subsequent quotations and summaries of Bob and Ruth are from this interview, unless otherwise noted.

21. Betty (pseudonym), interview by Rhoda Schuler, August 6, 2018. Subsequent quotations and summaries of Betty are from this interview, unless otherwise noted. For Betty (perhaps for Victoria as well) the small size of the congregation was a secondary factor. She described feeling "isolated and intimidated" at other churches and experienced their worship as "overwhelming." But St. Mary's worship was "so nice" and its size "not too much—just enough."

The Path of Conversion

As the interview questions moved to the stages of the catechumenate and enlightenment, the language of the Voyagers reflected a thicker sense of belonging. As they gathered weekly to reflect together on the Sunday Gospel readings in their small groups under the guidance of Pastor M and Pearl as catechist, Laura and Harry observed ways in which the process built community, shifting to familial language as they described the latter weeks. The shared meals were, they noted, how they "got to know people," and the circle prayer ending the weekly sessions brought them closer to one another. Laura stated that by the end of these weeks together, "at prayer time . . . we felt like St. Mary's was a *family*." They also reported that at one gathering the Voyagers collectively said of Pearl, "You're a *godmother* to us all."[22]

The presence of coaches at the weekly gathering began the process of weaving the familial thread of Voyagers into the fabric of the whole congregation. The rituals at the Sunday services during Lent, part of the pattern of the tapestry, also enhanced Voyagers' sense of belonging and identity. For Dayla, the friendliness of the congregation after these rituals made her feel "at home."[23] Stanley, the person with the most ambivalence about the Voyage process, reported an attitudinal shift around this time, saying, "I felt a bit more part of the community."[24] At the Vigil, full incorporation of the Voyagers into the life of the congregation was celebrated as part of the thanksgiving for baptism. Asked to describe how she felt about this service, Dayla said, "I love the idea of being brought officially into the family." Stanley "remembers the congregation praying openly" for all the Voyagers, which was an "affirmative" experience for him. Betty, who had attended Easter Vigils in Roman Catholic parishes, exclaimed, "It was incredible; beyond my expectations. How can I tell you? Such an experience!" About the formal congregational welcome, which included applause, she said, "The people were cheering at the end." As these comments express, the Voyagers recognized that the ritual at the Vigil marked the culmination of "belonging."

---

22. Laura and Harry (pseudonym), interview by Rhoda Schuler, August 7, 2018, emphasis added. Subsequent quotations and summaries of Laura and Harry are from this interview, unless otherwise noted.

23. Dayla (pseudonym), interview by Rhoda Schuler, April 20, 2019; and by phone June 2019. Subsequent quotations and summaries of Dayla are from this interview, unless otherwise noted.

24. Stanley (pseudonym), interview by Rhoda Schuler, August 6, 2018. Subsequent quotations and summaries of Stanley are from this interview, unless otherwise noted.

Part II: Common Themes across Uncommon Contexts

What of believing and behaving? Where is the simultaneity? Even as the shared prayer at the end of the Voyager sessions was creating a sense of belonging, the practice of praying for others was simultaneously forming the Voyagers' behavior. To listen carefully to others and to pray aloud in a personal way for one person shaped these individuals to move beyond themselves and their needs to care for others. Likewise, the public rituals during Sundays of Lent imbued a sense of belonging to and welcome by the whole congregation even as the presentation of the gifts were strong, concrete symbols of Christian beliefs—the Bible, the Apostles' Creed, Luther's *Small Catechism*, and the ELCA hymnal.[25] The prayers and blessings from these rituals also indicate expected behavior for Voyagers. As the Bible was presented, Pastor M exhorted the Voyagers to "Hear God's word with us. Listen and tell its stories. . . . Honor its commandments. Rejoice in its good news." As they received the hymnal, Pastor M said: "Receive this book of worship. We ask you to join us in prayer and song to God."[26] And they did. Throughout the entire process the Voyagers engaged in the core behavior of Christians, participation in corporate worship, joining with the congregation on Sundays "in prayer and song to God." Throughout the stages of catechumenate and enlightenment they listened attentively to biblical stories of Jesus both during Sunday worship and their weekly gatherings and, moved by the Spirit, their relationship with the Son and the Father who sent him was deepened. The Voyagers were woven into belonging, believing, and behaving disciples.

Ruth was the Voyager who critiqued the process for being "backwards" because the group did not delve into the "what" of believing until the stage of mystagogy. Only then did the group study Lutheran doctrine and learn more about the faith of the church, what the church confesses as true belief (*fides quae*). Her comment illustrates that the post-Reformation linear pattern of believing, behaving, and belonging noted by Bass is still a dominant model for some today. But in her desire for the *fides quae*, Ruth missed the intricate pattern of *fides qua* (the faith that trusts in Jesus as the

---

25. These words, emphasizing belief, were spoken as they received the catechism from the Rite of "Call to Renewal": "Receive this summary of the faith of [the] Church. Learn it. Pray it. Inwardly digest it. Join us in studying it." Copy provided by Pastor M; based on rituals she received as part of participation in Faith Forming Faith Workshop led by Paul Hoffman.

26. "Rite of Welcome" for First Sunday in Lent and "Rite of Commitment to Prayer." Copies provided by Pastor M; based on rituals she received as part of participation in Faith Forming Faith Workshop led by Paul Hoffman.

fulfillment of all of God's promises), that was woven into the lives of the Voyagers throughout the stages of catechumenate and enlightenment. In their small group gatherings, they responded to questions about how Jesus was drawing them from darkness into the light; of how Jesus' touch was healing their wounds and hurts; of how they themselves were on the road to the cross with Jesus. To stretch the weaving analogy further, the *fides quae* of the believing, the "what" that is believed, was not a separate strip added to the end of the finished fabric. Rather, the faith of the church is a border of an ancient, golden thread surrounding the finished tapestry. Only within that border can one question and explore the *fides qua*, of trusting in Christ as Savior and Lord; only within that border can one experience the true freedom of living a life of service to others; and only within that border will one discover the joy of belonging to Christ with all his saints. As Dayla, a cradle Lutheran in her eighties, said, the Voyage process "gave me a whole different and deeper understanding and reaffirmed everything."

REDEEMER: A HUGGING VINE

The three BEs all find expression in Redeemer's mission statement: Receiving, Teaching, Celebrating, and Sharing Christ Jesus. Instead of seeing the verbs parceled out into separate silos—believing with teaching; belonging with sharing; behaving with celebrating—one should see them as intertwined in the catechumenate and in the life of the congregation. As the people of Redeemer are receiving, teaching, celebrating, and sharing Christ Jesus, they are opening up belief, transforming behavior, and creating belonging. Certainly, belonging is the central characteristic of congregational life and how the catechumenate facilitates entry into the community. But catechumens experience belonging through believing and behaving. As Sandy describes their catechumenate, it is "like a vine hugging!"[27] Just as a vine hugs a tree or a pole, so the community of Redeemer surrounds and embraces the inquirers and catechumens who encounter the congregation. Sandy also says that the time the catechumens, sponsors, congregation, and Pastor Taylor and Deaconess Rojas spend together in group sessions, worship, and fellowship is all "structured but also informal to make space for community time. We want to lose our time in Jesus. As a community Redeemer seeks to address the needs in others' lives." All of this is deliberately

---

27. Sandy (pseudonym), interview by Kent J. Burreson, October 2, 2018. Subsequent quotations and summaries of Sandy are from this interview, unless otherwise noted.

PART II: COMMON THEMES ACROSS UNCOMMON CONTEXTS

intended to forge community and to welcome the inquirer and catechumen into that community.

Two stories of catechumens illustrate how Redeemer is a "hugging vine," creating the opportunity for belonging. The first is of Julie and Stewart, whom we encountered in chapter 5. From their words about the public nature of Redeemer's catechumenate it might appear that a sense of belonging was inhibited. Jennifer said that when they were brought forward for the rites of acceptance and election, and at other times when the catechumens were publicly before the congregation, "I felt exposed in front of the church. I was being made public. I'm not naturally comfortable in my own skin. I'm an introvert."[28] And Stewart felt similarly. "Every week in catechumenal class was introspective. It challenged me to look at my life and made me feel uncomfortable. I didn't feel judged. It was like a mirror, and I was able to look at it because of not being judged."[29] This introspection applied both to the shape of their believing and their behavior. As they both said, "We both question things. Why are things done in a particular way in this community?" Answers to their questions then allowed them to examine what they believed, why and how they were living, and what needed to change. The scrutinies in Lent were especially formative for Julie. She said of them, "We were back in front of the congregation. It was at that moment that I felt I gave birth to myself. We [had] talked about the meaning of the creed and the Lord's Prayer. We had never walked through them in that way. So, the prayers became more meaningful." Or as Stewart said, "Going through the Ten Commandments led to my absorbing and feeling them so as to live the Ten Commandments myself." This was another point of introspection encountered publicly within the congregation. The introspection shaped what they believed and recontextualized their behavior, and all of that intensified their sense of belonging to this community.

By surrounding Julie and Stewart, the Redeemer community created an environment of hospitality and welcome. Throughout the catechumenate, Julie says, "The congregation knew we were in it. They would ask how we were doing. If we needed support, they would provide it. They were very warm. It was important for the community to know where we were in the process." It was important for Redeemer to know that because it created

28. Julie (pseudonym), interview by Kent J. Burreson, October 4, 2018. Subsequent quotations and summaries of Julie are from this interview, unless otherwise noted.

29. Stewart (pseudonym), interview by Kent J. Burreson, October 4, 2018. Subsequent quotations and summaries of Stewart are from this interview, unless otherwise noted.

the opportunity to incorporate them into the community. And that was the intended result. As Stewart said, "It felt like we belonged to a group, and made it easy to connect. They provided encouragement and lots of support." They both said, "Building relationships with other members of the church takes time. We need longer to warm up. The length of the catechumenate gave us opportunity to know members of the church and of our catechumenate group. The congregation knew our names over time. [The time the catechumenate affords to build those relationships] may be why the church has been responsive to us." Creating the sense of belonging takes intentional effort on the part of the congregation, and Redeemer strives to own its responsibility to foster those opportunities.

Maura's story also reveals the importance of being welcomed into the congregation and embracing for herself a sense of belonging. Maura was born in the Bronx and raised there. She was baptized in the Methodist church but starting at age five grew up in the Lutheran church. Like many, she left the church in high school. However, there were familial expectations that she go to church. At the birth of her first child, she felt that something was missing from her life. As she said, "Life experience pushes you back to church."[30] After attending a baby shower, she had her daughter and son baptized at her old congregation. This led to the conviction that she needed to get her spiritual life in order. She asked herself, "Why do you want to get your child baptized? I felt it was important I bring up my children in the right way. But that meant *I* needed to do some self-exploration." She decided that Redeemer's life together provided the opportunity for that exploration. She had an immediate connection to Pastor Taylor, of which she said, "That meant so much to me!" Pastor Taylor told her there were no strings attached to her worshiping in the congregation. Maura described the congregation as "pristine, organized, open, and sincere," all qualities that were compelling to her for accepting their welcome. Eventually her husband would join her and, finding the church very authentic, would be baptized. They then both decided they needed to engage with the catechumenate.

The importance of the feeling of belonging is apparent in Maura's comments about the catechumenate. The catechumenate itself, she said, "felt authentic for me—a sum of all the parts. [Important were] the interactions with deaconess and pastor. It felt like an extension of family. I felt a unity of message and actions, of authenticity—with every member. This

---

30. Maura (pseudonym), interview by Kent J. Burreson, October 2, 2018. Subsequent quotations and summaries of Maura are from this interview, unless otherwise noted.

Part II: Common Themes across Uncommon Contexts

experience mirrors everything we were taught." Belief and belonging are intimately intertwined. The congregation lived as it believed, and Maura sensed and recognized that.

The intertwining of belief and belonging reached its culmination for Maura at the Rite of Election and at her confirmation. She said of signing the book, "It felt like I was getting married all over again. It always seemed like a natural progression. Seeing all that have signed before me created the sense of community. The entire community is supporting me and I'm joining them." Throughout all the rites and at her confirmation she could tangibly feel the welcome and embrace of the congregation. She said, "They are wonderful. People were supportive. They would say congratulations. They would extend their hands over me at the front of the congregation. They are participating. And after the service they are cheering you along the way." Belonging to Redeemer was how Maura experienced the catechumenate, belonging practiced by the assembly and fed by what they believe and how they behave with one another. That is authentic integration of belonging and believing.

Finally, behavior is a constitutive priority in Redeemer's catechumenate. Lydia, another catechumen we met in chapter 5, indicated the significant change of behavior that ensued for her through her baptism, the pinnacle event in her journey through the catechumenate. She reflected on this change of behavior in the following way, "I didn't feel confident telling people to pray. I now tell them that I pray for them. I *do*. I see that being a Christian, there are expectations. I will live so as to bring joy in my life. I heard the word 'taste' in my [confirmation] verse. You can taste sourness and negativity [in people]. I am here to bring joy into another person's life. You should serve God alone—I am going to walk in his waters—representing his foot soldier." The change in behavior for Lydia is palpable. Her manner of life has been reoriented 180 degrees through the encounter with the word in Redeemer's catechumenate and their life together. Lydia belongs to Redeemer, believes in the Redeemer, and now lives as one whose life is conformed to the Redeemer.

ENTICING LOVE ... GRAVITATIONAL PULL ... WEAVING A TAPESTRY ... A HUGGING VINE

The varied language and metaphors used in this chapter break open the many ways an adult catechumenate could be envisioned in other contexts

The Path of Conversion

to foster the lifelong process of becoming disciples of Jesus. To close this chapter, we return to Alan Kreider and Diana Butler Bass, whose historical analyses also pose salient questions regarding Christ's Great Commission, particularly the "how" of baptizing and teaching in a post-Christendom context.

Bass describes the experience of Vacation Bible School from her childhood, "when the women of the church and their children created [VBS] with construction paper, oilcloth, magic markers, yarn, buttons, and old socks." Now, she laments, "VBS has become a spiritual commodity, a religious experience that can be purchased," perhaps, she continues, because "people have forgotten how to do" it or "no one ever taught them," or "maybe it is just too hard." The same holds true for "spiritual practices" like prayer, according to Bass. There are canned programs for purchase, many of which are marketed according to the "attractional" model of outreach, "a kind of outsourced plan for transformation."[31] Bass identifies "two key elements" needed to move an activity like prayer "from the realm of external plan to internal transformation," namely, *"finding a teacher and time."*[32]

Pastors M and Droegemueller found lay teachers, Pearl and Daniel, in their midst; whom might the Spirit raise up in your congregation to serve in such a role? Time feels more elusive and precious, until one recognizes a key commonality among the stories in this chapter. Dayla, the octogenarian, cradle Lutheran at St. Mary's, for whom the catechumenate process deepened her faith; the carefully curated and crafted activities at St. John's, that reinforce a pattern of growing in mercy, generosity, and witness across generations; Oscar's multi-year struggle at Living Faith to find the truth that finally gave him joy. A purchased program cannot create the needed "time" for disciples of Jesus to deepen their spiritual practices, but in a lively, committed community, the time spent together engaging in spiritual practices and teaching the faith will bear fruit. As Sandy at Redeemer so eloquently said, "We want to lose our time in Jesus"!

Alan Kreider offers three "relevant clues" from the early church to inform a missional ethos in the church today. First, he notes that early Christians could feel the pulse and power of "conventional folkways" that "trapped people in deathly, demon-beset cages," and then asks, "What are the addictions of our time?" With good discernment (such as Justin Martyr had in the second century), Kreider says that "we might be able to announce

---

31. Butler Bass, *Christianity after Religion*, 160–63.
32. Butler Bass, *Christianity after Religion*, 163–64, emphasis in original.

with new winsomeness and grace the message of Jesus Christ, who sets people free and gives them life in all its abundance." Second, he challenges the patterns of modern evangelicalism, that "often place heaviest emphasis upon correct belief leading to overpowering experience." Might we see in the pattern of early Christianity, he asks (echoing Bass), "that learning is a product of action?" Third, he cites "the formative power of the catechetical process" and its revival in post-Christendom, when participants in the process "will be more aware . . . that they are dying to old options and rising to new opportunities" and that strong rituals will have transformative power for them. We agree with his final words: "Such churches, having learned from the past, would have something authentic to contribute to the future."[33]

---

33. Kreider, *Change of Conversion*, 101–7.

THE PATH OF CONVERSION

For Reflection and Discussion

1. With which narrative of the four congregations did you identify with most closely? Why?
2. For pastors: Reflect on your experience providing pastoral care to your flock; do the words of Pastor Bruzek resonate with that experience? Do your members manifest the feeling of "being alone and unloved"?
3. Reflect on the pattern of the three BEs in your congregation and current new member process.
    a. What is emphasized most? How does this emphasis relate to the context of your congregation and surrounding community?
    b. Which of the three is emphasized least? How might this aspect of discipleship receive more attention?
4. Consider asking your newer members what drew them into your congregation. Do their responses align with the priorities of the pastor and lay leaders who shape your new member process?
5. What changes could you make to your current process to emphasize lifelong discipleship?
6. In what way could a form of the adult catechumenate facilitate a process in your congregation that thoroughly addresses believing, belonging, and behaving as the path to authentic discipleship?

8

RITUAL

Enacting and Rehearsing the Christian Story

In our presentations and workshops on adult faith formation, we have approached the topic of ritual[1] with fear and trembling, wary of alienating some of our audience by our enthusiasm and fervor for robust ritual done with grace, reverence, and gravitas. Some church leaders (both from Lutheran and from other denominational traditions), especially those who resonate with language of "mission" and "discipleship," react to the phrase "liturgical worship"[2] on a continuum ranging from suspicion to hostility. Yet recent trends in philosophy and neuroscience, anecdotal evidence of changing attitudes toward worship within evangelical Christianity, and a fledgling movement in the business world give us hope that appreciation for ritual is on the rise.

First, consider this trend in philosophy. The Cartesian assertion that humans are primarily thinking, rational, independent beings that has

---

1. For the first half of this chapter, we use a clear and straightforward definition from Ramshaw, *Christian Worship*, 33: rituals are "defined actions that are repeated, communal, and symbolic." This definition is not limited to "religious" rituals, as some of our examples illustrate.

2. That is, worship that is centered in the classic Western liturgical structure of the Mass, of word and sacrament, with the fixed "Ordinary of the Mass" (Kyrie, Gloria, Credo, Sanctus, Agnus Dei) found in Mass settings from Mozart to Bernstein. All Christian worship, even "free" traditions that are not text-based, follow a set ritual pattern within their worship services.

dominated this discipline for centuries has been replaced with a more holistic, body-mind person who is shaped in and by a community.[3] This postmodern perception of the human person as embodied creates space for ritual as constitutive for how one comes to "know" and to make meaning in the world. The power of ritual knowledge lies in its participatory nature, an embodied way of knowing that engages all the senses and creates memory and knowledge through movement, gesture, and symbols. This turn in philosophy, a discipline concerned with some of the same topics and questions addressed in theology, gives us hope that ritual's value will gain currency among practitioners and pastors as they reflect on worship.

Second, we are heartened by anecdotal evidence within evangelical circles. For over a century and half, worship in evangelical Christianity in North America has privileged *ex corde* prayers and ad lib bridges between major parts of the worship service over the fixed texts of traditional "liturgical worship." The former is believed to be more authentic, heartfelt, and genuine than the latter, often characterized as rote, cold, and empty. Yet recent publications indicate a discovery of and appreciation for the historic Western liturgy.[4] This trend among American evangelicals includes a greater appreciation for fixed texts and prayers, which, by virtue of repetition, implant patterns of prayer, poetic language, images, and narrative within participants, as well as a new openness to ritual and its transformative power. We welcome this trend, and hope that this new, more positive view of the Western liturgical tradition on the part of our brothers and sisters in American evangelicalism will strengthen ecumenical conversations about worship and foster cross pollination of ideas for strong adult faith formation and the role of worship in that endeavor.

And a third, curious turn to ritual in secular settings hints that the human longing for ritual continues, as the subtitle of this *New York Times* story from 2020 declares: "Divinity consultants are designing sacred rituals for corporations and their spiritually depleted employees." The article describes theologically trained spiritual entrepreneurs who are crafting rituals to build community, mourn losses, and create meaning for and in

---

3. This is the major argument of James K. A. Smith, outlined in his Cultural Liturgies trilogy. This chapter draws on volume 2, *Imagining the Kingdom*.

4. See, for example, Winfield, *Ever Ancient, Ever New*; Webber and Ruth, *Evangelicals on the Canterbury Trail*; and The Center for Baptist Renewal website, "What Can We Learn from the Ancient Church?" The interest extends to a greater appreciation for the liturgical year and its lectionary and many other "treasures" from denominations with a liturgical tradition.

PART II: COMMON THEMES ACROSS UNCOMMON CONTEXTS

the workplace. The titles listed in the article illustrate the strange juxtaposition of the word "ritual" with milestones in the busyness of creating a business: "A ritual for purchasing your domain name (aka your little plot of virtual land up in the clouds)" and "A ritual for when you get the email from LegalZoom that you've been officially registered as a Limited Liability Company."[5] The words of one spiritual consultant quoted in the article inspire both fear and hope in us: ". . . the fact is that people are showing up in the workplace with these big deficits in themselves when it comes to belonging and connection to the beyond." We fear that such endeavors will fill these spiritual voids with that which cannot satisfy; yet we hope that people with "these big deficits" might find the bread without price in Christian congregations, places where there is a solid adult faith formation process that will draw those hungering for meaning into a relationship with Jesus Christ.

THE CLAIMS OF RITUAL SCHOLARS

Scholars of ritual studies make some sweeping claims about the power of ritual; for our purposes, we'll examine three such claims that correspond to the journey of discipleship summarized by the three BEs—believing, belonging, and behaving—detailed in chapter 7, providing evidence for each with examples from history and daily life as well as from our research. The second half of the chapter explores the role of the Sunday liturgy in shaping a community's and individuals' *habitus* of "desiring the kingdom" through the work of James K. A. Smith.

Ritual Has the Power to Shape What People Believe

During the fourth century, the Arian heresy—that is, the belief that the Son was a second-class god—had many adherents in Constantinople; Sozomen, a church historian writing in the early fifth century, reported that the Arians gathered outdoors, sang hymns expressing heretical Arian beliefs, and then "marched in procession, singing those hymns, to the places in which they held their assemblies." John Chrysostom, bishop of Constantinople, fearing other Christians would be "led astray" by joining their processions and singing heretical hymns, fought ritual with ritual by organizing

---

5. Bowles, "God Is Dead. So Is the Office."

his own. Sozomen comments, "The orthodox, being more numerous and more wealthy than the Arians, soon surpassed them in pomp and splendor of their procession; for they had silver crosses and lighted torches borne before them."[6] Good ritual, involving sung texts, movement of participants, and concrete symbols of the faith, shaped the beliefs of early Christian laity, bringing into their hearts, minds, and bodies the theological truths of the Council of Nicaea, that the Son is begotten, not made.

As liturgists researching current examples of the adult catechumenate, we assumed that the Easter Vigil would be the crowning ritual for those completing the process. Thus, for our interviews we had crafted several questions about people's experiences of the Easter Vigil and were eager to hear about their recollections. It was surprising then, to discover that some St. John interviewees remembered more about the party following the Vigil than the Vigil itself, and few could offer details of the rite within the Vigil that welcomed them into membership at St. John. The analysis of one couple provides interesting insights into this lacuna of memory.[7] Ken and Phyllis compared the Easter Vigil with a confirmation service for their nephew at another congregation. The latter was a two-hour service on a Saturday, at which the entire focus was on the youth confirmands. St. John's Vigil was also a long service that included confirmation of the youth, but by contrast, in the words of Ken, it is "98 percent high feast day, 2 percent acceptance of new members," consisting of a rite that took "less than five minutes." Phyllis added that the Vigil is "very religious," "done up" with music and vestments, and is "as high as the [Sunday morning] Easter service, higher than Christmas." They experienced the Easter Vigil as a feast day about Christ's triumph over death through his resurrection, the central belief of the Christian faith, and not about new members joining the congregation. For Ken and Phyllis, this focus on Christ's resurrection was right and salutary.

As noted in chapter 2, St. John's in Wheaton has no public rituals for those in the catechumenate prior to Holy Week. Alongside the Vigil is the Holy Thursday service, which stands out as an exemplar of powerful ritual that reinforces the other side of the "coin" of Christianity's central belief—Christ's atoning death on the cross. Without benefit of a researcher's prompt,

---

6. Sozomen, *Ecclesiastical History*, book VIII, chapter 8.

7. Ken and Phyllis (pseudonyms), interview by Rhoda Schuler, August 8, 2018. Subsequent quotations and summaries of Ken and Phyllis are from this interview, unless otherwise noted.

Part II: Common Themes across Uncommon Contexts

Ken followed his 98/2 percent comment by saying, "Maundy Thursday is the big service; catechumens are invited to help." Other interviewees also spoke of their involvement in the stripping of the altar at the end of this service with deep reverence. Curt said that Maundy Thursday is "my favorite," describing it as "somber" and "a stunning service—that's why people remember it."[8] He and Lucille had been so moved by their participation in it the first time, that they asked and were able to help the following year.

From the lens of ritual studies, there are several factors that likely contribute to the memorable quality of this service: first, as one of a series of services that marks this most holy time of year for Christians, it is carefully planned and rehearsed; second, it involves movement and prominent use of symbols by the lay participants—an unusual opportunity in St. John's worship, which is highly clerical in worship leadership. Through all these factors—time of year in the Christian calendar, careful rehearsal to ensure the somber nature of the service, movement by and handling of symbols by the laity—the ritual draws people to contemplate on the saving work of Jesus Christ on the cross, solidifying the core belief of Christianity through their kinaesthetic participation.

Val Gaede, the preschool director, invites those in the catechumenal process to participate in this service and rehearses with them earlier in the week.[9] She begins the gathering with prayer, a ritual cue that this is a rehearsal for a holy event, and reminds them that what they are doing is "all about Jesus Christ." On Holy Thursday, as Psalm 22 is chanted, Val and two members of the altar guild guide participants forward to receive with reverence the communion vessels, candles, and paraments from the chancel area, solemnly bearing these items to the sacristy. As Keith said of the services on Thursday and Friday of Holy Week, he was moved by the "solemnity" of the services that evoked "a sense of spirituality," and that "brings you closer to the Lord; it's the death he went through [that] makes you reflect on your life, the life hereafter."[10] The ritual movement of the slow procession up the center aisle, the solemn gestures receiving the altar furnishings, and the touching and handling of these holy objects

---

8. Curt and Lucille (pseudonyms), interview by Rhoda Schuler, August 8, 2018. Subsequent quotations and summaries of Curt and Lucille are from this interview, unless otherwise noted.

9. Val Gaede, interview by Rhoda Schuler, January 19, 2019. Subsequent quotations and summaries of Val are from this interview, unless otherwise noted.

10. Keith (pseudonym), interview by Rhoda Schuler, August 7, 2018. Subsequent quotations and summaries of Keith are from this interview, unless otherwise noted.

as a single voice chants the plaintive words of Psalm 22 all contribute to the "solemnity" as the assembly collectively ponders Jesus' holy passion for the redemption of the world. In contrast to many key rituals at Redeemer and St. Mary, which are (appropriately) centered on the participants in the catechumenate, this ritual, a liminal moment for participants at St. John, is not about them. Rather, it draws them into the central story of salvation history, particularly from a Johannine perspective, the moment of "glory," when the Son of Man is lifted up on the cross to draw all people to the God is who is love (John 12:32; 1 John 4:16).

As chapter 3 demonstrated, Living Faith's catechumenate focuses on belief as the formative factor for incorporation into the body of Christ. Ritual at Living Faith brings the centrality of belief to focused expression. This was certainly true for Oscar; for him baptism and the Lord's Supper were particularly potent and powerful experiences. Because of his background (growing up a Methodist minister's son, engaging with cultural Christianity, then radio preachers; joining a nondenominational Baptist church, and then a Reformed Baptist church) he knew when he came to Living Faith that the sacraments—as means of grace—were going to be doctrinal thresholds that he would have to cross at some point. Both sacraments represented fundamental elements of believing and belonging for Oscar. They were, in his words "especially the Lord's Supper, signs of correct belief and belonging."[11] Baptism was the first hurdle. For him, baptism in a magical way[12] "was not constitutive of being a Christian. But I did a lot of listening first. Passages show clearly that baptism is the work of God." Note how the Scriptures led to right belief as construed at Living Faith. It was important for Oscar that Scripture lead to this change of belief. The culmination in this threshold experience was when "I was led to the font for confirmation at the Easter Vigil. This was very meaningful, and I [was] fixated on the moment. I knew that I was entering a new stage of life, a place of rest from my constant searching, especially for the true teaching."

The next hurdle after baptism was the Lutheran teaching on the Lord's Supper. Lutherans believe that the sacraments effectively convey God's grace and that they do so realistically with elements of creation—water, bread, and wine—as the vehicles for participating in that grace. By virtue

---

11. Oscar (pseudonym), interview with Kent J. Burreson, August 15, 2018. Subsequent quotations and summaries of Oscar are from this interview, unless otherwise noted.

12. This is how Oscar described sacraments as encounters with God, as means of grace, prior to his change in belief.

Part II: Common Themes across Uncommon Contexts

of Jesus' words, his body and blood are truly present in the bread and wine of the Lord's Supper and, in Luther's words from his *Small Catechism*, they bring "forgiveness, life, and salvation" to those who believe the words associated with the bread and wine.[13] For Oscar, "This was harder... if this is not simply a symbol." In order to address this doctrinal obstacle, he "walked through with pastor [often outside of class on the phone] Zwingli's objections to Luther's teaching in the Marburg Colloquy."[14] That debate, and his conversation with Pastor Droegemueller about it, "Gave me a proper understanding of the Lord's Supper." After struggling with the Lutheran teaching on the Lord's Supper, his final doctrinal threshold, at the Easter Vigil he "just wanted to run to the altar." And, for whatever reason, he did not realize that he was going to receive the Lord's Supper at the Easter Vigil. It was for him unexpectedly a "wonderful gift at that moment." As he said to himself then, and still does, *"This feast is what you are coming to believe."* From that moment at the Easter Vigil he realized, "When I participate in Jesus' body and blood, I feel strengthened. It invigorates me here and now." Believing the word that he heard at Living Faith was at the crux of Oscar's experience of the catechumenate. Believing and belonging were intricately interwoven, and the unity of the two reached its pinnacle at his first ritual experience of receiving the Lord's Supper at the Easter Vigil. As Oscar said, "I found community in the teaching. My wife and I did not go to the reception after the end of the Easter Vigil. Instead, we stood and talked with pastor for half an hour about what had just happened at the font and the altar. We shared in the joy of the event." Through the ritual of the Lord's Supper, they embraced their newfound belief and were fully incorporated into the body of Christ at Living Faith.

In Oscar's case it was the focused experience of the Lord's Supper liturgy and of receiving the body and blood of Christ that brought to fulfillment his change of belief. In Lily's case (we met her in chapter 5 about Redeemer), it was the cumulative effect of the Easter Vigil that concentrated the primary experience of faith. All of the ritual experiences of Redeemer's Vigil—the Service of Light, the anointing of confirmation, the hearing of the word, the touch of the community—embodied the very nature of faith. "I didn't realize the magnitude. It started with the bonfire. The pink papers

---

13. Luther, *Small Catechism*, 362.

14. For the curious interested in this sixteenth-century reference, details of Zwingli and Luther's dispute on the topic are laid out in "Marburg Colloquy and the Marburg Articles" (1529) in *Luther's Works*, vol. 38, 5–89.

were part of the centrality [of the ritual moment].[15] The struggle with lighting the candle,[16] *[it captured Jesus' call] to believe in me. All five of my senses were awake. From darkness to light. I had support, felt support, felt the body of warmth. The oil, the smell of it, the touch of pastor. Amazing. At my confirmation, kneeling, receiving my psalm verse, and being prayed over personally [by pastor and the community]. This is the thing I cling to.*"[17] There is an echo in her words of Martin Luther in his *Large Catechism*, critiquing the Anabaptists of his day: "But these leaders of the blind are unwilling to see that faith must have something to believe—something to which it may cling and upon which it may stand."[18] The ritual of the Easter Vigil elicited that faith in Lily, something she could cling to, someone in whom she could place her faith.

Ritual Creates Identity, Forms People into Community, and Imbues a Sense of Belonging

Military service is a powerful cultural example of ritual that creates identity and community. At boot camp, one sheds civilian clothing for the military uniform; that word, "uniform," evokes the goal of forming a disparate group of people into one. The shared living space, shared meals, shared experiences of training that pushes people to the limits of their strength and endurance are experiences that form a bond intended to sustain them as a community in battle. These shared ritual experiences are marked with formal rites that reinforce the chain of command and military discipline—the inspections, roll call, and playing of taps to end the day.

Those who leave active service do not leave behind this identity. Consider the ubiquitous VFW halls present in small towns across the country, where those bonds continue in civilian life. The death of Rhoda's father-in-law, who served in World War II, illustrates the strong sense of belonging and community enacted through ritual. Although never active in VFW activities or other programs for veterans, at his committal service a group

---

15. On the pink papers members of Redeemer had written sins at the start of Lent. They were invited to toss the papers into the bonfire as a sign of the burning away of the dross of human sin.

16. It was a challenge to get the paschal candle lit from the bonfire due to the wind.

17. Lily (pseudonym), interview by Kent J. Burreson, March 9–10, 2019. Subsequent quotations and summaries of Lily are from this interview, unless otherwise noted.

18. Luther, *Large Catechism*, 460.

of total strangers arrived in dress uniform, solemnly lined up in formation on either side of the walkway leading to the cemetery chapel, and stood at attention as his casket was carried past them. At the close of the service, the family witnessed the ritual folding of the flag and its presentation to a grandson. Even in death, his military identity defined him, and members of the military community honored him for his service. Ritual creates identity and a sense of belonging, forming individuals into community.

The faith formation at St. Mary's included numerous rituals for the participants within the Sunday liturgy to create that sense of community and belonging: a rite of welcome on the first Sunday in Lent; rites on subsequent Sundays in Lent with a blessing by their sponsors and a gift (for example, a Bible, hymnal, and catechism); and the affirmation of baptism at the Easter Vigil. St. Mary's has a moveable font which is placed in the center aisle just inside the entrance to the nave of the church for most of the church year. For the Easter Vigil, the font is moved forward in the nave and placed in front of the railing of the chancel area. One participant, Bob, articulated the impact these rituals had on him; his recollections demonstrate how deep meaning is enacted through ritual action, movement of participants, and prominent symbols.[19] When asked about the rite of welcome which took place on the First Sunday in Lent, Bob remembered that they first gathered at the font (located inside the entrance to the nave throughout the season of Lent), and then they moved into the nave of the church (during the gathering hymn). The pastor began the service with these words: "Dear friends, we are gathered at this door today to meet these persons who have been called by God's Spirit to affirm their baptism into Christ. Together, let us welcome them to this time of preparation and renewal." The participants' names were read, questions were addressed to them and to the gathered community, which was asked, "Will you help them hear the gospel of Christ and be strengthened as members of the household of faith?" followed by a brief prayer and culminating with these words "Now, [names], come into St. Mary's and hear the word of God with us."[20]

When asked about the Easter Vigil, Bob spoke not only about the affirmation of baptism at the Vigil, which takes place at the font relocated to

---

19. Bob and Ruth (pseudonyms), interview by Rhoda Schuler, April 19, 2019; and by phone June 11, 2019. Subsequent quotations and summaries of Bob and Ruth are from this interview, unless otherwise noted.

20. St. Mary's church bulletin, Sunday, March 10, 2019, First Sunday in Lent; based on *Welcome to Christ: Lutheran Rites*, 9.

RITUAL

the front of the nave; his words from the interview indicate that the ritual during the Vigil triggered his memory of the rite of welcome:

> The part [at the Vigil] that I took to [came when] they prayed for us after the water coming ritual; [we were] in the back with the font [when we experienced] our first going on this journey. From water to water—it's symbolism I remember from English literature—water as a symbol of birth. Yeah, born again in Christ. And the congregation was going to pray for you in the next step of this voyage.

The baptismal font; prayer; moving in procession; metaphoric, poetic language of journey; a "water coming ritual"—two multisensory ritual experiences so powerful that the latter evoked memories of the former for Bob, recalling that at both rituals the congregation had prayed for them.

The font, as focal center of both the rite of welcome and the affirmation of baptism, seemed to trigger in Bob key aspects of each. At the welcome conducted by the font, the "first going on this journey," he recalled that "the congregation was going to pray for you in the next step of this voyage"—a practice the congregation did throughout the season of Lent and at the Vigil. Bob's phrase, "the water coming ritual," are his words for the rite of aspersion, during which an evergreen branch was dipped into the baptismal water and sprinkled on the whole assembly, a ritual gesture done "in remembrance of our Baptisms" as the rubrics from the service folder of the Vigil reads. Or as Bob said, to remember that all those gathered have been "born again in Christ" through the waters of baptism. At the Vigil Pastor M walked the length of the center aisle, sprinkling everyone in the pews as the whole assembly sang "I'm going on a journey." In the interview, Bob repeated both "journey" and "voyage," the latter word that which St. Mary's used for their catechumenal process. At the rite of welcome on the first Sunday in Lent, they embodied their "journey" as they processed from the font at the entrance to the nave into their place near the front of the nave within the congregation. The journey culminated near the chancel on the night of the Vigil, again before the font filled with the water of new birth, witnessed by the whole assembly. Ruth, Bob's wife, drawing on her ritual experience as a youth, said, "It's like confirmation; *you don't go on this journey alone*" (emphasis added). They entered the Voyager process as devout Christians; the journey created in them a sense of community within the congregation.

PART II: COMMON THEMES ACROSS UNCOMMON CONTEXTS

Both Bob and Ruth mentioned the water theme when asked what was most meaningful from the Vigil. For Ruth, it was the remembrance of baptism, "a rebirth with Christ" that was connected "with this congregation, with this area." The couple had recently purchased their first home and were expecting their first child; they were putting down roots in the community, and finding a church home was important and had a sense of urgency for them. Ruth noted that the whole series of rituals "being in front of the congregation so many times . . . *provided us an identity* [that] gave and cemented our identity in the church" (emphasis added). Bob again made a ritual connection to that identity and belonging, noting "the water [in the aspersion rite]—*the whole congregation was sprinkled along with us*" (emphasis added).

Highlighting the ritual experiences of Bob and Ruth is ironic, for although they were Lutheran, they had been raised in a small "free church" Lutheran denomination with nonliturgical worship. I interviewed them over dinner in their home, and Ruth offered a beautiful, well-crafted *ex corde* table prayer, a practice she learned growing up in her home congregation. I commented on it, and she said that she had "read Scripture in church, and when you did that, you prayed your own prayer." She, who early in the interview said, "I don't like change," openly shared that she found the text-driven liturgy at St. Mary's "mindless" and merely "going through the motions." Bob said of printed prayers: "That's not praying; it's reciting." There were other barriers that made St. Mary's, as an ELCA congregation, less than an ideal fit for them.[21] They both (but especially Ruth) struggled with the structure of the faith formation process. Ruth wanted to know what the ELCA believed and expected to be asked what *she* believed; St. Mary's process, which covers Lutheran teachings in the final stage, mystagogy, was, according to Ruth, "backwards." Although first drawn to St. Mary's by Pastor's M personal welcome and the strong connection they felt with her, it was the rituals associated with the adult catechumenate that created in them a sense of belonging. As Ruth said, "Being in front of the congregation so many times . . . cemented our identity in the church." Ironic, yes, but also a testament to the transforming power of ritual to create identity and community.

---

21. The ELCA has practices that differ from the more theologically conservative denomination from whence they came; Pastor M was their first experience with a female pastor, and the denomination's open position on the LGBTQ+ issues was also a stretch for them, although it did not prevent their decision to join the congregation.

Redeemer also offers two more examples of ritual's formative role in shaping identity and community. The first is catechumen Lily's experience of her confirmation through anointing and the laying on of hands at the Easter Vigil. Her language to describe this ritual includes language of relationship, community, and support, all experienced through the ritual. She says of that experience,

> During the anointing before the altar, I knew the church was behind me, my sponsors were there, my mother and my brother were there. There is community here. It was like a graduation of sorts. We [those in the catechumenal cohort] had all journeyed together. There were congratulations and welcome shared by all. It felt like a culmination. This is the personality of the church. Redeemer congratulated me. [Throughout the process] people learned my name. They were intentional about it. I am excited about my daughter growing up here. There is a strong sense of community. For anyone's family—if there are complexities [in family life]—bring it in here.

Lily experienced the ritual reality of the psalmist:

> How very good and pleasant it is when kindred live together in unity!
> It is like the precious oil on the head, running down upon the beard,
> on the beard of Aaron, running down over the collar of his robes.
>   (Ps 133:1–2)

Her anointing was the very blessing of community in the body of Christ at Redeemer, brothers and sisters living together in love and unity.

Gifts can be tangible expressions of the ritual moment, points of remembrance of the concretized experience of grace and life. Redeemer, like Living Faith and St. Mary's, gifts the catechumens with various things to mark those ritual moments of passage. At the culmination of their journey through the catechumenate they receive a crucifix on a neck chain. The crucifix is a reproduction of the cross that hangs over the altar in Redeemer's sanctuary, a primary symbol of the congregation that receives, teaches, celebrates, and shares Christ Jesus. After their anointing Deaconess Rojas places the cross over the heads of the newly confirmed. Members hold these crosses close to their hearts, both realistically and figuratively. They not only wear them to worship, but also to work, when with their neighbors, and when they travel. It is a tangible sign of the community to which they belong and of the One to whom their lives are devoted. It is a marker of identity for the baptized of Redeemer, an indication that they have made the journey through the catechumenate and that the rituals of the catechumenate have shaped them to be and live as a child of God.

Ritual Can Be Transformative, Reshaping Behavior

Harry Truman's "whistle-stop tour" weeks prior to the 1948 presidential election is illustrative of ritual's claim to be transformative, for this "Hail Mary" political gamble changed the hearts and minds of enough voters to deliver a narrow victory for Truman. In September, with his opponent leading in the polls by 10 to 12 percentage points, Truman left Washington, traveling 22,000 miles over thirty-three days and repeating a political ritual at venues large and small. A high school band played the national anthem as the train pulled into the station; Truman would appear on the platform at the rear of the train with several local politicians, one of whom would introduce the president. After a stump speech tailored to the local context, and with the crowd cheering "give 'em hell, Harry," he would introduce his wife and daughter, the latter of whom would toss roses to the crowd as the president leaned over the car railing to shake a few hands; the band would begin to play, and the Truman family would wave as the train pulled out of the station. It was a powerful ritual that not only transformed hearts and minds to favor Truman over his opponent but also inspired the behavior of enough people who made the effort to vote on election day.[22]

We offer here some examples from Redeemer and St. Mary's, the two congregations with rich ritual we studied—ritual examples that encompass the Sunday worship of the whole community and that illustrate the transformative power of ritual within the catechetical process as well.

One of the most transformative ritual experiences in the catechumenate is Redeemer's Rite of Acceptance/Welcome, often on the First Sunday in Advent. The signing of the candidates with the cross on various parts of the body is a moving and richly symbolic experience. This marking with oil indicates that the candidates belong to Christ and are willing to begin carrying the cross in their life of witness to Jesus. The signing of the senses claims every part of the body and all the senses as redeemed by Jesus' death and resurrection, oriented in service to his kingdom, and directed toward the final renewal in the new heaven and new earth. The basic pattern at Redeemer (following the RCIA) is as follows: the candidates are invited forward and addressed by the presiding minister; their foreheads are signed

---

22. McCullough, *Truman*, 653–64.

with the congregation responding in thankful acclamation, then each of the senses is signed: ears, eyes, lips, heart, shoulders, hands, and feet, accompanied by appropriate texts linked to the biblical narrative with a concluding signing of all the candidates together. Commenting on this rite at one of our online conferences, Pastor Taylor said, "It is extremely intimate, and the catechumens understand that the good touch [they receive] is part of the way God is working with them for the rest of their lives."[23]

The rite begins with Pastor Taylor saying, "Receive the sign of your new life as catechumens" as sponsors place their right hands on the shoulders of the catechumens.[24] Then he proceeds to anoint each of the parts of the body, starting with "Receive the sign of the holy cross on your forehead. It is Christ himself who now strengthens you with this sign of love. Learn to know him and learn to follow him." Pastor Taylor comments on this anointing: "Right on our brains . . . so beautiful that the sign of the cross is made right on the part of our brains where the religious imagination actually happens—that's the creative part."

The ears follow with the words: "Receive the sign of the holy cross on your ears, that you may hear the voice of the Lord." And then follows the eyes: "Receive the sign of the holy cross on your eyes, that you may see the glory of God." The intimacy of touch is most poignant here for Pastor Taylor: "How intimate that can be, how they allow their eyelids to close, there can even be a little hesitancy. We do it so that the person may be able to see the glory of the Lord." And if the eyes were not intimate enough, how about the lips: "Receive the sign of the holy cross on your lips, that you may respond to the word of God." For the presider this is a powerful ritual indicating the willingness of the catechumen to receive the pastor's touch: "One that is powerful for me is the sign of the holy cross over people's lips. I am intrigued by what people do with their lips. Do they keep them the same? Do they fold them in? Are they nervous and afraid? Usually by the time we get to the lips they can be more relaxed, recognizing this is a gentler sign, validating the [overall] response that a person is going to have. They [can] remember that pastor actually touched my lips. The book of James must be very, very true: better keep track of that tongue! Better make sure that rudder doesn't take us awry into crazy zones." These ritual actions with

23. Burreson and Taylor, "Transforming Power of Robust Ritual Practices," January 12–14, 2021. Additional commentary by Pastor Taylor on the ritual anointing in subsequent paragraphs is also from this source.

24. Texts quoted here and following are adapted from *Rite of Christian Initiation of Adults*, 58–60.

accompanying texts embody the change of behavior that the catechumenate calls forth in the catechumens.

The next two actions focus on the centrality of Christ for the life of faith in God. Pastor Taylor touches the heart and says: "Receive the sign of the holy cross on your heart, that Christ may dwell there by faith." The union between Christ and the believer, which will reach its culmination at the Easter Vigil through baptism, confirmation, and communion, is symbolized here. As Pastor Taylor notes, signing the heart helps them to realized that "physically someone is touching them and saying Christ is dwelling there." Being united to Christ leads to the next action, that one in him can bear his yoke: "Receive the sign of the holy cross on your shoulders, that you may bear the gentle yoke of Christ." Through this ritual act, Pastor Taylor says, "They are able to remember that Jesus touches them and reaches them right there to carry and bear the gentle yoke of Jesus Christ. How intimate."

The last two body parts signed are those engaged in action and motion, agents that express the movement of the Christian life. First, the hands: "Receive the sign of the holy cross on your hands, that Christ may be known in the work which you do." Work is now oriented toward making Christ known. Pastor Taylor is quite intentional here: "I do the outsides of the hands and then I do the insides of the hands. [I do] the outside that the person might be able to see how the cross is made. [I do the] inside, a very intimate part of a person's life and work, reminding them of everything that person is touching and doing. It's [faith and behavior] all now connected with this new life that we're seeking." Second, the feet: "Receive the sign of the holy cross on your feet, that you may walk in the way of Christ." This is a sign of the continual journey the person is making toward the kingdom of God. Pastor Taylor points to the power of the ritual: "How powerful it is to get down to someone's feet that they may walk in the way of Christ. Everywhere that person is going, is going to be signed in the life of the Lord."

The Rite of Acceptance culminates with one large sign of the cross over all the catechumens: "I now sign you with the sign of eternal life in the name of the Father, and of the Son +, and of the Holy Spirit." Pastor Taylor communicates the nature of this final signing and of all the touches of the body with the sign of the cross: "One large, gracious, gigantic holy cross upon them in the end, the sign of eternal living—the Father, the Son, and the Holy Spirit. How beautiful [all this] can be and how needed that is when one can feel so disconnected, so disintegrated, so not invited, so not received." The catechumen belongs to this community, can live in conformity to this community's life, can live in the faith of this community. As Pastor Taylor concludes, "Now the hands have been placed upon you in all these parts of your body that you might know that you are being welcomed and accepted with all your questions, and with all your queries, and with all the things that have been on your mind. You are given a chance to understand that you are given space here and the community is affirming and supporting that together." The impact of the Rite of Acceptance is that catechumens are beginning to be changed, to live differently in faith. As Preston said, "Impact on who you are—makes me want to be a better person than I was and to be a better person than I am. To do better than I did the day before. I asked you [Jesus] into this life. It's hard!"[25] But the transformation is apparent, as Lydia said, "We bloomed, we were in the dirt. We bloomed. I bloomed in the church. Jesus planted the seed in me."[26]

In contrast to the Rite of Acceptance before the whole congregation, Laura and Harry's experience of the intimate rituals within the catechumenal process at St. Mary's had a profound impact on them.[27] Through the prayer ritual at the end of their weekly gatherings they were drawn into community with others. As described by Pearl, they would join hands and pray for the person on their left or right (decided by Pearl). Laura articulated the sense of belonging, saying, "At prayer times by the end [of the process] we felt like St. Mary's was a family." Her memories of the rituals at the Vigil were conflated with their marriage service; she remembered "we said 'I will' stuff [at the font] . . . it's all one big blur . . . we said 'I will' at the Vigil and our wedding." Just as they made vows to one another at their wedding, they made vows before the congregation. Pastor M asked, "Do you intend to continue in the covenant God made with you in holy baptism; to live among God's faithful people, to hear the word of God and share in the Lord's Supper, to proclaim the good news of God in Christ through word and deed, to serve all people, following the example of Jesus, and to strive for justice and peace in all the earth?"[28] Comments during their interview

---

25. Preston (pseudonym), interview by Kent J. Burreson, October 2, 2018. Subsequent quotations and summaries of Preston are from this interview, unless otherwise noted.

26. Lydia (pseudonym), interview by Kent J. Burreson, March 9–10, 2019. Subsequent quotations and summaries of Lydia are from this interview, unless otherwise noted.

27. Laura and Harry (pseudonyms), interview by Rhoda Schuler, August 7, 2018. Subsequent quotations and summaries of Laura and Harry are from this interview, unless otherwise noted.

28. St. Mary's service folder, Resurrection of Our Lord: Vigil of Easter, April 20, 2019.

PART II: Common Themes across Uncommon Contexts

confirmed their commitment; they expressed a desire to serve as coaches for the Voyage process; they had helped with VBS for the previous two summers; and three years later Laura had been elected president of the congregation.[29] Their words express the transformation of behavior wrought by a catechumenal process rich with ritual: "Now we know how we want to live as Christians."

Redeemer wants to be a visible presence in the Bronx, the people known as those who pray for and serve their community. One way in which they ritually enact this visible presence is through their Palm Sunday procession. On that day they parade through their community waving palm branches, with many of the assembly wearing red as they observe Passion Sunday and the entrance into Holy Week. The catechumens, who will be baptized and confirmed the next Saturday at the Easter Vigil, lead the way. This ritual act embeds in their bodies the self-understanding of being a people sent into the world immediately around them. They understand themselves to be sent as God's missionaries into the places where they live, work, play, and serve. It forms Redeemer to live incarnationally, to live Christ's presence in the world visibly. As Hirsch says, "By living incarnationally we not only model the pattern of humanity set up in the incarnation but also create space for mission to take place in organic ways. In this way mission becomes something that 'fits' seamlessly into the ordinary rhythms of life, friendships, and community and is thus thoroughly contextualized."[30] God has moved into the neighborhood to live among his people. The catechumenate creates the opportunity for Redeemer to see itself as a sent people. This ritual shapes the catechumens to live as sent people. As we heard from Maura in chapter 6: "I truly feel a member of the church. There is a commitment I have undertaken. I have an understanding of the mission of the church, of the mission of God. I integrate it all into my life. I pray all the time. I am a Christian *all the time*."[31] The Palm Sunday procession forms behavior by which the people of Redeemer live as missionaries in the world.

Believing, belonging, behaving—each of these facets of "making disciples"—can be accomplished in part through ritual, "defined actions that

---

29. Phone conversation with Rhoda Schuler and the current pastor of St. Mary's, September 28, 2021.

30. Hirsch, *Forgotten Ways*, 135.

31. Maura (pseudonym), interview by Kent J. Burreson, October 2, 2018. Subsequent quotations and summaries of Maura are from this interview, unless otherwise noted.

are repeated, symbolic, and communal." As the examples from daily life illustrate, whether the "spiritual" entrepreneurs described in the *New York Times* article or the funeral rituals for miliary veterans, in one form or another, people encounter ritual and, though they may not realize it or can articulate it with the clarity of Oscar, or Lily, or Bob, or Laura and Harry, or Maura, the lives of many are profoundly shaped by ritual experiences. Robust and frequent rituals marking the stages of the catechumenal process, though not essential, serve to enhance faith formation in multiple ways. They have the capacity to deepen beliefs and practices, to strengthen communal bonds, and to inspire disciples to lives of service and witness. We move from these thick descriptions of rituals specific to the catechumenal process to a consideration of Sunday worship as the overarching, "ur-ritual" for the lifelong process of becoming a disciple of Jesus.

FROM MICRO TO MACRO: SUNDAY LITURGY AS THE HEART OF CHRISTIAN FORMATION

James K. A. Smith argues for a deep and broad power of ritual: "I emphasize that there is a unique 'understanding' that is 'carried' in Christian practices, particularly the practices of Christian worship. It is in such practices that our love is trained, disciplined, shaped, and formed."[32] Smith, a Christian philosopher, operates from the first of the three signs of "hope" we named to open this chapter: recent trends in philosophy and neuroscience challenging the assumption that humans are primarily thinking, rational, independent beings.[33] With one pithy sentence, Smith summarizes the three themes of his book: "In short, the way to the *heart* is through the *body*, and the way into the *body* is through *story*."[34] According to Smith's "liturgical anthropology,"[35] humans are defined and define themselves primarily by what they love (the heart), not by what they "think" rationally; how humans come to know and make sense of the world is a preconscious, embodied

---

32. Smith, *Imagining the Kingdom*, 13.

33. Smith sees this move in philosophy as a necessary corrective, especially within the context of the Christian university; Smith, *Imagining the Kingdom*, 5–6; 10–11, 31–38. In the area of cognitive neuroscience, he draws on the work of Mark Johnson; see 110–24. He also uses cognitive science of literature to support the "poetics" of his thesis; see 130–37.

34. Smith, *Imagining the Kingdom*, 14, emphasis added.

35. Smith, *Imagining the Kingdom*, xvii (first use); it is a recurring phrase throughout the book.

process (the body), not an intellectual exercise; and it is narrative (story), "as a kind of pretheoretical compass," not logic and propositional truths, "that guides and generates human action."[36] His anthropology "is rooted in both a kinaesthetics and a poetics" because humans are embodied beings (kinaesthetics), which "primes us to be oriented by story, the imagination (poetics)."[37]

The second of his themes, the preconscious, embodied process, needs to be unpacked in greater detail, for this theme includes philosophical jargon that one must understand to grasp the radical nature of Smith's assertion that "our love is trained, disciplined, shaped, and formed" through "liturgy." First, Smith uses the word "liturgy" very broadly; a liturgy may be "secular" or "Christian," but both have the power to shape what humans love and "thus ultimately govern our actions."[38] Second, Smith rejects the binary distinction that human action is "*either* conscious, deliberate, chosen action *or* mere bodily reflex and instinct," making a case instead for "a kind of third space: a bodily know-how that guides and drives much that deserves to be called 'action.'"[39] He is making an epistemological case—how humans come to know—but argues that "perception" is an essential aspect of coming "to know." He writes, "Perception is not clumsy unreflective judgment. It is something different altogether and is the background that makes judgment, analysis, and 'knowledge' possible."[40] Perception is, as he says, "the background," operating on a preconscious level that honors the mind-body nature of the human person: "we *are* being-in-the-world—embedded, embodied actors at home in an environment that we navigate with a kind of intentionality that precedes knowledge and whose locus is in the body."[41]

Third, Smith also rejects an anthropology of autonomous individuals freely making rational decisions independent of their context; humans, existing in this "third space" in between intellect and instinct, are at the same time "embedded . . . in an environment" that is communal and social,

36. Smith, *Imagining the Kingdom*, 14.

37. Smith, *Imagining the Kingdom*, 101.

38. Smith, *Imagining the Kingdom*, 15. In chapter 3 of *Desiring the Kingdom* Smith discusses at length the threat of secular liturgies constituted by "a web of practices and institutions associated with consumerism," 93n6.

39. Smith, *Imagining the Kingdom*, 32n3, emphasis in original.

40. Smith, *Imagining the Kingdom*, 42; "perception" comes from the French philosopher Merleau-Ponty.

41. Smith, *Imagining the Kingdom*, 44, emphasis in original.

affecting how individuals make meaning of and act in the world. When one understands Smith's "liturgical anthropology," then, he says, one can "understand how *habits* are acquired," habits that govern human action.⁴² Smith uses Aristotle's definition of habit: "those dispositions that incline us to a certain end," but expands the meaning of *habitus* as "shorthand to refer to those 'dispositions' we have to constitute the world in certain ways—the habitual way that we construct our world," and this *habitus* "is always sort of bigger than me—it is a communal, collective disposition that gets inscribed in me."⁴³

Finally, regarding the "poetics," Smith claims that the human's identity and action in the world are formed through narrative working on our imagination: "We come to 'see' ourselves in a certain way . . . because we have absorbed a narrative that now functions as the background drama of our existence."⁴⁴ Thus, the human's desire is formed through the imagination: "It is because I *imagine* the world (and my place in it) in certain ways that I am oriented by fundamental loves and longings."⁴⁵ Smith's themes of the heart, the body, and story, of the shaping of one's desires through the imagination and a narrative that work within an embodied person, resonant with our understanding of how the Sunday liturgy, over time, constitutes and shapes people into disciples of Christ.

To approach the task of adult faith formation in this post-Christendom context, we also need to pay attention to Smith's assertion that secular "liturgies" are grounded in "rival" narratives with the same "metaphoric power [that will] seep into our bones" by operating "under the radar of awareness," and forming within us disordered desires.⁴⁶ Gail, a newly baptized member of St. John, showed some remarkable insights that reflect Smith's "liturgical anthropology" and confirm his claim about rival narratives. Gail's husband George, raised by devout Roman Catholic parents, studied music at a Lutheran university, where he was introduced to Lutheran theology. As a young adult living in a community near Wheaton, Illinois, he was searching for a church home and found St. John's; seven years and two moves later, he was still there when he and Gail were interviewed. He loves

---

42. Smith, *Imagining the Kingdom*, 57, emphasis added.

43. Smith, *Imagining the Kingdom*, 81. Smith's discussion of *habitus* here draws on the work of French sociologist Pierre Bourdieu.

44. Smith, *Imagining the Kingdom*, 127.

45. Smith, *Imagining the Kingdom*, 124–25, emphasis added.

46. Smith, *Imagining the Kingdom*, 141.

the law/gospel dialectic he hears in the preaching at St. John, and the "high church" liturgy of St. John is similar to that which he experienced growing up in the Catholic Church.[47]

Gail's story is in stark contrast to George's. As she said, "I was not raised Christian ... but felt something was missing. I've always been a spiritual person." At the time of the interview, she had been attending worship with George for three years, going back to when they had started dating, because, she said, "I knew his faith was important to him." As Gail herself might have said, during those three years they had experienced several "rites of passage."[48] They were married by Pastor Buchs; they had had a baby (a toddler at the time of our interview); four months before our interview they started attending St. John's catechumenate; and Gail and her daughter had been baptized at St. John.[49] Were James Smith to reflect on her story, he would observe her navigating her way through two rival "narratives." Having been habituated into one way of construing her world, for the past three years she was being reformed by a different *habitus*, one that was training and shaping her through the Sunday liturgy, as "an alternative imaginary, a way that the Spirit of God invites us into the Story of God in Christ reconciling the world to himself."[50]

Her path had not been smooth and easy. Smith, as he comments about acquiring "a *new habitus*," warns that the process will "bump up against my prior ... formation."[51] Before deciding to enter into the catechumenate, Gail talked with Pastor Buchs. She spoke of "all the questions floating in my head that I haven't had time to think about," indicating the seriousness of this decision for her. Later she referenced additional conversations with the pastor, saying, "It's safe talking about my doubts and challenges; I never felt like I would be rejected." She also said, "I had to eliminate doubt before my baptism." Unlike Fritz (from the Introduction), who was baptized at

---

47. Gail and George (pseudonyms), interview by Rhoda Schuler, January 20, 2019. Subsequent quotations and summaries of Gail and George are from this interview, unless otherwise noted.

48. Gail used the term "rite of passage" when asked what was most meaningful about the catechumenal classes. Rhoda was surprised by this language and asked her about it later; she majored in sociology and minored in anthropology at university, which gave her the language of ritual and the lens through which she interpreted her experiences.

49. Gail and George are a blended family; the oldest child is George's; the daughter who was baptized is Gail's; and the toddler (presumably baptized as an infant) is theirs.

50. Smith, *Imagining the Kingdom*, 150.

51. Smith, *Imagining the Kingdom*, 93, emphasis in original.

the Easter Vigil at the end of the catechumenal process, Gail had made a sudden decision to be baptized with her daughter, saying that "on lunch break I called Pastor Buchs" and said to him, "One of my kids is getting baptized—then I ought to be doing this for myself" as well. Yes, she admitted, her daughter's imminent baptism was "a catalyst," but being baptized herself was "something I had been thinking about for a long time." Because she had consented to the baptism of her own child and understood that meant raising the child as a Christian, she realized that she, too, had to be claimed by Christ in this initiation ritual.

With her background in sociology and anthropology, she framed her formation process through various rituals. Although her first response to the question "What led you to enter the catechumenate," was "all the questions floating in my head," she followed up by saying, "My daughter was baptized here. Pastor Buchs married us," implying that these rituals had already bound her to St. John. When asked what was most meaningful about the catechetical classes, George responded by speaking of the content of the classes that he enjoyed most. Gail, however, replied that "meaningful" for her was on "a higher level." The whole catechumenal process for her is "a rite of passage—like marriage." At her baptism, she continued, "I'm formally establishing a relationship with God," and through participation in the catechumenal classes she was "formally establishing a relationship with St. John and these pastors. I take these rites of passage very seriously."

Gail, by virtue of her college study, had the vocabulary to understand and articulate St. John's adult catechumenal process as a "rite of passage," a particular kind of ritual that brings about a change of status and creates a new identity. And with her "higher level" understanding, Gail was acutely aware of her internal struggle. Smith, engaging with experts in neuroscience, writes about the human acquisition of neural maps and "*primary repertoires*" that are "formed by 'normal' environmental conditions." By receiving the most stimuli, one repertoire becomes dominant, while others go dormant.[52] Gail, speaking again of her struggles, describes herself in a similar manner, saying "My default setting was 'not Christian'—the bar was so high for me." Then referencing their young son, baptized as an infant, she said, "for him the default setting 'is Christian,'" and she anticipates he would struggle less "when he hits those doubts." As Smith might point out, her son's neural mapping was being constituted in a Christian environment. In this moment Gail, articulating her primary repertoire (her "default setting"

---

52. Smith, *Imagining the Kingdom*, 115, emphasis in original.

as "not Christian"), supports what Smith extrapolates from neuroscience: "secondary repertoires that become dormant can also be reactivated, and ... if the balance of competing rituals shifts—there also seems to be the possibility that the ordering of primary and secondary repertoires could be reversed... What Johnson gives us is an embodied way to think about the dynamics of conversion, initiation, and sanctification."[53]

What is striking about Gail's story is the role of the Sunday liturgy "inscribing" a new *habitus* within her, operating, in the language of Smith, "under the hood."[54] At the time of the interview, she had been attending worship with George for *three years*, while their total time attending the catechetical classes was only four months. Here Smith's work on the importance of story and imagination comes into play: "Liturgies are formative because ... they tap into our imaginative core. As compressed narratives and tactile poems, the formative power of liturgies ... is bound up with their aesthetic force. Such liturgies are pedagogies of desire that shape our love because they *picture* the good life for us in ways that resonate with our imaginative nature."[55] Liturgy, an embodied practice, and the Christian narrative were at work reforming Gail's imagination and desires.

The worship life at all four of our research congregations align with Smith's description of formative liturgies. Sunday liturgy at all four congregations follows a similar, consistent structure or pattern with a narrative arc (gathering, word, meal, sending),[56] centered in the proclamation of Holy Scripture and in the sharing of Holy Communion: in Lutheran shorthand, word and sacrament. The narrative arc begins with a confession of sin—of our disordered loves, as Smith would say—and forgiveness through Christ as part of the assembly's *gathering* as the preparation to hear the *word*, with the reading from one of the four Gospels as the apex. The *meal* or Holy Communion follows, when sung and spoken liturgy culminate with the embodied ritual of sharing in the holy food. The liturgy concludes with a *sending* through prayer, hymn, and blessing, to encourage the assembly's witness to the world. When carefully planned, the Sunday liturgy will

---

53. Smith, *Imagining the Kingdom*, 115–16. Smith references here the philosopher Mark Johnson, who delves into aesthetics and cognitive sciences; see Johnson, *Meaning of the Body*.

54. Smith, *Imagining the Kingdom*, 83.

55. Smith, *Imagining the Kingdom*, 137, emphasis in original.

56. For details of this "shape of the rite," see *With One Voice*, 8–9.

express the "Story of God in Christ reconciling the world to himself,"[57] drawing participants away from their disordered loves and toward the God who is Love, revealed in the Word made flesh.

The Sunday liturgy is not ultimately about our story and what we do in worship. Rather, through human liturgical action it is the work of God offering grace upon grace through the forgiveness of sins, through the good news of Christ proclaimed and unpacked in preaching, and through sharing the body and blood of the very One who laid down his life for the world.[58] Smith critiques social media, declaring that "it inculcates in us dispositions and inclinations that lean toward a configuration of the social world that revolves around *me*."[59] In contrast, he says, "Christian worship is an intentionally decentering practice, calling us out of ourselves into the very life of God."[60] Gail embodies the "decentering," disruptive quality of Christian worship, expressed profoundly in these words: "my default setting was 'not Christian'; the bar was so high for me." While she certainly had other interactions with St. John, its pastors, and people, the ritual moments were most significant and meaningful for her and enabled her to clear "the bar," to move from being "spiritual" to "formally establishing a relationship with God," a God she had come to know by encountering him regularly through the proclaimed and preached word in worship.

The recentering work of the Sunday liturgy happens not only through the narrative arc of the structure. In our research congregations (and many in Lutheran and "mainline denominations" as well as Roman Catholic parishes worldwide), the Scriptures read weekly unfolds the story of God's reconciling work throughout history. These parishes follow a common lectionary—readings appointed for every Sunday throughout the calendar year.[61] Gail had heard the story of salvation through Christ—his birth, min-

---

57. Smith, *Imagining the Kingdom*, 150.

58. The priority of God's action in worship is evident in the introductions of *Evangelical Lutheran Worship*, the hymnal of the ELCA, and of *Lutheran Service Book*, the hymnal of the LCMS. *ELW*: "God gives the Word and the sacraments to the church and by the power of the Spirit thereby creates and sustains the church . . . ," 6. *LSB*: "Our Lord serves us today through His holy Word and sacraments," viii.

59. Smith, *Imagining the Kingdom*, 148, emphasis in original.

60. Smith, *Imagining the Kingdom*, 149.

61. The development of a lectionary is an ancient practice, dating back to at least the fifth century. The three-year lectionary, pioneered by the Roman Catholic Church, was introduced in 1969; it was quickly adopted (with some adaptations) by most mainline denominations in the US. The most recent revision, the Revised Common Lectionary, was an ecumenical endeavor. Distinctive to all versions of the three-year lectionary is

istry, passion, death, resurrection, and sending of the Spirit—three times. The repetition of salvation history in Scripture alongside of liturgical texts packed with metaphors and poetic language works in the imagination, so that the narrative, in the words of Smith, "seeps into our bones."[62]

Smith's interest in Christian liturgy is not merely a matter of aesthetics for its own sake nor an academic exercise to "Christianize" twentieth-century philosophy and social theory. He writes of the shared end (*telos*) of the church and Christian universities as "formation *for* mission." Of worship and its *telos*, he says, "Drawn into union with Christ, the 'end' of Christian worship is bound up with our sending for Christian *action*, . . . the creational task of making and remaking God's world."[63] In a final chapter he returns to this missional *telos* of formation through liturgy, reiterating his claim that Christian formation works on the heart through stories "that recruit the imagination through the body,"[64] as "a matter of . . . rehabituation of our desires and loves."[65]

Our research demonstrates that while rich and abundant rituals such as we witnessed at Redeemer and St. Mary's do enhance and strengthen a robust adult catechumenate, a successful catechumenal process is not dependent on these rituals. A decision to incorporate such rituals in one's parish requires a close examination of the congregation's and community's context and a careful, pastoral process to introduce new practices into parish life. As a case in point, the ritual signing of body parts by Pastor Taylor in the Bronx would most likely not be well received by the people of Living Faith in Georgia. But gathering for Sunday worship defines what it means to be Christian, to which the uproar and angst of March 2020 attests, when churches closed their doors due to the pandemic. Thus we, embracing the wisdom of James K. A. Smith, invite pastors and all involved in worship planning to consider how to captivate the hearts, bodies, and imaginations of those in the pews with grace-filled, poetic speech and with graceful

---

the focus on a particular Gospel for each year; in Year A most Gospel readings are from Matthew; Gospel readings for Year B are predominantly from Mark; and Year C has readings from Luke; readings from the Gospel of John predominate during the Easter Season in all three years.

62. Smith, *Imagining the Kingdom*, 14.
63. Smith, *Imagining the Kingdom*, 4–6, emphasis in original.
64. Smith, *Imagining the Kingdom*, 20.
65. Smith, *Imagining the Kingdom*, 166.

RITUAL

gesture and movement "centered in Christ" that will "intentionally carry, embody, enact, and rehearse the normative shape of the Christian Story."[66]

---

66. Smith, *Imagining the Kingdom*, 163.

Part II: Common Themes across Uncommon Contexts

For Reflection and Discussion

1. Working with Ramshaw's definition of ritual as "defined actions that are repeated, communal, and symbolic,"[67] reflect on and/or discuss with others one or two rituals from your family life, your broader cultural experiences, or civic sphere. How has this ritual shaped your beliefs, identity, and/or actions?

2. Which rituals in your congregational context shape

    a. What parishioners believe?

    b. Parishioners into a community?

    c. Transformative behavior?

3. Are there rituals in your adult formation or youth confirmation that shape

    a. What the participants believe?

    b. Participants into a community?

    c. Transformative behavior?

4. How does the Sunday liturgy in your congregation "intentionally carry, embody, enact, and rehearse the normative shape of the Christian Story"?

5. Are there aspects of the Sunday liturgy in your congregation that obscure the narrative arc of the Christian Story? If so, what are these?

---

67. Ramshaw, *Christian Worship*, 33.

9

EPILOGUE

Catechumenal Signs of Resilience

Most generations have major markers, worldwide watershed events, that shape their generation's thinking and the trajectory of their lives. And many of us can recount personal narratives of where we were on a particular day, be it the assassination of John F. Kennedy or Martin Luther King Jr. in the 1960s, or September 11, 2000, when two hijacked planes slammed into the Twin Towers of the World Trade Center. For Kent and me, the long gestation process for this book began in March 2020, as the COVID pandemic spread its way around the globe. In fall 2019 we had summarized our proposed project to the Calvin Institute of Christian Worship with these words:

> Kent Burreson and I will analyze the field research data on the adult catechumenate from our [Vital Worship Grant for Worshiping Communities] to develop workshops on catechumenate practices for the purpose of sharing our findings primarily with Lutheran pastors and laity.... We also see the analysis of our field research as the next step toward publication of our findings.[1]

---

1. Vital Worship Teacher-Scholar Grant, 2020–2021, Project Summary. This was our second grant proposal submitted to CICW. On November 26, 2019, Rhoda received an email informing us our grant proposal had been approved.

Part II: Common Themes across Uncommon Contexts

We expected to be developing a workshop and taking it on the road, presenting the lessons from our research congregations in person to pastors and laity around the country. And here begins my personal narrative surrounding the pandemic and the grant. On March 12, one day after the World Health Organization declared a worldwide pandemic, I boarded a plane from Minneapolis to Chicago to attend the Fine Arts Festival at my goddaughter's junior high; Tessa, an eighth grader, was singing in the girls' choir. Before my ride at Midway Airport in Chicago had picked me up, Tessa's concert—indeed, the entire Fine Arts Festival—had been canceled. Institutions of higher education were making difficult decisions with a paucity of information. Later that evening I learned that Concordia University, St. Paul, where I was teaching, had canceled classes on Friday, ordered students home, and announced that online instruction would begin on Monday. The next day, March 13, President Trump declared a national emergency. Fortunately, planes were still flying on March 15, and I made my flight home to the Twin Cities in time to muddle through the challenges of online teaching—and to discover the first installment of the grant money in my campus mailbox.[2]

The hands-on, in-person workshops we had envisioned morphed into (of course) a series of online conferences conducted over Zoom that included the pastors from three of our four research congregations.[3] My Google Calendar shows a Zoom meeting with our pastor collaborators on May 19, 2020, titled "Calvin Grant: Re-imagining the project." Kent took notes as I moderated the "reimagining" discussion with the pastors, during which Pastors Bruzek, Droegemueller, and Taylor reflected on the current mood of their flocks. Pastor Bruzek spoke of an "unnatural calm" at St. John and theorized that the catechumenate had "shaped the congregation in this way." Pastor Droegemueller agreed with the language of "calm," saying, "People were trained for this. The word of God has formed them to be a learner, bearer, doer of the word. They were prepared for this and are well-grounded to respond appropriately. If they believe in the process of training for lifelong catechesis, then they are prepared for this." Pastor Taylor framed the power of the catechumenate for this kairos time by contrasting the certainty Christians have through Christ with the uncertainties of life:

---

2. Email from Rhoda Schuler to Lesley Erickson, director of donor relations, Concordia University, St. Paul, March 20, 2020.

3. Pastor M had left St. Mary's in 2020. One of the pastors from our "mentored" congregations, Dan Eggold, joined the pastoral collaborators for the online conferences.

Epilogue

> It [the catechumenate] is a model of mystery, of certainty and uncertainty—certainty of Christ and his blessings, and of how the Spirit moves, but not how you want to design it. It doesn't follow the "plan" [as] the Spirit moves. This is part of the pattern of the catechumenate, [which] prepares the space and opportunity for this uncertainty, . . . to live in the plan of the Lord. It is both challenging and liberating [and] allows us to adjust to one of the great things about Christianity, an adjustment [and a realization that] it's about God! The catechumenate has allowed us to embrace and weather change.

Four years later, those words of wisdom from the pastors of our research congregations still held true. While each congregation had made some adjustments to their adult faith formation process in the early days of the pandemic, the power of months-long, in-person gatherings, of time for questions and community building, of shaping a *habitus* through weekly liturgies of word and sacrament has endured, and each congregation has shown the resilience necessary "to embrace and weather change." With their permission, we share some of the pastors' reflections on then and now. Of "then" Pastor Bruzek wrote,

> Those were indeed strange days. With everybody else around here, we were shut down after our Liturgies on March 15, 2020. . . . From March 22 until June 1, 2020, our Liturgies were offered online—but only the audio. We purposely did not offer video because we did not want folks developing the habit of staying home for church once the pandemic was over. Our pastors remained available for pastoral care, hospital calls, and baptisms as needed. By the time we were closed down in mid-March 2020, our catechetical instruction for 2020 had ended, except for receiving our catechumens into membership. The catechumens of 2020 were received as members at the Easter Vigil in 2021. From Lent 2020 until the Vigil of 2021, those catechumens received care from the pastors as if they were indeed members.
>
> We reopened on June 8, 2020, with the recommended rubrics . . . [which] stayed in place until they were removed by the State in 2021.[4] We returned to regular Liturgies without restrictions on June 6, 2021. . . . Our plate giving actually increased throughout COVID, which was pretty remarkable. More amazing was that giving to our Manna Fund—alms given above and beyond plate

---

4. Those rubrics included "masks, distancing, hand sanitizer, a maximum of 100 persons in a Liturgy, no large gatherings before or after the Liturgy."

giving, and then distributed solely by the pastors to anyone in need, whether inside [or] outside our congregation—increased substantially during the COVID years. That was a comforting mark of love in and from our community.[5]

Pastor Droegemueller from Living Faith wrote about "then," saying:

> On Lent 5 when the world shut down, we continued to teach them in person with masks on. We had less than 10, so we were not breaking the law! The world stopped, but the catechumenate rolled on! We went to online gatherings for a few weeks, and then we put together an online Divine Service without Holy Communion for everybody to watch online, but then gave Absolution and Holy Communion to all of our members 10 people at a time. That lasted for two months, and we called it the greatest gifts format. After that time, we then asked everyone to wear masks in love for your family in Christ so that we could be together.
>
> The total shutdown of church and ministry affected us all greatly. Of course, we all need God's word and the sacraments. We would die without them! But these gifts are given to a community of the faithful to enjoy together. We have life together at the altar, love for each other, we suffer together . . .[6]

Pastor Taylor provided similar details about Redeemer's move to online worship via Zoom and to outdoor worship when permitted, but the experience of Redeemer in the Bronx, in the early epicenter of the pandemic as it swept across the US, was markedly different:

> The City of New York and the borough of the Bronx were hit particularly hard with COVID-19; the first east coast outbreak was in our geography in the north Bronx. Many died, especially in the Wakefield section of the Bronx . . . Hospital emergency rooms overflowed onto sidewalks. Streets once known for the sounds of global music, conversation, and commerce had only the eerie sounds of rushing ambulances and hearses as refrigerated trucks containing the bodies of those deceased dotted the streets once full of people in our neighborhood. Grateful that the State recognized the importance of spiritual leaders, theology-of-the-cross-work-in-the-trenches with those who were ill, those who were

---

5. Email from Scott Bruzek to Rhoda Schuler and Kent J. Burreson, May 15, 2024. Additional quotations of Pastor Bruzek are from this source, unless otherwise indicated.

6. Email from Timothy Droegemueller to Rhoda Schuler and Kent J. Burreson, May 9, 2024. Additional quotations of Pastor Droegemueller are from this source, unless otherwise indicated.

Epilogue

attending to those who were ill, and those who bring the gifts of God to people provided little opportunity for the kind of armchair philosophical debate afforded to others in different geographical settings. The pandemic was a time for action and Redeemer was up to it.[7]

Redeemer chose online, live services via Zoom, "because it allowed for visual and audio contact with people as opposed to other formats that could make people spectators or observers." Along with the online worship, the congregation added "creative visitations with people to ensure that the ties that bind our hearts in Christian love were not forgotten or neglected." When the law allowed, "Redeemer was one of the very first congregations in the neighborhood to facilitate in-person gatherings outside that followed all the protocols given. People who ventured from their homes appreciated this and would join the worship services that were offered."

Regarding the catechumenate, Pastor Taylor wrote:

> On the Feast of Christ the King in 2020, Redeemer was delighted to have the confirmations that had been scheduled for the Vigil of Easter. Rituals were not adversely affected. Sponsors stood behind the candidates during the rites. Caution was observed with the wiping of the kneeler after each confirmation and the cleansing of pastor's hands. Touch, even though regarded by some in the society as taboo during the pandemic, still was sought by many, especially in the catechumenate's rites, so proper precautions and protocols were followed so that this could be done appropriately.

The importance of touch, "sought by many," speaks again of the different context of Redeemer, located in a neighborhood where refrigerator trucks filled with the deceased—many of whom died alone, without the touch of family—were parked on the streets. The "delight" of Redeemer as the congregation marked the confirmations that Sunday was in contrast to the many funerals during those days.[8]

Pastors Bruzek and Droegemueller report that current giving levels are strong, and attendance is at or "exceeds pre-pandemic levels. The Catechumenate is back to normal and going strong," says Pastor Bruzek. Living

---

7. Email attachment from Dien Ashley Taylor to Rhoda Schuler and Kent J. Burreson, May 27, 2024. Additional quotations of Pastor Taylor are from this source, unless otherwise indicated.

8. Pastor Taylor reported that "Redeemer lost twenty-four members to death as a result of COVID-19. This does not include others who may have been regular attendees or friends and loved ones of parishioners."

Part II: Common Themes across Uncommon Contexts

Faith, according to Pastor Droegemueller, has "planted two churches since then." Pastor Taylor's reflections are more nuanced and sober, writing that "since we were 'first affected' by the pandemic [it should be expected] that we would be among the 'last to return' as it subsided. Financial giving remained strong during the pandemic. In-person attendance, however, has not yet returned to pre-pandemic levels."

In response to our query about any "signs of resilience" because of the catechumenate, Pastors Bruzek and Droegemueller wrote similar yet distinctive replies:[9]

> Our greatest sign of resilience is the joy of our community. Folks who treasured each other before the pandemic cherish each other doubly now. The things that held us together—Christ, Scripture, Prayer, Liturgy and Eucharist, Tithing and Alms, a Thorough Mercy, and a Winsome Witness (Acts 2)—were the things instilled by our Catechumenate. Sharing the same Holy Gifts—and so, embracing the same holy orbit around our Lord Jesus Christ—bestowed a common identity that endured throughout the pandemic challenges and continues today. That joy remains attractive to members and visitors alike.

> Signs of resilience? The beloved saints of God cannot be stopped. Jesus knows his way out of a grave, and so does his bride. All the texts of the Bible are now at hand to us and are whacking us with complete applicability, whereby previously we glossed over them, especially when they talk about suffering for the faith. The frying pan of persecution moved from simmer to low heat, and so we are finally waking up, and realizing our need for discipleship, prayer, God's service (the incarnate Feast!), accountability, fellowship, stewardship, and witness. It's time to be our baptized selves! All day, every day, till the final day! We are daily seeing people respond to the call to action! Men and women [are] beginning joyful and meaningful service in one way or another.

Pastor Taylor's words focus on hope rather than joy, as he described upgrades to Redeemer's classrooms, meeting spaces, and offices "to foster better work for a new future. This is a sign of resilience and an insistence on a hope-filled future." Of the catechumenate, he says that "Redeemer continues to have inquirers who are youth and adults who want to join the catechumenate and the congregation continues to see how that model

---

9. The first quote is from Pastor Bruzek; the second from Pastor Droegemueller, which should come as no surprise to anyone who's read the rest of the book.

Epilogue

helps contribute to the stable rhythm that characterizes our liturgical life together." His is a more cruciform description of resilience, writing, "The numerical loss of people in addition to the post-traumatic stress experienced by people who lived through the pandemic with comorbidities, deaths of loved ones, and the experience of death around them contribute to the parish's understanding not only of the reality of the Law and death but of the sweetness of the Gospel and new life that does not always seem evident on our timetables."

At a time when many pastors are struggling to find contentment and joy in ministry, when the grim statistics about the decline of adherents to the Christian faith looms over the faithful, these pastors' dedication to Christ and to the care of the flocks entrusted to them and zeal to welcome others in Christ's sheepfold is remarkable. Are their words "proof" of the adult catechumenate as "the answer" to the malaise of the church? While we make no such claim, we commend to our readers their deep wisdom, infectious joy, and confidence in the power of the gospel that permeates their reflections. We, too, believe that Jesus knows his way out of a grave, and so does his bride, the church.

Feast of the Holy Trinity, 2024

Appendix 1

RESEARCH DESIGN AND METHODS

The genesis of this book traces back to 2016 when Kent invited Rhoda to partner with him on a research project studying effective adult catechumenate models in Lutheran congregations, made possible in 2018–19 when we were awarded a Vital Worshipping Communities Grant from the Calvin Institute of Christian Worship (CICW).[1] For academic geeks and others curious about the process by which we chose these particular four congregations from the 14,900 Lutheran congregations of the ELCA and LCMS as the research subjects for this book,[2] we offer this narrative of our research design and methods. We are trained as theologians, not as social scientists, but like many of our colleagues in the field of liturgical studies, our research interests, and this project in particular, require some basic knowledge about research practices in the social sciences.[3] That, from our viewpoint, the social sciences are "handmaids" to theology[4] is clear from the placement of this material in an appendix, not in an opening chapter, as it would be for an author whose primary field is, for example, education or

---

1. Our research was made possible through two grants from the Calvin Institute of Christian Worship, Grand Rapids, Michigan, with funds provided by Lilly Endowment Inc. First, a Vital Worship Grant for congregations was awarded in 2018–19, and second, a Vital Worship Teacher-Scholar Grant was awarded in 2020–21.

2. According to their website, ELCA congregations number approximately 8,900. According to their website, there are "more than 6,000" LCMS congregations.

3. Examples of similar research by liturgical scholars include the following: Ross, *Evangelical Worship*; Ross, *Evangelical versus Liturgical?*; Scharen, *Public Worship and Public Work*; Anderson, *Worship and Christian Identity*.

4. Thomas Aquinas, *Summa Theologia* I.1.5.

sociology. Yet we respect our colleagues in the social sciences, have relied on their knowledge and wisdom as we developed and refined our research design, and have appreciated this kind of detail in the writings of our colleagues in liturgical studies.

We earnestly wrote in our CICW grant proposal that our goal was "to reshape and renew congregational life for American Lutherans." We self-identified "[a]s 'cradle Lutherans' of the boomer and buster generations, [who] are deeply committed to the church's life. Our academic study and personal experiences suggest that the catechumenate, a holistic conversion process of formation for adults into Christian discipleship, has the potential to engage the millennial generation to explore the Christian faith and to be drawn into the Christian community."[5] Fortunately for us, the ideal of the researcher as one who is unbiased and neutral toward the research question is a relic of the past. As one author notes, "Formerly, an 'expert knowledge' model of the social scientist was seen as justifying . . . [research] that was conducted autonomously by a researcher, an outsider to the community being studied, who operated in ways akin to those of a field biologist. Today, the adequacy and legitimacy of that research stance have been seriously challenged, with . . . researchers being members themselves of the communities whose everyday lives and meaning perspective are being studied . . ."[6] With gratitude to the social sciences for recognizing that researchers bring their own values and meaning to their endeavors, we draw on the work of Sue McGregor for the topics covered here.[7]

Our work falls into the broad category of qualitative (vs. quantitative) research, defined as "studies [that] are concerned with understanding and interpreting participants' lived experiences with a particular phenomenon and the meanings people attach to these experiences."[8] The primary research method we used is the case study; that is, a detailed exploration "of a social process, organisation or collectivity . . . seen as a social unit in its own right and as a holistic entity."[9] Our "social unit" is the Lutheran congregation, with chapters 2 through 5 "interpreting participants' lived

---

5. Vital Worship Grant Proposal Form, response to question 2, January 2018.

6. Erickson, "History of Qualitative Inquiry," 53.

7. McGregor, *Understanding and Evaluating Research*, 228–52; Figure 9.1, "Major Components of the Qualitative Methods Section of a Research Paper" on page 228 was a particularly helpful summary for organizing this material.

8. McGregor, *Understanding and Evaluating Research*, 227.

9. Payne and Payne, *Key Concepts in Social Research*, 31.

Research Design and Methods

experiences" of the adult faith formation process in the four congregations selected for the project. Unlike quantitative research, often associated with "random samples," our research called for "purposeful case selection strategies" that are "concerned with . . . capturing insider meanings and complex contextuality."[10] We chose to do case studies "because [this strategy] can best provide information required to answer the research question."[11] Selection of four congregations was a practical choice based on the time limitations and financial constraints of the grant. While the number of cases may seem small, calling into question the validity of our conclusions, the value of qualitative research derives "from thick and dense descriptions of lived experiences, social processes, cultures, and narrative accounts."[12] We are confident that our work provides the necessary "thick and dense descriptions" of congregational life and of the experiences of those involved in their adult faith formation.

As a first step to identify congregations, Kent worked with the Council of Presidents comprised of the thirty-nine district presidents of the LCMS, soliciting from them names of congregations they were aware of that had a strong adult catechumenal process. Nine district presidents, representing a diversity of geographic regions of the US, responded with the names of twenty-three congregations. We contacted the ELCA church-wide director of worship and received from him a list of seven congregations, and through other informal connections, increased the list to ten ELCA congregations. The pastors of these thirty-three congregations were contacted via an email explaining the purpose and scope of our grant and, if the pastor and congregation were interested in participating in the grant, inviting them to complete a survey about current adult faith formation practices in their congregation. The pastors of four ELCA congregations and ten LCMS congregations expressed interest in the project, and twelve completed the survey, giving us a pool of three ELCA and nine LCMS congregations from which to choose four model and four mentored congregations.[13] The survey had asked the pastor to self-select either the model or mentored category

---

10. Schwandt and Gates, "Case Study Methodology," 348–49.
11. McGregor, *Understanding and Evaluating Research*, 238.
12. McGregor, *Understanding and Evaluating Research*, 240.
13. As described in our Vital Worship Grant [for congregations] Proposal Form (Foundation and purpose, question 2), the "model congregations"—those with "robust [adult] catechumenates"—were chosen to be part of the research design; in contrast, we offered "guidance and resources to four congregations with an interest in developing an adult catechumenate" and called these the "mentored congregations."

for their congregation; five expressed interest in participating as a model congregation; five chose the mentored category; one did not answer, and another indicated openness to either model or mentored.

For both the model and mentored congregations, we sought diversity by geography, size of congregation and its staff, and by denomination,[14] and we also considered the racial and ethnic composition of the congregation and community. For the model congregations, we favored congregations with longer track records of an adult catechumenate and those at which one of us had personal knowledge of the pastor; and we deliberately chose two of the four congregations because of the strong ritual component to their catechumenate process.[15] When selecting mentored congregations, we gave weight to those pastors who had indicated prior interest in and knowledge of adult catechumenate practices and who expressed a desire and motivation to move forward toward implementation. We have no representation in either the model or mentored category from west of the Rocky Mountains only because we had no congregations in that geographic area that were willing to be part of our grant process. All eight of our initial choices agreed to be participants in the project.

Our next step was to determine which of the principal investigators would be assigned to which congregations; this was particularly important regarding the model congregations, as we would be traveling to them, working closely with the pastor, who would not only be an interview subject but would be the "gatekeeper" (selecting the laity we would contact to interview), and who would inform the entire congregation of our presence at the church and provide follow-up information as needed. Even with our limited experience at the collaborative process of case study research, we intuitively knew it was vital that we develop a relationship of trust with these pastors and assigned a model congregation to each researcher because of our personal knowledge of and prior relationship with the pastor. For the remaining two model congregations, we agreed that pairing by gender (female researcher with female pastor at an ELCA congregation; male researcher with male pastor) would facilitate the process of building trust. Greater flexibility and overall balance informed the assignments of

14. We chose one ELCA and three LCMS congregations in each category, model and mentored.

15. The grant budget included visits to two of the four model congregations during Holy Week to observe the rituals associated with the catechumenal process. Thus, it was essential that we have two congregations with robust ritual practices to fulfill this aspect of our grant.

the mentored congregations. So that each principal researcher worked with a congregation of the ELCA, Kent was paired with that congregation from the mentored group, and a pastor whom both researchers knew was assigned to Rhoda. The remaining two were assigned randomly.

As professors in higher education, our research on human subjects required us both to seek approval for our research through the Institutional Review Boards (IRB) of our respective institutions. The application materials required by the IRB included submitting the list of questions we would ask the interviewees. We are grateful for the consulting work of Dr. Alisa Potter-Mee, a sociologist, for her help in crafting questions that addressed the topic of our research, and for the IRBs at Concordia University, St. Paul and Concordia Seminary, St. Louis that reviewed and approved our research plan.[16]

We have received permission from three of the four congregations to use the real congregational names and locations and names of the pastors; these pastors participated in Zoom conferences funded by our second grant, so their names and that of their congregations was made public then.[17] Due to a variety of factors, we decided to maintain the anonymity of the fourth congregation, St. Mary's, and used a pseudonym for the pastor. She is no longer serving the congregation, and the current pastor has not continued the adult faith formation model of her predecessor. It was also the smallest of the model congregations, and therefore more difficult to maintain the anonymity of participants. We are not the first among liturgical scholars to make such a choice. In her most recent book, Melanie Ross made a similar decision, naming those congregations that "are well established . . . and are capable of bearing the burden of academic inquiry" while keeping anonymous three of the seven congregations she studied "because of the small size of the congregation and/or the sensitive nature of the topics disclosed."[18]

---

16. We developed two sets of questions, one for pastors, other church professionals, and lay leaders involved in the leadership of the catechumenate, the other for "neophytes," those people who were participating in the catechumenal process or who had recently completed the process. Married couples were interviewed together; Kent conducted one group interview or "focus group" with neophytes who were nearing completion of the process. Rhoda did follow-up phone conversations after the period of mystagogy was completed for those interviewed in spring 2019.

17. When we reached the publishing stage of our research, we consulted with Concordia University's IRB and received approval for revised consent forms that have been signed by participants from these congregations.

18. Ross, *Evangelical Worship*, 4.

Appendix 1

We visited all four model congregations to conduct interviews in the summer and fall of 2018. We returned to St. Mary and Redeemer, the two congregations with strong ritual components as part of their adult catechumenal process, in spring 2019 to conduct additional interviews and to observe and participate in their Holy Week services. At the invitation of the senior pastor, Rhoda was invited back to St. John (at the congregation's expense) to attend their women's retreat in January 2019 and witness firsthand the welcoming ethos of the congregation.[19] She was also able to sit in on a Saturday morning adult catechumenate class and conduct interviews with several people who were in the current catechumenal process; thanks to the generosity of St. John, these additional interviews helped to identify the strengths of St. John's catechumenal process and provided a richer portrait of congregational life. Kent, as ordained clergy, was invited by the pastor of Redeemer to participate in the worship leadership of the congregation's Holy Week services, giving him a privileged perspective on the worshiping community and their participation in the rituals relating to the catechumens. We are grateful for the warm hospitality we received from the pastors and laity of all four model congregations, and especially that of St. John and Redeemer.

Faced with a plethora of rich, raw data, we returned to CICW in 2019 for a second grant in a new category, the teacher-scholar grant. The summary in the grant proposal stated that we would

> analyze the field research data on the adult catechumenate from our [first grant] to develop workshops on catechumenate practices for the purpose of sharing our findings primarily with Lutheran pastors and laity. A deep analysis of our field research will shape the content of workshops to help pastors and congregations envision an adult catechumenal model that could transform their congregations. We also see the analysis of our field research as the next step toward publication of our findings.[20]

The second grant supported the data analysis phase of the project, which focused on three key data sources: interviews with the pastors, other lay and church professional leaders, and the "neophytes" who were currently participating or had recently participated in the adult catechumenate,

---

19. In this situation Rhoda started as a participant-observer, that is one who "may assume a variety of roles within a fieldwork situation and may actually participate in the actions being studied." Yin, *Case Study Research*, 115.

20. Vital Worship Teacher-Scholar Grant, 2020–2021, project summary.

Research Design and Methods

participant observation of worship services, and congregational documents.[21] Methods derived from grounded theory informed the analysis of all three sources, particularly the primary data source, the interviews.[22] The use of multiple strategies of data collection contributes to triangulation,[23] defined as "a process whereby researchers ... use multiple methods together so they can examine convergence, expansion, and complementarity of the data sets."[24]

Throughout all stages of this project, we have safeguarded research integrity to the extent possible, striving for research authenticity and credibility. Authenticity "refers to the extent to which participants' voices and agency are ensured, and it strives for assurances that the researcher has represented all views of all participants."[25] We have shared sections of the manuscript with individuals whose stories are told in greater detail and also respected their edits and changes. We have striven for transparency and noted the limitations of our findings. The goal for us is to "create a faithful accounting of people's lived experience."[26] We attempted to give voice to the individuals we interviewed while also seeking the common threads within each congregation, forming what we are confident is a credible picture of the particular ethos of each congregation. All four pastors reviewed and approved the draft chapter on their congregation; Dr. Laura Wangsness Willemsen reviewed early drafts of memos to confirm the method for

---

21. Examples of documents are primarily the texts of public rituals that are part of the catechumenal process; Redeemer Lutheran also generously shared some of their "swag" gifted to catechumenate participants; for example, they give to each person a cross wall hanging that is a replica of the cross with the risen Christ in the chancel of Redeemer Church and a small version that can be worn as a necklace. Both gifts—and their reported use by Redeemer members—illustrate ways in which their Christian faith permeated the everyday lives of those who had participated in Redeemer's catechumenate.

22. See Charmaz, *Constructing Grounded Theory*, chapter 7, "Memo Writing," 162–91. This process helped analyze the data already gathered; we were not able to return to the congregation for additional data collection to reach the level of "data saturation," McGregor, *Understanding and Evaluating Research*, 243; Charmaz also writes of "Saturating Theoretical Categories," 213–16.

23. McGregor, *Understanding and Evaluating Research*, 242.

24. McGregor, *Understanding and Evaluating Research*, 377.

25. McGregor, *Understanding and Evaluating Research*, Table 9.5, "Criteria to Ensure High Quality Qualitative Research," 248.

26. McGregor, *Understanding and Evaluating Research*, Table 9.5, "Criteria to Ensure High Quality Qualitative Research," 247.

Appendix 1

transforming interview data into a narrative and affirming the interpretive work of the memo.[27]

As those who come laden with our own Christian values, Lutheran beliefs, and ecumenical hopes for the church, we are called to evaluate regularly the extent to which our desires and biases might overshadow or skew the interpretation of the data. Through our regular conversations about our data and its interpretation, ongoing collaborative work with the pastors, and consultations with other professionals about our data analysis process, we have a high degree of confidence that we met the "ultimate objective," namely, "to provide evidence that the participants' voices were privileged rather than the researcher's."[28]

---

27. Dr. Wangsness Willemsen is associate professor of education and dissertation coordinator in the department of doctoral studies in education at Concordia University, St. Paul.

28. McGregor, *Understanding and Evaluating Research*, 241.

Appendix 2

SCRIPTURE STUDY/REFLECTION

An Aural Method/The African Method

GATHERING AND LOGISTICS

- The space should be private and welcoming, ideally lacking in clutter that can distract hearts and minds and that can detract from spiritual engagement with Scripture.
- To welcome folks, consider having some simple refreshments available as people gather.
- After an informal time of gathering, the group settles at a table or tables to hear and respond to the word of God. Six to seven people per table is the maximum, one of whom (ideally) is a church professional or trusted lay person of mature faith with the right skill set for this task. This facilitator is usually called a catechist. Most resources recommend that someone other than the pastor facilitate the small groups during the stage of inquiry, as the pastoral presence can often intimidate the "seekers," preventing them from verbalizing their questions.
- If the group is split into more than one table, separate rooms are the best practice.
- Some sources recommend having a candle to light on the table to transition from casual conversation to reading and reflecting on Scripture. The catechist would do this task and offer a brief prayer or exhortation to begin.

Appendix 2

THE PATTERN OF READING, REFLECTION, AND SHARING[1]

- The biblical text is the Gospel reading for the "current" Sunday (that is, if the group gathers on Sunday, they will use the text from that day). The same reading is used throughout the week, Monday through Saturday, on whatever day the group meets.
- The Gospel text is read three times, each time with a different prompt for individual reflection. This is one example of the "prompts."
    - First reading, reflection, and sharing
        - The catechist gives the first prompt, "Listen for a word, phrase, or image that captures your attention," pauses for a brief time of silence, and then reads the text slowly.
        - After the reading and a short silence, each person shares the word, phrase, or image; no one comments on what others have said.
    - Second reading, reflection, and sharing
        - The catechist gives the second prompt, followed by silence, before the text is read slowly a second time by someone else at the table.
        - Second prompt (two variations)
            » How is God speaking to you in this story? Or
            » What theme or concerns do you hear in this text?
        - After the reading and a short silence, each person shares briefly; no one comments on what others have said.
    - Third reading, reflection, and sharing
        - The catechist gives the third prompt, followed by silence, before the text is read slowly the third time by someone else at the table.

---

1. This method is described in a similar way in *Go Make Disciples*, 140–41; our composite resource also borrows from "Aural Method of Experiencing Scripture (The African Method)," JBL website.

Scripture Study/Reflection

- Third prompt
  - » Where does this passage touch your life today? Or
  - » A question crafted by the catechumenal team specific to the Gospel reading. These questions were written for Matthew 21:23–27.
    - With whom do you identify in the story?
    - What good news did you hear in this story that can support you in your daily life?
    - How are you challenged or affirmed by this story?
- Optional addition after the second reading: The catechist may offer a voice from tradition that illuminates the passage in some way (i.e., scriptural teaching and/or catechesis); this "voice from tradition" should be prepared in consultation with the pastor or may be one or two points from the Sunday's sermon.

THE GROUND RULES[2]

Confidentiality is always observed.[3] Whatever is said of a personal nature is not to be repeated outside of the group, not even with the individual involved. "What is said here stays here."

- Participants are free to pass at any time if they cannot think of a response or do not wish to share.
- When a person is speaking to the group, the group simply listens with no response. No one is to discuss what someone else has said, though sometimes another person's response may trigger a similar thought.
- Insights generated by others' reflections may be shared with the group.

---

[2]. These "ground rules" are verbatim from "Aural Method."

[3]. Exceptions to this "ground rule" would be leaders who are mandated by law to report possible neglect or abuse of minors, should such a matter be revealed by a participant.

APPENDIX 2

CLOSING PRAYER

- First option: If appropriate for the group, the catechist will invite them to stand in a circle, join hands, and pray for the person on their left (or right—at the discretion of the catechist).
    - The participants are encouraged to shape the petition in response to the person's reflection on the final question/prompt.
    - Or the participant may speak a general prayer such as: "Christ, may your blessing go with _____. Fill her/him with your love."
    - Participants may pray silently for the person, indicating when the prayer has been offered by squeezing the person's hand.
    - The catechist closes with a gathering up of the prayers in a final petition, which may lead into . . .
    - . . . the group joining together in the Lord's Prayer. Note: this should only be done if everyone in the group is familiar enough with the Lord's Prayer to do so.
- Second option: If all are familiar with the Lord's Prayer or if the group remains seated at the table and have easy access to a copy, they may close by praying it together. The catechist may dismiss the group with these or similar words: "Let us all depart in peace and joy." Or "May Christ be with you throughout the coming week."

VARIATIONS OF PROMPTS/QUESTIONS

- Option Two of prompts and questions
    - First prompt: Listen for a word, phrase, or image that catches your attention.
    - Second prompt: Where does this passage touch your life today? Sharing begins "For me . . ."
    - Third prompt (one of these two choices), with sharing that begins "For me . . .":
        - From what you have heard and shared, what does God want you to do or be this week?
        - How is God inviting you to change?

Scripture Study/Reflection

- Option Three of prompts and questions (adapted from "An Aural Method")
    - First prompt: What does this reading say to you about God?
    - Second prompt: What does this reading say to you about who you are?
    - Third prompt: What do you hear God asking you to do or be this week?

- Option Four of prompts and questions (adapted from *Go Make Disciples*)
    - First prompt: A word or phrase or image that speaks to your life at this time.
    - Second prompt: How the text speaks to your life in a way that is deeper or wider.
        - Deeper means reflecting on some aspect of their life that is challenged, questioned, or affirmed by the text.
        - Wider means reflecting on how it speaks to relationships with family, work, and world.
    - Third prompt: Invite participants to speak a prayer that grows out of the text and their reflection, either praying for themselves or for others in the group.

- Option Five of prompts and questions[4]
    - What word or phrase stands out to you? Why?
    - With whom in the reading do you most identify? Why?
    - Do you feel attracted to anything in today's reading? Do you feel resistant to anything? Do you know why?

---

4. Verbatim prompts from Ralph, *Breaking Open the Lectionary*, 13.

The Stages of the Adult Catechumenate and the Ritual Transitions

In present-day adult faith formation, there are four distinct stages or periods, each punctuated with a public ritual marking one's passage from one stage to the next.

Stages of the Catechumenate	Ritual Transitions
The **stage of inquiry**, as an opportunity for the seeker to begin exploring Christianity and for the church to introduce the seeker to Christ, is a very open-ended and informal period. Its inspiration comes from early church practices when adult baptism was normative, and catechesis, that is, formal instruction in the faith, preceded the rite of baptism. The length of this stage ranges from several weeks to several months, depending on the local context. The transition to the next stage is marked by …	… the **Rite of Acceptance or Welcome**, which moves those who have been exploring the Christian faith into structured formation as disciples (the catechumenate). Through this rite the congregation publicly welcomes the seekers as catechumens. The new catechumens accept the assembly's call to follow the way of Christ, indicating their desire to enter this period of formation in faith; the assembly confesses its willingness and desire to enfold the person into their midst through prayer and the witness of Christ's saving power proclaimed through Scripture.
Through the Rite of Acceptance or Welcome, those ready to commit to the full faith formation process enter into **the second stage, the catechumenate.** As catechumens, they are now ready to be instructed in faith of the church and formed to be a disciple of Jesus Christ by its practices. It may last from two to six months, and the weekly gatherings may shift to include more formal teaching about the Christian faith and intentional formation in the practice of prayer and regular worship with the community of faith. The transition to the next stage happens through …	… the **Rite of Election or Enrollment,** which confirms the readiness of the catechumens for journeying toward initiation into the life of the church, the Body of Christ, through the sacraments of baptism and the Lord's Supper. This rite marks their liminal passage from catechumens to the Elect, those chosen and selected by the Lord through the church to become members of his family. In this rite the catechumens express their desire to be baptized and to join in the fellowship of the Lord's Supper. They may do so ritually by signing the Book of the Elect which contains the names of all the saints who have journeyed into the assembly's life through the catechumenate at this congregation.

Stages of the Adult Catechumenate

Stages of the Catechumenate	Ritual Transitions
With the Rite of Election or Enrollment, one moves into **the third stage, purification and enlightenment,** so named from early church sources that describes an intense time of daily instruction during the forty days of Lent. This term has been adopted by the Roman Catholic RCIA. Gathering weekly with their sponsors, catechist, and pastor for study and discussion, "the Elect" seek to purify disordered desires and to be enlightened by the Holy Spirit toward the shape of the life of faith. The transition to the next stage happens at …	… the **Vigil of Easter**, which is not only the culmination of Holy Week but the culmination of the journey to the font, where the Lord through his church baptizes new brothers and sisters, bringing them through death to new life by the water and the Word. They are sealed with the gift of the Holy Spirit in baptism, which may be symbolized by their anointing with chrism. From the font, the newly baptized and the entire assembly gather around the table of the Lord to receive the Bread of life and Cup of salvation. The neophytes have made the journey to a new life that they now live forever. For those already baptized, a thanksgiving for baptism can be used to mark the transition.
Following the Vigil of Easter, the **fourth and final stage is called mystagogy**, again drawing on the language of the early church, where the focus of this stage was teaching about the "mysteries," or sacraments, as we in the Western church call them. Having experienced baptism or thanksgiving for baptism at the Vigil and, for some, partaking in the Lord's Supper for the first time, the mystagogical gatherings reflect on the meaning of the sacraments for the life of these disciples of Jesus. These gatherings reinforce the reality that the Christian life is not a goal but a journey, marked by …	… the ongoing dying to sin and rising to Christ (that Martin Luther speaks of as the daily power of baptism) and lived out ritually through **Confession and Absolution.**[1] The gatherings highlight the power of **Holy Communion**, through which faith in the Triune God and love for others are strengthened. The weekly rhythm of the Divine Service deepens the faith of Christians and empowers them through the work of the Spirit for the daily life of witness, prayer, fellowship, and service to the church and world.

---

1. Luther, "Large Catechism," in *Book of Concord*, paras. 64–86, 464–67.

GLOSSARY

Anointing—the ritual application of olive oil on individuals in the adult catechumenal process, usually by a pastor. A small amount can be applied by dipping one's thumb into the oil and making a sign of the cross on the recipient's forehead (or other part of the body). Some baptismal rites include an anointing after the baptism with water; the presider anoints the neophyte by pouring a generous amount of scented olive oil on the neophyte's head.

Aspergillum—a brass wand that can be filled with water and has holes on the top; or a short, round brush of hair or fibers that retains water, used in the aspersion rite (see next entry); a pine branch can also be substituted.

Aspersion—the sprinkling of water on the worshiping assembly as a reminder of baptism and God's promises in and through this sacrament. If using the brush or pine branch, water is transferred from the baptismal font to a smaller bowl, which is carried in procession throughout the nave of the church. The sprinkling by the presiding pastor is done by dipping an aspergillum into the bowl (carried by an assistant) and then releasing the water on to the people with a sweeping gesture of the arm. At the Vigil of Easter, this ritual can be done as part of the Service of Baptism.

Baby boomers—the generation of people born between 1946 and 1964 that makes up about 20.5 percent of the US population.[1]

Catechist—a leader in the adult faith formation process; the word comes from the Greek verb *katēcheō,* which means to teach or instruct, and in Pauline epistles is used in a way that "may even be regarded as a technical term for 'to instruct in the faith.'"[2] The term is commonly used for

---

1. See Statista, "Population Distribution," for this and other generational statistics.
2. Wegenast, "Teach," 771.

a lay person of mature faith with teaching and listening skills who provides leadership in a congregation's adult faith formation process.

Catechumen—one who is being instructed and formed in the Christian faith; the term is used in most literature on the adult catechumenate only for those seeking baptism. It is used in some denominations for baptized youth who are preparing for the rite of confirmation; thus, it can also be applied in the same way to adults in a faith formation process.

Catechumenal director—in Roman Catholic parishes, the director oversees the entire catechumenal process, both organizing the weekly gatherings and planning the rites and ritual details. The director may also serve as a catechist.

Catechumenate—broadly defined as a process to prepare adults for baptism and baptismal living as members of the body of Christ in the world; in this book, the term applies both to those preparing for baptism as well as to those already baptized who desire to return to active discipleship and/or who seek to renew and strengthen their Christian faith. The process forms people by their participation in the corporate worship of the church; through regular gatherings to hear and reflect on Scripture; by exposure to and engagement in the practice of prayer; through instruction in the teachings of the church; and through active service on behalf of others.

Catechumenate, stage of—more narrowly, the word is used for the second stage in the catechumenal process, for those "seekers" who, after participating in the stage of inquiry, desire to be instructed in the faith of the church and formed to be disciples of Jesus Christ.

Chancel—the front section of a church's worship space, usually a raised platform on which is the altar, pulpit, and lectern. It may include chairs for worship leaders, the baptismal font, and/or organ and choir seating or space for other musicians. In many churches, it is bounded on the front by a communion rail at which the assembly receives the Eucharist.

Chrism—the oil designated for use in the post-baptismal, episcopal (that is, by the bishop) anointing in many Christian traditions' baptismal rites. Chrism is made from a base of olive oil and then fragranced with various aromatic substances such as balsam and myrrh. It is often associated with the gift of the Holy Spirit and the use of the gifts of the Spirit.

Divine Service—term used by the LCMS for Sunday worship that includes preaching and celebration of the Lord's Supper. It is a way of translating the German word *Gottesdienst*, which was Martin Luther's preferred term for worship; the German can also be translated as "service of God."

Glossary

Elect—the Elect are those in the traditional process of the catechumenate who have entered into the final period of preparation for baptism, the period often referred to as the period of enlightenment and purification. In the ancient mystagogy of the church fathers, the Elect became such when they "gave in their names" indicating their request to be baptized. The catechumens were presented for election by their sponsors, who testified to their commitment and desire to become disciples of the Lord Jesus. Through the sponsors the community discerned that the catechumens were elected for participation in the body of Christ.

Enlightenment, stage of—the third stage in the adult catechumenate, encompassing the final weeks before baptism or affirmation of baptism, when catechumens seek to purify disordered desires and to be enlightened by the Holy Spirit toward the shape of a life of faith.

Eucharist—term for the Christian sacrament also known as Holy Communion, the Lord's Supper, and the Sacrament of the Altar; the word comes from the Greek verb *eucharisteō*, give thanks, used by Jesus in the accounts of his last meal with his disciples in the synoptic Gospels and in 1 Corinthians by Paul for the meal shared by early Christians. The noun form became the common terms of early Christians for this ritual meal.

Faith formation—the authors' preferred term for "the catechumenate" and "catechesis" for two reasons: 1) this phrase is more accessible to the general population; and 2) it emphasizes the holistic nature of becoming a disciple of Jesus Christ, which involves more that intellectual assent to a body of teachings. Faith formation shapes the mind, heart, and one's whole being into a person who trusts Jesus as the One who reveals the Father.

Gen X—the generation of people born between 1965 and 1980 that makes up approximately 19.5 percent of the US population.

Gen Z—the generation of people born between 1997 and 2012 that makes up approximately 21 percent of the US population.

Habitus—term from the discipline of sociology and made popular by Pierre Bourdieu to describe the way a person understands and responds to the social world that the person inhabits; how one responds to that world evokes the person's character, skills, and habits. In faith formation, the person's "social world" may be radically altered by entering the world of Christians; a new "*habitus*" or way of responding to the world is formed through the catechumenate.

Inculturation—the predominant post-Vatican II term describing the process by which the liturgy of the church actively takes on forms that are appropriate to the cultural context in which the local church resides. This first entails a dialogue with the culture, so as best to understand the identity of the culture and its primary modes of expression. Elements from the culture are incorporated into Christian worship so that it communicates effectively and forms Christian disciples appropriately without compromising the gospel and its narrative arc.

Initiation, rites of—In the Roman Catholic church, rites of initiation (or sacraments of initiation) include baptism, confirmation/anointing, and first Eucharist. The term expresses the theology of the Second Vatican Council and the accompanying liturgical reforms that reasserted the unitive ritual practice of the early church at the Vigil of Easter: baptism followed by anointing, and the neophytes then joining with the worshiping assembly to partake for the first time in the Holy Eucharist.

Inquiry, stage of—this first stage of the adult catechumenate is an opportunity for the seeker to begin exploring Christianity and for the church to introduce the seeker to Christ; it is very open-ended and informal, intended to welcome newcomers and allow them to explore their questions about God, Jesus, and the church.

Kinaesthetics—a term paired with "poetics" by Christian philosopher James K. A. Smith, which he describes in this way: "an appreciation for the bodily basis of meaning (kinaesthetics) and a recognition that it is precisely this bodily comportment that primes us to be oriented by story, by the imagination (poetics)."[3]

Liminal—a term from the discipline of ritual studies related to rites of passage that result in a change of status for the participant; the rite of marriage is a good example. One begins the rite as a single person but ends it in a different state or status, married. In ritual studies, this liminal, "in between" time is one of disorientation and ambiguity.

Millennials—the generation of people born between 1981 and 1996 that makes up approximately 21.5 percent of the US population.

Mystagogy, stage of—the fourth and final stage in the adult catechumenate; the word comes from the Greek word, *mystērion*, used by the early church as a term for the sacraments of baptism and Eucharist. In the early church, mystagogy took place in the days following the Vigil of Easter, when the newly baptized were instructed in the meaning of the sacraments they had participated in for the first time.

---

3. Smith, *Imagining the Kingdom*, 101.

Glossary

Nave—the section of a church building where the laity gather for worship; until the Middle Ages, the nave had no pews or chairs, and Christians stood for worship; from the Latin *navis*, for ship, so called because the long, narrow shape of many large churches resembled the shape of a ship; the early church also used the metaphor of a ship as a place of safety and security from the tempests of the world.

Neophyte—literally, the newly planted, from the Greek; term for those who are newly baptized used during the stage of mystagogy to indicate the new status of these people as fully part of the body of Christ.

OCIA—See RCIA.

Oils—Christian tradition has often designated the use of three different types of oils for different purposes. 1) The oil of the sick is a pure olive oil base with no added aromatic substances. Used as part of the church's ministry to the sick, it is intended for healing purposes; 2) the oil of catechumens, often employed prior to baptism, and also a pure olive oil base with no added aromatic substances, is often associated with the exorcism of evil, sin, and satanic powers from the catechumen's life; 3) For chrism, see above.

Paschal candle—the preeminent symbol of Easter and of the Easter season. First lit at the Easter Vigil, it remains lighted throughout services during the Easter season and at all baptisms. In various traditions it is extinguished either on Ascension Day or on the Day of Pentecost. At the Easter Vigil in the West it is lit during the Service of Light at the beginning of the Vigil. Throughout the Vigil it is associated at various points with the Word of God and creation, the incarnation of Jesus, and the resurrection of Jesus (thus, the Pascha).

Poetics—see kinaesthetics, above.

Post-Christendom—Christendom is defined as "the dominion or sovereignty of the Christian religion."[4] Given the decline of adherents to the Christian faith in the US, most scholars consider the present time to be post-Christendom; that is, the dominance of Christian culture has given way to religious pluralism in the US.

RCIA—Rite of Christian Initiation of Adults is a series of rituals marking stages in the adult catechumenate developed by the Roman Catholic Church as mandated by the Constitution on the Sacred Liturgy, a document approved at the Second Vatican Council in 1963; the text reads that the "catechumenate for adults, comprising several distinct steps" should

---

4. Hall, *End of Christendom*, ix.

"be restored and brought into use at the discretion of the local ordinary [bishop]."[5] Under the direction of Liturgiam Authenticum, the Roman Catholic Church issued a new English translation published in 2024. The result is the *Order of Christian Initiation of Adults* (OCIA), which supplants the former translation, the *Rite of Christian Initiation of Adults*.

Sacristy—a room, usually located directly off or near the chancel, used to store communion vessels, bread and wine, altar linens, vestments, and other items used in worship services; the room, equipped with a closet for vestments, storage cabinets, and sink, is used to prepare the vessels for Holy Communion and clean up afterwards. Clergy and laity use the space to don their vestments for worship.

Scrutinies—the initiatory practice of the early church points to the use of three scrutinies in Lent. These scrutinies in fourth-century practice allowed the Christian community to examine the Elect's commitment and readiness, as exemplified in their way of life, toward becoming disciples of the Lord Jesus Christ through baptismal initiation and to engage in spiritual warfare against sin and evil. The scrutinies in the RCIA on the third, fourth, and fifth Sundays in Lent are not primarily intensive examinations of the Elect's lives. Instead, they allow the Elect to renounce sin and evil and to confess faith. They function as rites of purification as the elect learn about sin, especially their own, and the Holy Spirit elicits in them the desire to be delivered from sin and evil.

Sponsor—a mentor assigned to an adult catechumen to accompany the catechumen on their faith journey; mentors typically attend the catechumenal gatherings with their assigned catechumen and meet separately with the catechumen throughout the process, providing a mature Christian role model for the person.

Silent generation—the generation of people born between 1928 and 1945 that makes up approximately 5.5 percent of the US population.

Vigil of Easter—the oldest annual liturgical feast of Christianity, dating to the second century; originally an all-night vigil ending at dawn on Easter Sunday, the service included readings from the Hebrew Scriptures and baptisms of those completing the catechumenate, concluding with a celebration of the Eucharist for the whole assembly. The liturgical movement of the twentieth century revived the Vigil of Easter in the Roman Catholic Church, and it spread to mainline Protestant denominations in the latter part of the century. Most Easter Vigil services include four distinct

---

5. Constitution on the Sacred Liturgy, para. 64.

parts: a service of light (including procession of the Paschal candle), service of readings (all from the Hebrew Scriptures), service of baptism and/or remembrance of baptism, and celebration of the Eucharist.

Bibliography

Anderson, E. Byron. *Worship and Christian Identity.* Collegeville, MN: Liturgical, 2003.
Aquinas, Thomas. *Summa Theologia* I.1.5. "Whether sacred doctrine is nobler than other sciences?" https://www.newadvent.org/summa/1001.htm#article5.
Bourdieu, Pierre. *The Logic of Practice.* Translated by Richard Nice. Stanford, CA: Stanford University Press, 1990.
Bowles, Nellie. "God Is Dead. So Is the Office. These People Want to Save Both." *New York Times,* August 28, 2020. https://www.nytimes.com/2020/08/28/business/remote-work-spiritual-consultants.html.
Bradshaw, Paul F. *The Search for the Origins of Christian Worship: Sources and Methods for the Study of Early Liturgy.* 2nd ed. New York: Oxford University Press, 2002.
Brunner, Peter. *Worship in the Name of Jesus.* Translated by M. H. Bertram. St. Louis: Concordia, 1968.
Burreson, Kent J., and Dien Ashley Taylor. "The Transforming Power of Robust Ritual Practices." Plenary presentation. Treasures Old and New: A Conference on Adult Faith Formation, online format. January 12–14, 2021.
Butler Bass, Diana. *Christianity after Religion: The End of Church and the Birth of a New Spiritual Awakening.* New York: HarperOne, 2012.
Byassee, Jason. "From the Sacristy: The Christian War on Christmas." *Homily Service* 43:1 (2009) 168–70.
Calvin Institute of Christian Worship. https://worship.calvin.edu/grants/.
Calvin Vital Worship Grant. Capstone Event for Leaders. Concordia Seminary, St. Louis, June 6–8, 2019.
The Center for Baptist Renewal. "What Can We Learn from the Ancient Church?" https://www.centerforbaptistrenewal.com/blog/2018/6/2/retrieving-the-early-church-to-renew-the-modern-church.
Charmaz, Kathy. *Constructing Grounded Theory.* 2nd ed. Los Angeles: Sage, 2014.
Constitution on the Sacred Liturgy. The Vatican. https://www.vatican.va/archive/hist_councils/ii_vatican_council/documents/vat-ii_const_19631204_sacrosanctum-concilium_en.html.
Cyril of Jerusalem. "Five Catechetical Lectures to the Newly Baptized." https://ccel.org/ccel/schaff/npnf207/npnf207.ii.xxiii.html.
DeSilver, Drew. "The Concerns and Challenges of Being a U.S. Teen: What the Data Show" Pew Research, February 26, 2019. https://www.pewresearch.org/fact-

tank/2019/02/26/the-concerns-and-challenges-of-being-a-u-s-teen-what-the-data-show/.

Erickson, Frederick. "A History of Qualitative Inquiry in Social and Educational Research." In *The Sage Handbook of Qualitative Research*, 5th ed., edited by Norman K. Denzin and Yvonna S. Lincoln, 36–65. Los Angeles: Sage, 2018.

Erlander, Daniel. *Baptized, We Live: Lutheranism As a Way of Life*. Minneapolis: Augsburg, 2020.

Evangelical Lutheran Church in America. "Congregations." https://www.elca.org/About/Congregations.

Evangelical Lutheran Worship. Minneapolis: Augsburg Fortress, 2006.

Ferguson, Everett. "Catechesis and Initiation." In *Origins of Christendom in the West*, edited by Alan Kreider, 229–68. ProQuest Ebook Central. London: Bloomsbury, 2001.

Go Make Disciples: An Invitation to Baptismal Living. Minneapolis: Augsburg Fortress, 2012.

Hall, Douglas John. *The End of Christendom and the Future of Christianity*. Eugene, OR: Wipf and Stock, 2002.

Hansen, Byron. "The Emmaus Journey: Mystagogy for God's People." Workshop Presentation, NAAC Conference, Niagara Falls, ON, 2004. https://journeytobaptism.org/wp-content/uploads/sites/17/2023/05/Workshop_Mystagogy.pdf.

Hirsch, Alan. *The Forgotten Ways: Reactivating the Missional Church*. Grand Rapids: Brazos, 2009.

———. Website. https://www.alanhirsch.org/.

Hoffman, Paul E. *Faith Forming Faith: Bringing New Christians to Baptism and Beyond*. Eugene, OR: Cascade, 2012.

Huck, Gabe. *The Three Days: Parish Prayer in the Paschal Triduum*. Chicago: Liturgy Training Publications, 1992.

"I Know that My Redeemer Lives." https://hymnary.org/text/i_know_that_my_redeemer_lives_what_joy.

JBL Website. "An Aural Method of Experiencing Scripture (The African Method)." https://journeytobaptism.org/wp-content/uploads/sites/17/2023/05/BibleStudies_AuralMethod.pdf.

Jennings, Theodore W., Jr. "On Ritual Knowledge." In *Readings in Ritual Studies*, edited by Ronald L. Grimes, 324–34. Upper Saddle River, NJ: Prentice Hall, 1996.

Johnson, Mark. *The Meaning of the Body: Aesthetics of Human Understanding*. Chicago: University of Chicago Press, 2007.

Jones, Jeffrey M. "U.S. Church Membership Falls Below Majority for First Time." Gallup News, March 29, 2021. https://news.gallup.com/poll/341963/church-membership-falls-below-majority-first-time.aspx.

Just, Arthur A., Jr. *Heaven on Earth: The Gifts of Christ in the Divine Service*. St. Louis: Concordia, 2013.

Kavanagh, Aidan. "Christian Initiation in Post-Conciliar Catholicism: A Brief Report." In *Living Water, Sealing Spirit: Readings on Christian Initiation*, edited by Maxwell E. Johnson, 1–10. Collegeville, MN: Liturgical, 1995.

Kinnaman, David. *You Lost Me: Why Young Christians are Leaving Church and Rethinking Faith*. Grand Rapids: Baker, 2011.

Kreider, Alan. *The Change of Conversion and the Origin of Christendom*. Eugene, OR: Wipf & Stock, 1999.

Bibliography

Living Faith Lutheran Church website. https://www.livingfaithlutheran.com/im-new.

Luther, Martin. *The Freedom of a Christian*. Translated and introduced by Mark D. Tranvik. Minneapolis: Fortress, 2008.

———. *The Large Catechism*. In *The Book of Concord: The Confessions of the Evangelical Lutheran Church,* edited by Robert Kolb and Timothy J. Wengert, 377–480. Minneapolis: Fortress, 2000.

———. *Luther's Works*. Edited by Jaroslav Pelikan and Helmut T. Lehmann. 56 vols. Philadelphia: Fortress Press; St. Louis: Concordia, 1955–86.

———. *The Small Catechism*. In *The Book of Concord: The Confessions of the Evangelical Lutheran Church,* edited by Robert Kolb and Timothy J. Wengert, 345–75. Minneapolis: Fortress, 2000.

The Lutheran Church–Missouri Synod. "About Us: The LCMS Today." https://www.lcms.org/about; "Rosters and Statistics." https://files.lcms.org/file/preview/oP6YfWqhIvpvei9cTShodBsbgoWy78VV.

Lutheran Service Book. Prepared by the Commission on Worship of The Lutheran Church–Missouri Synod. St. Louis: Concordia, 2006.

Lutheran Service Book Agenda. Prepared by the Commission on Worship of The Lutheran Church–Missouri Synod. St. Louis: Concordia, 2006.

Lutheran Service Book Altar Book. Prepared by the Commission on Worship of The Lutheran Church–Missouri Synod. St. Louis: Concordia, 2006.

Macalintal, Diana. *Your Parish Is the Curriculum: RCIA in the Midst of the Community*. Collegeville, MN: Liturgical, 2018.

McCullough, David G. *Truman*. New York: Touchstone, 1993.

McGregor, Sue L. T. *Understanding and Evaluating Research: A Critical Guide*. Los Angeles: Sage, 2018.

McLeod, Hugh, and Werner Ustorf, eds. *The Decline of Christendom in Western Europe: 1750–2000*. New York: Cambridge University Press, 2003.

Merleau-Ponty, Maurice. *Phenomenology of Perception*. Translated by Colin Smith. New York: Routledge Classics, 2002.

Murray, Stuart. *Post-Christendom: Church and Mission in a Strange New World*. 2nd ed. Eugene, OR: Cascade, 2018.

"Our Epidemic of Loneliness and Isolation." The US Surgeon General's Advisory on the Healing Effects of Social Connection and Community, 2023. https://www.hhs.gov/sites/default/files/surgeon-general-social-connection-advisory.pdf.

"Painting a Vision for Forming Lutheran Christians." Panel discussion with Pastors Scott Bruzek, Timothy Droegemueller, and Dien Ashley Taylor. Treasures Old and New: A Conference on Adult Faith Formation, online format. October 20–22, 2020.

"Painting a Vision for Forming Lutheran Christians." Panel discussion with Pastors Scott Bruzek, Timothy Droegemueller and Dien Ashley Taylor. Treasures Old and New: A Conference on Adult Faith Formation, online format. January 12–14, 2021.

Payne, Geoff, and Judy Payne. *Key Concepts in Social Research*. Los Angeles: Sage, 2004.

The Pilgrimage of Egeria. Translated by Anne McGowan and Paul Bradshaw. Collegeville, MN: Liturgical, 2018.

Portals of Prayer. St. Louis: Concordia, 1937–present. https://www1.cph.org/portals/default.aspx.

Ralph, Margaret Nutting. *Breaking Open the Lectionary*, Cycle A. New York: Paulist, 2007.

Ramshaw, Gail. *Christian Worship: 10,000 Sundays of Symbols and Rituals*. Minneapolis: Fortress, 2009.

Bibliography

Redeemer Lutheran Church website. https://www.redeemerlutheranbronx.org/.

Rite of Christian Initiation of Adults. Study ed. Prepared by International Commission on English in the Liturgy. Chicago: Liturgy Training Publications, 1988.

Rojas, Raquel A., and Rhoda Schuler. "Called in Christ for Witness and Service." Plenary presentation. Orbiting Christ: Belonging, Believing, Behaving, online conference, June 1–3, 2021.

Ross, Melanie C. *Evangelical versus Liturgical? Defying a Dichotomy*. Grand Rapids: Eerdmans, 2014.

———. *Evangelical Worship: An American Mosaic*. New York: Oxford University Press, 2021.

Saint John Lutheran Church, Wheaton, IL. https://www.stjohnwheaton.org/#home.

Scharen, Christian. *Public Worship and Public Work*. Collegeville, MN: Liturgical, 2004.

Schwandt, Thomas A., and Emily F. Gates. "Case Study Methodology." In *The Sage Handbook of Qualitative Research*, 5th ed., edited by Norman K. Denzin and Yvonna S. Lincoln, 341–58. Los Angeles: Sage, 2018.

Smith, Gregory A. "About Three-in-Ten U.S. Adults Are Now Religiously Unaffiliated." Pew Research, December 14, 2021. https://www.pewforum.org/2021/12/14/about-three-in-ten-u-s-adults-are-now-religiously-unaffiliated/.

Smith, James K. A. *Desiring the Kingdom: Worship, Worldview, and Cultural Formation*. Grand Rapids: Baker Academic, 2009.

———. *Imagining the Kingdom: How Worship Works*. Grand Rapids: Baker Academic, 2013.

———. Website. https://jameskasmith.com/about/.

Sozomen. *The Ecclesiastical History of Sozomen: comprising a history of the church from A.D. 324 to A.D. 440*. Translated by Edward Walford. London: Henry G. Bohn, 1855. https://ia802701.us.archive.org/15/items/theecclesiastica00sozouoft/theecclesiastica00sozouoft.pdf.

Statista. "Population Distribution in the United States in 2022, by Generation." https://www.statista.com/statistics/296974/us-population-share-by-generation/.

Substance Abuse and Mental Health Services Administration. *Key Substance Use and Mental Health Indicators in the United States: Results from the 2020 National Survey on Drug Use and Health* (HHS Publication No. PEP21-07-01-003, NSDUH Series H-56). Rockville, MD: Center for Behavioral Health Statistics and Quality, Substance Abuse and Mental Health Services Administration, 2021. https://www.samhsa.gov/data/sites/default/files/reports/rpt35325/NSDUHFFRPDFWHTMLFiles2020/2020NSDUHFFR1PDFW102121.pdf.

This Far by Faith: An African American Resource for Worship. Minneapolis: Augsburg Fortress, 1999.

This is the Night. Produced by Victoria M. Tufano. VHS. Chicago: Liturgy Training Publications, 1992.

Tufano, Victoria M., Paul Turner, and D. Todd Williamson. *Guide for Celebrating Christian Initiation with Adults*. Chicago: Liturgy Training Publications, 2017.

US Census Bureau. "Forsyth County, Georgia, Decennial Census, P1: Race." https://data.census.gov/table/DECENNIALPL2020.P1?g=050XX00US13117.

———. "QuickFacts: Forsyth County, Georgia; Bronx County, New York; United States." https://www.census.gov/quickfacts/fact/table/forsythcountygeorgia,bronxcountynewyork,US/PST045223.

BIBLIOGRAPHY

———. "QuickFacts: Wheaton (city), Illinois. https://www.census.gov/quickfacts/wheatoncityillinois.

Webber, Robert E., and Lester Ruth. *Evangelicals on the Canterbury Trail: Why Evangelicals Are Attracted to the Liturgical Church*. Rev. ed. New York: Morehouse, 2013.

Wegenast, K. "Teach." In *The New International Dictionary of New Testament Theology*, edited by Colin Brown, 3:659–772. Grand Rapids: Zondervan, 1976.

Welcome to Christ: A Lutheran Catechetical Guide. Minneapolis: Augsburg Fortress, 1997.

Welcome to Christ: Lutheran Rites for the Catechumenate. Minneapolis: Augsburg Fortress, 1997.

Whitaker, E. C. *Documents of the Baptismal Liturgy*. Revised and expanded by Maxwell E. Johnson. Collegeville, MN: Liturgical, 2003.

Winfield, Bevins. *Ever Ancient, Ever New*. Grand Rapids: Zondervan, 2019.

With One Voice: A Lutheran Resource for Worship. Minneapolis: Augsburg Fortress, 1995.

Yarnold, Edward. *The Awe-Inspiring Rites of Initiation: The Origins of the R.C.I.A.* 2nd ed. Collegeville, MN: Liturgical, 1994.

Yin, Robert K. *Case Study Research: Design and Methods*. 5th ed. Los Angeles: Sage, 2014.

Index

Bold *items are also in the glossary.*

absolution, 29, 31–32, 48, 127, 172, 191
acceptance, 27–28, 61, 83, 145
adult catechumenal process, x, 4, 56, 78, 97, 126, 163, 182, 192
adult catechumenate, ix–xii, 2–3, 5, 9–10, 13–15, 17, 19–20, 23–24, 26–27, 60, 96, 104–5, 112–13, 116–17, 119–20, 122–23, 179–80, 182, 190–91, 193–96
adult faith formation, 2–3, 5–6, 9–10, 13–15, 19, 115, 117, 179, 190, 192–93, 199, 201
affirmation of baptism, 7–8, 62–63, 150–51, 194
allegiance, 43, 46, 48–49, 51, 54, 130
altar, ix, 26, 34, 50–51, 80, 146, 148, 153, 172, 193–94
anointing, 83, 88, 153, 155, 191–93, 195
Apostles' Creed, 29, 48, 85, 87–88, 134
apostolic environment, 100, 110–11, 114, 122
Apostolic Genius, 99–100, 111, 120–21
apprenticeship, 7, 76, 101
authenticity, 78, 103, 105, 137, 183

baptism, ix–xii, 6–10, 27–29, 31–32, 42–44, 46, 48, 50–51, 53, 62–63, 80, 84–89, 101–6, 120–21, 124–25, 128, 147, 150–52, 156–57, 162–63, 190–98
baptismal font; *see* font
behavior, 13, 38–39, 54, 61, 124, 126–27, 129, 136, 138, 154, 156, 158
belief, 39, 46–47, 49, 51–53, 61, 63, 124, 127, 129–31, 134–35, 138, 144–45, 147–48
believing, xii, 13, 15, 37, 54, 61, 64, 96, 123, 126, 130, 132, 134–36, 138, 141, 144, 147–48
belonging, xii, 13, 15–16, 20–21, 37–39, 49, 52–54, 56–57, 60–62, 64, 70–71, 93–94, 96, 123–27, 130–38, 141, 144, 147–50, 152, 157–58
Butler Bass, Diana, 13–14, 38, 61, 64, 96, 123–25, 134, 139–40, 199

Calvin Institute of Christian Worship (CICW), xi, 169, 177, 182, 199
candidates, 6–8, 26, 51, 83–84, 87–88, 93, 102, 113, 117, 124–25, 154–55
catechesis, ix, xii, 6, 10, 28, 31, 46, 51, 60, 64, 91, 127–28, 130, 170, 187, 190, 194
catechism, xii, 29, 48, 51, 62–64, 91, 124, 134, 150
catechist, 7–8, 40, 57, 60, 75, 107, 114, 133, 185–88, 191–93

Index

catechumenal process, 15–16, 20–23, 25, 27, 37–38, 67, 69–71, 101, 104, 106–7, 124, 127–29, 157–59, 163, 166, 180–81, 183, 193

catechumenate, x–xiii, 6–8, 14–15, 20–21, 23, 37, 42–46, 49–53, 72–76, 78–84, 88–91, 93–94, 100–104, 112–14, 116–17, 121–22, 124–25, 127–38, 147–48, 153–54, 162–63, 170–74, 178–79, 190–91, 193–94, 196–97
  ancient, xi–xii, 15, 73, 78
  classes, 25, 52, 116, 131

catechumens, xii, 6–7, 16, 21–22, 34, 36, 45–46, 48–51, 53, 62, 76, 78–79, 81–87, 89–94, 101–2, 120–21, 135–36, 155–58, 171, 190, 193–94, 196–97

child of God, 55, 103–4, 154

chrism, 88, 191, 193, 196

Christian
  community, 4–6, 8–9, 51, 79, 85, 102, 104, 178, 197
  faith, 3, 6, 37, 43, 47, 83, 85, 91, 178, 183, 190, 193, 196
  life, 36–37, 44–45, 48, 55, 83, 86, 105, 129, 156, 191

Christian Initiation, Rite of . . . of Adults; *see* Rite of Christian Initiation of Adults

CICW; *see* Calvin Institute of Christian Worship

classes, 14, 21, 25, 29–30, 36, 47, 57, 90–91, 93, 131–32, 148
  catechetical, 20, 28, 31–33, 36, 163–64
  catechumenal, 27–28, 46, 136, 162–63

communitas, 100, 117–18, 121

community, xi–xiii, 6–8, 10, 13–16, 37–39, 41–42, 52–53, 56–57, 60–62, 65–67, 76–78, 81–84, 89–91, 93, 100, 103–4, 106–7, 117, 121, 133, 135–38, 143–44, 148–54, 156–58, 172, 178

confession of faith, 26, 88, 112

confession of sins, 29–32, 48, 104, 118, 127, 164, 191

confirmation, 44, 50–51, 53, 83, 87–89, 93, 125, 138, 147–49, 151, 153, 156, 173

congregational life, 15, 49–50, 73, 75–76, 88, 91, 102, 104, 112, 115, 117, 120, 122, 179, 182

context, 13–17, 20–95, 120, 122, 138, 141, 159–60

conversion, 4, 13, 21, 39, 64, 76, 82, 96, 123–41
  process, 61, 123–24

devil, 14, 40, 42, 45, 48–49, 52, 87

disciples, 7–10, 19–21, 24, 35–36, 38, 68–71, 85, 100, 103–7, 109, 116, 119, 121–22, 128–30, 139, 159, 161, 189–91, 193–94, 197

discipleship, 10, 16, 46, 52, 76, 83–84, 96, 104–6, 127–29, 141–42, 144

Divine Service, 31–32, 50, 80, 113, 118, 191, 193, 200

early church, xi, 3, 5, 8, 13, 60, 63, 80, 124, 139, 191, 195–96

Easter, 6, 8, 24, 27, 52, 63, 83, 86, 103, 191–92, 195–97
  Season, 27, 44, 166, 196
  Sunday, 40, 51, 71, 75, 86, 88–89, 197
  Vigil of, 6, 8, 26–28, 34–35, 50–51, 62–63, 66–68, 83, 85–87, 89, 104, 106, 133, 145, 147–53, 156–58, 171, 173, 191–92, 195–97

Egeria, 6, 201

ELCA; *see* Evangelical Lutheran Church in America

ELCA congregations, 125, 152, 179–80

Elect, 8, 51, 85–88, 190–91, 194, 197

election; *see* Rite of Election

Index

enlightenment; *see* period of enlightenment *or* stage of enlightenment
enrollment; *see* rite of enrollment
Eucharist, xii, 31–32, 35, 37, 51, 58, 63, 67–68, 79–80, 193–95, 197–98
Evangelical Lutheran Church in America (ELCA), xi, 56, 74, 152, 165, 177, 179–81, 200–201
experience, 9, 32–36, 38–39, 48, 50, 52–55, 62, 64–66, 68, 84, 86–90, 92–94, 96, 101–2, 106, 112, 126–28, 141, 148–49, 178–79

faith communities, x, 1–2, 7–8, 63–64, 67, 121, 124, 190
faith formation, xi–xiii, 7–8, 10, 14–16, 48–49, 56–57, 59–62, 66–67, 75–76, 85, 92, 96–97, 101–2, 116–17, 120–22, 126, 129–30, 150, 162–63, 190, 193–94
faith journey, 1, 16, 59, 65, 197
fides qua, 30, 37, 128, 134–35
fides quae, 30, 37, 128, 134–35
font, 50, 52, 72, 87, 106, 131, 147–48, 150–51, 157, 191–93
forgiveness, 7, 37, 76, 127, 129, 131, 148, 164–65
Friendlies, 21, 29, 35–36, 116, 128–29

Good Friday, 34, 37, 44, 51, 86, 94
grace, 23–24, 26, 41, 74, 80, 88, 94, 128, 131, 140, 142, 147, 165
Great Commission, 11, 19, 42, 101

habitus, 71, 96, 101–21, 144, 161–62, 164, 171, 194
hands, laying on, 62, 68, 85, 88–89, 138, 153
Hansen, Byron, 9, 200
Hirsch, Alan, 96, 99–100, 102–3, 105, 107–12, 114–15, 117–18, 121, 158, 200

Hoffman, Paul, 13, 56–57, 60–62, 101, 116, 122, 134, 200
Holy Communion, 22, 31, 44, 49, 164, 172, 191, 194, 197
Holy Spirit, 8, 84–85, 90, 128, 156, 191, 193–94, 197
Holy Thursday, 21, 33–34, 44, 146

identity, 50, 62, 64, 100, 103–4, 114, 118, 121, 126, 133, 149–50, 152–53
imagination, xi, 117–18, 122, 160–61, 164, 166, 195
incorporation, 8, 43–44, 50, 54–55, 126, 133, 147
initiation, 7, 78, 82, 85–88, 106, 164, 190, 195, 203
inquirers, 6–7, 60, 79, 81, 135–36, 174
inquiry; *see* stage of inquiry

journey, xi–xiii, 1–11, 40–41, 44–45, 72, 74, 81–83, 86, 88–89, 102, 104, 124–74, 191
catechumenal, 44, 50, 73, 82, 104
justification, 33, 35, 37, 47, 80, 101, 129

kinaesthetics, 160, 195–96
kingdom, 5, 7, 52, 84, 97, 130, 143, 154, 159–67, 195, 202
Kreider, Alan, 4, 13, 39, 61, 96, 123–24, 139–40, 200

Large Catechism, 9, 31, 45, 79, 91, 105, 149, 191, 201
LCMS; *see* Lutheran Church–Missouri Synod
LCMS congregations, 31, 44, 74, 109, 118, 125, 177, 179–80
leadership, 13, 48, 58, 71, 76, 110–11, 181, 193
apostolic, 111, 113–14
lectionary, 50, 60, 114, 143, 165, 189, 201

Index

Lent, 7–8, 48–49, 62–63, 66, 68, 71, 82, 84–86, 133–34, 136, 149–50, 171–72, 197
   first Sunday in, 48, 51, 62, 84–85, 134, 150–51
   season of, 16, 44, 150–51
liminal, 23, 26–27, 33, 117–19, 127, 147, 190, 195
liturgy, 3, 6, 14, 16, 31–33, 35, 38, 48, 50, 85, 87, 91, 93, 124, 127–29, 160–61, 164, 166, 171, 174
loneliness, 4, 125–26, 201
Lord's Prayer, 8, 29, 45, 48, 85, 92, 136, 188
Lord's Supper, 26, 29, 31–32, 48–51, 79–80, 83, 87–89, 125, 131, 147–48, 190–91, 193–94
Luther, Martin, 15, 29–33, 36–37, 40, 43–45, 48, 50–51, 63, 79. 91–92, 105, 129, 134, 148–49, 191, 193
Lutheran Church–Missouri Synod (LCMS), xi, 24, 26, 37, 40, 50, 74, 80, 83, 85, 91, 109, 112–13, 118, 125, 165, 177, 179, 193, 201
Lutheran congregations, 3, 10, 13, 77, 92, 177–78
Lutheran theology, 15, 28, 113, 161
Lutheran tradition, 30, 36–37, 44, 69, 105, 114, 120

Maundy Thursday, 33–34, 86, 104, 146
McGregor, Sue L.T., 178–79, 183–84, 201
mDNA, 100, 102, 115, 122
membership, 26–27, 44, 51, 65–66, 70, 74, 76, 83, 102, 104, 113, 119, 125
mentored congregations, 116, 170, 179–81
mentors, 36, 93, 101, 120, 197
mercy, 14, 35–37, 54, 128–30, 139, 174

mission, xi–xiii, 42, 74, 77, 80, 96, 100–102, 104, 107–8, 111–12, 115–17, 120–22, 158
missional, 63, 96, 101–21, 166
   church, 117, 121, 200
   ethos, 17, 62–63, 69–70, 99, 113, 120, 139
   identity, 101–2, 112
   mindset, 10, 99, 102, 110, 121
missional-incarnational impulse, 100, 107–10
mission of God, 42, 102, 107, 111, 121, 158
mission statement, 37, 41, 57, 64, 74, 119–20, 129
mystagogy, 8–9, 21, 27, 31, 55, 60, 63–64, 69, 89, 91, 191, 195–96, 200

narrative arc, 164–65, 168, 195
nave, 31, 87, 150–51, 192, 196
neophytes, 9, 15, 50, 54, 63, 76, 89, 91–93, 181–82, 191–92, 195–96

OCIA; *see* Ordo of Christian Initiation of Adults
oil, 88, 94, 149, 154, 192–93, 196
Ordo of Christian Initiation of Adults (OCIA), ix, 3, 196–97

pandemic, xi, 71, 116, 166, 170–75
paschal candle, 87, 149, 196, 198
Passion Sunday, 86, 103, 158
pastoral care, 14, 19–20, 23–27, 35, 112, 126–27, 141, 171
period of
   catechumenate, 8, 78, 83–84
   enlightenment, 8, 60–61, 78, 84–85, 194
   inquiry, 59–60, 64–65, 78–79, 83
   mystagogy, 63–64, 69, 78, 89, 181
poetics, 159–61, 195–96
post-Christendom, 4, 97, 139–40, 161, 196, 201
power of ritual, 5, 62, 97, 144, 159

Index

practices, 3, 5, 7–8, 22, 24, 26, 60–61, 63, 86, 122, 125, 128, 139, 151–52, 159–60
pray, 33, 43, 61–63, 93, 102, 111, 134, 138, 151, 157–58, 188
prayer, 7, 9, 14, 16, 33–35, 37–38, 49–50, 61–62, 65, 83–84, 93, 109–10, 128–29, 133–34, 136, 139, 143, 150–52, 174, 188–91
preaching, 3, 15–16, 20, 30, 32–33, 41, 43, 52, 68, 162, 165
procession, 31, 87, 89, 144–45, 151, 192, 198

RCIA; *see* Rite of Christian Initiation of Adults
research congregations, 96–97, 102, 104–5, 112, 126, 164–65, 170–71
research design, 177–79, 181, 183
right belief, 45, 47, 51, 130, 147
Rite of Acceptance, 51, 78, 83, 136, 154, 156–57, 190
Rite of Christian Initiation of Adults (RCIA), ix, 3, 5, 7–8, 73, 78, 83–85, 101, 154–55, 196–97, 200–202
rite of confession and absolution, 31, 104
Rite of Election, 7, 84, 93, 136, 138, 190–91
rite of enrollment, 62–63, 66, 69, 190–91
rite of welcome, 7, 62, 120, 134, 150–51
Rites of Initiation, 78, 82, 85–89, 195
rites of passage, 162–63, 195
ritual action, 34, 68, 150, 155
ritual experiences, 9, 97, 148, 151–52, 159
rituals, 3, 5–10, 16, 23, 27–28, 34–35, 62, 66–67, 81, 94, 96–97, 121, 124, 133–34, 142–68, 180, 182
powerful, 21, 145, 154–55

public, 6, 23, 25–26, 63, 134, 145, 183, 190
ritual studies, 144, 146, 195, 200
ritual transitions, 9, 27, 78, 190–91
Roman Catholic, ix–x, 3, 5, 8, 27, 64, 101, 133, 165, 193
Church, 23, 86, 165, 195–97

sacrament of baptism; *see* baptism
sacraments, 8–9, 31, 33, 35, 38, 67–68, 84, 113, 127–29, 131, 147, 164–65, 171–72, 191–92, 194–95
sanctification, 33, 37, 129, 164
Satan, 47, 55, 87–88, 130
Scripture, 6–7, 9, 14–15, 30, 33, 35, 37–38, 62, 64, 128–29, 131, 147, 165–66, 185, 190, 193
scrutinies, 84–87, 136, 197
Second Vatican Council, 3, 5, 194–96
seekers, 6–7, 10, 33, 58, 60, 69, 96, 185, 190, 193, 195
sign, 34–35, 38, 50, 83, 85, 121, 124, 126, 131, 147, 149, 153, 155–56, 159
signing, 7, 23, 74, 85, 88, 138, 154–56, 190
simultaneity, 96, 126, 128–29, 134
sins, 30, 37, 40, 46, 48, 85, 87, 117–18, 127, 130, 164–65, 191, 196–97
Small Catechism, 15, 29–30, 44, 48, 51, 63, 79, 85, 91–92, 134, 148
Smith, James K.A., 2, 5, 97, 143–44, 159–67, 195, 202
Sozomen, 144–45, 202
spiritual battle, 14–15, 44, 46, 48, 50–52, 130
sponsors, 7–8, 53–54, 84–85, 87–89, 93–94, 101, 116, 120, 150, 153, 191, 194, 197
stage of
  catechumenate, xi, 7, 25–26, 83, 133–35, 190, 193
  enlightenment, xi, 26, 84–85, 124, 133–35, 191, 194

209

Index

stage of (*continued*)
   inquiry, xi, 6, 23, 82, 185, 190, 193
   mystagogy, xi, 8–9, 21, 27, 134, 152, 191, 195–96
stories, 10, 21, 23, 35, 37–38, 56, 59–60, 64, 67, 70, 109, 111–12, 117, 119, 122, 134, 136, 159–62, 164–66, 186–87
Sunday liturgy, 7–8, 21–22, 29, 31, 127, 150, 159, 161–62, 164–65, 168
Sunday worship, 16, 23, 25, 31–32, 48, 61, 134, 154, 159, 166, 193

teaching, xi, 8–9, 11, 14, 16, 20, 28–30, 35, 37, 41, 47–50, 59, 80, 90–92, 112–14, 124, 129, 135, 139, 193–94
   catechetical, 21, 28, 31
theology, sacramental, 9, 32, 128
transformation, 68, 94, 101, 106, 120–21, 139, 157–58
transformative power, 10, 71, 140, 143, 154
transition, 7, 16, 23, 26, 43–44, 50–51, 53, 81, 83–85, 185, 190–91
truth, 5, 42, 45, 49, 94, 129–30, 132, 139

vigil; *see* Easter, Vigil of
vocation, 42, 52, 55, 101
vows, 35, 88, 157
voyage process, 56–57, 61–63, 65–71, 106, 133, 135, 151, 158
Voyager process, 120, 132, 151
Voyagers, 57, 62–65, 67, 70–71, 120, 133–35

water, 33, 79, 86–87, 127, 138, 147, 151–52, 191–92
witness, 6–7, 9–10, 14–16, 35–38, 40, 42–44, 74, 76, 84, 86–87, 89, 101, 103–4, 107–10, 113, 128–30, 174, 190–91
word and sacrament, 25, 31, 68, 113, 127, 142, 164, 171
worship, 2–3, 7, 9, 32–33, 46–47, 78, 80, 83, 90, 92–93, 126–27, 132, 134–35, 142–43, 165–66, 177, 179, 196–97, 199, 201–3
worshiping community, 25, 65, 70–71, 120, 169, 182
worship life, 21, 28, 35, 129, 164
worship services, 74, 83, 89, 92, 142–43, 173, 183, 197

www.ingramcontent.com/pod-product-compliance
Lightning Source LLC
Chambersburg PA
CBHW052214240426
43670CB00037B/566